PROJECT OF CRISIS

Writing **Architecture** series

A project of the Anyone Corporation; Cynthia Davidson, editor

PROJECT OF CRISIS

MANFREDO TAFURI AND CONTEMPORARY ARCHITECTURE

MARCO BIRAGHI
TRANSLATED BY ALTA PRICE

THE MIT PRESS

CAMBRIDGE, MASSACHUSETTS

LONDON, ENGLAND

This work first appeared in Italian as *Progetto di crisi: Manfredo Tafuri e
l'architettura contemporanea*, © 2005 Christian Marinotti Edizioni, Milan.
This translation was made possible in part by a grant from the Graham
Foundation for Advanced Studies in the Fine Arts and with the support of
the Milan Polytechnic University.

This book was set in Filosofia and Trade Gothic by the MIT Press.

Library of Congress Cataloging-in-Publication Data
Biraghi, Marco, 1959–
    [Progetto di crisi. English]
    Project of crisis : Manfredo Tafuri and contemporary architecture /
    Marco Biraghi ; translated by Alta Price.
    pages cm — (Writing architecture)
    Includes bibliographical references and index.
    ISBN 978-0-262-51956-4 (pbk. : alk. paper)
       1. Tafuri, Manfredo—Criticism and interpretation. 2. Architectural
    criticism—Italy—History—20th century. 3. Architecture, Modern—
    20th century. I. Price, Alta L., translator. II. Title.
NA2599.8.T34B5413 2013
720.92—dc23

                                                      2012046606

CONTENTS

CONTENTS

PREFACE

The subject of this volume is the "project of crisis," or *progetto di crisi*, of the architectural historian Manfredo Tafuri (Rome, 1935–Venice, 1994). *Progetto di crisi* is a quintessentially Tafurian term that can assume many different, nuanced meanings. *Progetto*, often translated as design, is more broadly used in Italian, and can mean project, plan, and even architecture. It can also imply a projection or an intention. Hence *progetto di crisi* cannot be literally translated, but alludes to the productive possibilities of crisis. It is a condition, but also a chance. This multiplicity of meanings also allows me to make an immediate disclaimer here: I have no pretense of painting an exhaustive picture of Tafuri's world, nor do I intend to confront the intellectual biography of one of the most complex and influential figures of the late twentieth century.[1]

Anyone who knows Tafuri from having read his numerous books or listened to his university lectures understands that his interests ranged from the Renaissance to the years in which he lived, and that he did not limit himself to architecture alone but included all that constitutes architecture's inseparable (though too often de facto separate) context and foundation—its lifeblood of society, the economy, culture, and the thinking of the time. More than the work of other historians, and despite his involvement in a variety of subjects and periods, Tafuri's work possesses a coherence, supported and illuminated by a lucid line of thinking. Accordingly, there is no contradiction between Tafuri the Renaissance historian and Tafuri the contemporary critic, only the greatest possible integration between the two. As I will try to demonstrate, a common thread motivates both facets, and the subdivision between historian and critic becomes, in any case, beside the point.

Rereading Tafuri's historiographic definition of contemporary architecture is in no way equivalent to reducing his work to this period alone—his work cannot be conveniently divided into separate fields, self-sufficient and distinguished by their independent logic—nor is it the equivalent of acritically confusing these fields with one another; nor does it mean to deprive each of its own specificity. Rather, rereading Tafuri means circumscribing the field of inquiry to only one part of a vaster terrain—one that nevertheless contains the many problems (or at least a good number of them) with which Tafuri dealt from the early 1960s until his untimely death in 1994. It also means moving on to a historicization of his writing on the contemporary period, in search of evolutions, second thoughts, and fertile contradictions interlaced throughout—in search of more or other Tafuris within Tafuri.

Trying to focus on the crucial points, on the critical and the more productive moments of his specific historical construction of contemporary architecture—his *progetto di crisi*—is not to be understood as a demanding piece of historical bravura on a problematic period by a notoriously difficult author. I have no intention of creating any sort of short guide to Tafuri's thinking. The best explanations of his thought remain his own work—which I can only strongly suggest be read.

Rather, the inspiration for this book is something else entirely. To propose today an analysis of Tafuri's interpretation of contemporary architecture is to suggest some value beyond mere academic or historiographic interest. After all, to embark on such a weighty endeavor, so fraught with peril, would be senseless unless there were some sort of urgency. My deeply rooted conviction is that something within that project of crisis speaks to the present, without in any way rendering it banally current. For this reason, I aim to relate this project of crisis to what, in many ways, seems to descend from it. My conviction is that Tafuri's project of crisis, in the chronological terms specified here, is fundamentally important in understanding the present-day architectural condition.

I must extend my heartfelt thanks to many people for the counsel they so generously provided during the many years I worked on what is here reduced to a rather inconspicuous little volume. That I do not list specific names should in no way be read as unwarranted ingratitude, but rather reflects a more specific desire to avoid any errors in reception on my part.

I would thank Cynthia Davidson for her strong faith in this book, and her editorial team, Tina Di Carlo, Taylor Davey, and Luke Studebaker. I also thank Alta Price for her dedication to translating this book from the Italian. Because the existing English translations of Tafuri's work are notoriously inconsistent in quality, she has translated anew the quotations from his Italian texts unless otherwise noted.

INTRODUCTION

This book is about Manfredo Tafuri's historical construction of contemporary architecture. Why construction as opposed to reconstruction? To understand this we must take a step back from Tafuri and turn to those before him who addressed such historical issues, along with the complex problems they pose. Nikolaus Pevsner, in his book *An Outline of European Architecture*, writes:

> It can indeed not be avoided that the historian turns advocate if he chooses to lead his history up to current events. Yet there is a great temptation to do so. History writing is a process of selection and of valuing. To avoid its being done arbitrarily the historian must never forget Ranke's ambition to write of events "as they really were" (wie es wirklich gewesen ist). This ambition, taken seriously enough, includes selection and valuation upon criteria of the age one deals with rather than one's own age. Should not a lifetime spent in adhering to these criteria equip a historian safely to cope with the case in which the age he deals with is also his own? It must be left to the reader of this book to decide whether the last few pages are a fair treatment of architectural problems and solutions "as they really are."[1]

From Pevsner's point of view, the period of architectural history closest to the present, even more than the history of other periods, is exposed to the dangers of arbitrariness and subjectivism. In this sense, to become an advocate appears to be more than a simple possibility for the contemporary historian; it is an almost inevitable certainty. It is not entirely clear if this is due to the difficulty of obtaining the tools necessary to write history—the measure for judging one's own time, as well as for judging the period of history in question—or to a coincidence in contemporary history between the two measures. But since Pevsner is guided by Leopold von Ranke's positivist history, it can be presumed that what transcendentally impedes creating an acceptable contemporary history is, in his view, the impossibility of reconstructing, exactly as they happened, yet-to-be concluded events, or events which, despite being concluded, are not yet crystallized into a definitive, completed, perfect configuration. In short, and from a historicist's point of view, in order to make history, death must reign over the field in question. Or, in other words, to carry out a historical reconstruction there must be an already written, extant plot that predates the reconstruction and upon which it can be modeled.

For those who believe that "to articulate the past historically does not mean to recognize it 'the way it really was,'"[2] history's work is never reduced to a mere reconstruction, as much as it represents an original construction. "History is the subject of a structure,"[3] writes Walter Benjamin in the fourteenth thesis—a *project*, regardless of whether it considers a more or less recent period of time.

To conceive of history as a *project* necessarily implies a reversal, subverting the principles of historicism espoused by Ranke. It means considering the past as an open, unconcluded time to which the present provides form, albeit an ever-changing and indeterminate form.

The greatest contribution to such a Copernican revolution in this way of historical thinking lay in the reflections of Benjamin—an author with whom Tafuri maintained a special intellectual affinity throughout his life. But the first man to formulate such a revolution was Friedrich Nietzsche in his second essay in *Untimely Meditations*, "On the Use and Abuse of History for Life."[4] If for Nietzsche it is in the vital living realm that history is essentially written, that does not exclusively regard its utility. It is precisely the falsely objective perspective of historicism, in which things give the illusion of having been captured exactly as they were, that wields a mortifying power. As Nietzsche writes, "A historical phenomenon, known clearly and completely and resolved into a phenomenon of knowledge, is, for him who has perceived it, dead."[5]

In contrast to a dead history of objective reconstructions exactly as they occurred, then, is a history constructed with attention to hidden things, to almost erased traces and palimpsests—or, rather, polysests: a history that "can and should never become a pure science."[6] In order to interpret the past, history needs "the fullest exertion of the vigour of the present"[7] and an equally strong—if not stronger—capacity for analysis. "When the past speaks it always speaks as an oracle: only if you are an architect of the future and know the present will you understand it."[8]

The distance that separates these two types of historian—Nietzsche's oracular response to the past, and Pevsner's advocate, before the uncertainties of the immediate present—represents two highly antithetical conceptions of history.

To those like Tafuri, who intend to get as close as possible to the history of architecture of the recent past and the immediate present with the necessary deep conscience this demands, the sole remaining task is to work meticulously on his own construction to offer a vision of articulate (yet uncertain and unreliable) historical projects rather than incontestable facts, detached stories, objective descriptions, or, even worse, unsubstantiated subjective impressions.

But how does one present such a construction—in what way does one construct the historical project? Certainly not as a monolithic edifice, an unassailable fortress poised atop the sturdy foundations of a presumed Truth. On the contrary, the historical project is made up of "little unpretentious truths which have been discovered by means of rigorous method,"[9] and therefore is easily exposed to the risks associated with what Tafuri calls the "shocks, accidents, points of weakness or resistance that history itself presents."[10] Its material, he writes, comprises "the event in its most unique and acute character,"[11] the "event in its devastating character";[12] its structure is discontinuous, lacking its own calming unity, but at the same time resistant to the spells of a naïve plurality. What matters is the "profound disassociation of all that is real"[13]—the internal breakup of the real into incoherent, different, and often contradictory multiplicities. This dynamic disassociation is called upon to reflect or, better still, to embody, but in any case, never to mediate. Its paradoxical glue is the absence of any and all "nostalgia for dialectic synthesis,"[14] for the conciliation or pacification of opposites. "There is the possibility of constructing history . . . only by destroying, step by step, the linearity of that history and its autonomy."[15] Tafuri continues: "Operating on its own constructions, history uses a scalpel to cut into a body whose scars cannot be marginalized: but at the same time, analogous scars, when not marginalized, mangle the compactness of historical constructions, turning them into problems, preventing them from presenting themselves as 'truths.'"[16]

Of course, if history is constructed, and if the product of the historian is a project, then such projects must be evaluated according to their ability to relate or not to the bumpy terrain of facts, dates, data, and eyewitness accounts, with a keen awareness that these factors play a determining role in the historical field, and that their value is never absolute. In any case, their very *sense* can be measured only by the meter of interpretation. Faced with this problem it is worth mentioning the work of Ludwig

Wittgenstein, who in many respects is quite close to Tafuri, as we can see in his *Philosophical Investigations*. Wittgenstein writes: "Every interpretation hangs in the air together with what it interprets, and cannot give it any support. Interpretations by themselves do not determine meaning."[17] To this proposition one could add a second, from Tafuri's *The Sphere and the Labyrinth*: "At the origin of criticism there is always the act of destruction, separation, disintegration of the given structure. Without such a disintegration of the subject to be analyzed . . . no later rewriting of that subject is possible."[18] While these two statements appear substantially contradictory, both question the relationship between a given fact and the way of reading it. Wittgenstein's subject of interpretation is Tafuri's given structure and subject of analysis; the interpretation of Wittgenstein is the criticism of Tafuri. Profoundly different, however, is the relation of each to the other. For Wittgenstein, the subject of interpretation and the interpretation float, suspended in the air next to one another, with no point of contact. The subject of interpretation can therefore not support itself on the interpretation, and the interpretation cannot, in turn, find support within the interpreted subject. Between the two there is only proximity without justification. Indeed, interpretations alone do not determine meaning.[19]

What, then, connects one to the other? What makes us favor one interpretation over another? According to Wittgenstein, it is the existence of stable use—of habit. The relationship between interpreted and interpretation, the frequency with which they appear together, determines meaning. Yet far from constituting an effective support of one another, such a relation continues to leave them both in suspension, a suspension that weighs as heavily upon the given fact as on its reading.

In Tafuri, interpretation, or criticism, meddles with the given—and not in a painless way, as is implied. Between interpreted subject and interpretation, or between a given structure and criticism, a polarity, a tension, is established, which depends on and defines their relationship. One feeds on the other, taking possession of the material that constitutes it. That this assimilation implies a fragmentation, destruction, or disintegration of the subject of analysis is only partially justified by the very nature of criticism itself—which is indeed a *krínein*, a separating, a distinguishing, a discerning, but not yet an absolute disintegration.[20]

In criticism, then, Tafuri sees something more than what is naturally there. It is not only an analytical, organized dissection, a hacking to bits that nevertheless leaves each element in its place, as much as it is a crushing that remixes, transforms, and results in a new version of the given. "There isn't any critique that doesn't follow the same process that gives life to the work, and rearranges the work's materials in a different order," he writes.[21] In this sense, disintegration and rewriting are, for him, equivalent. They are simply two different moments of a singular process—inasmuch as interpreted and interpretation, seen from this viewpoint, represent two different states of a single phenomenon. Certainly one could object: the former is always supreme, it is a firstborn's right; without it criticism would not have any material with which to shape itself, any structure to dismantle and rewrite. But that is not the real problem; the kink that needs undoing consists instead in identifying what binds (or leaves free) criticism and the given. How much does the critical act manage to detach itself from the given? In the final analysis, is criticism made up of the very same material? And how, and to what extent, can the critical relate to the given if its rewriting brings about a radical metamorphosis?

Wittgenstein poses these same questions. Yet Tafuri's answer is much less unequivocal and reassuring (even if Wittgenstein's only appeared to be such). Tafuri writes:

> Here begins what one might call the bifurcation of cri-
> tique. The simple linguistic analysis of an architecture
> that speaks only of its being a language stripped bare
> would result in pure description. It couldn't escape the
> magical circle the work casts round itself, it could do
> nothing but manipulate the selfsame constitutive pro-
> cess of the text, repeating its axiomatic nature. The only
> external reference (point) of such an entirely "internal"
> reading of the subject of analysis would be pointed out
> in the cracks, in the interstices of the linguistic subject.
> The "bifurcation" carried out by criticism must therefore
> be something other than the construction of a "second
> language," floating above the original text.[22]

This condition of floating a critical text above the original is at
once similar and different to that prefigured by Wittgenstein.
Tafuri's discourse, then, can be linked not so much to a critique
of language in a logical sense, à la Wittgenstein, but rather to a
critique of language in an ethical sense, à la Karl Kraus. In fact,
the pages of Tafuri in which this discourse appears are explicitly
"in a Krausian tone."[23]

If not as a second language, in what other way can the language
of critique emerge and present itself? That is, in what way must
one view—and practice—its bifurcation?

To respond to such questions we must inevitably return to the
first page of *The Sphere and the Labyrinth*, where Tafuri explains
the book's scope and his own historical project:[24] "To those who
deal with the subject of architectural *writing* . . . we will introduce
the subject of critical writing: isn't it perhaps criticism that constitutes the historical (and therefore real) specificity of artistic
writings?"[25]

Right from the start Tafuri presents criticism not as a simple comment, an ornament of artistic/architectural writing, or

emblematic of Henri Focillon's luxuriant wilderness that "may spring up beside a work of art: flowers of interpretation that do not adorn, but completely conceal."[26] Criticism is not a second language limited to doubling or at best retranscribing the original source writing of the work; rather, criticism is writing in its own right, writing that, given the "untranslatability of architecture in linguistic terms"[27] different from its own, has full autonomy with respect to the given that provokes it.

Still this solution cannot suffice as a reply, even if partial, to one of the questions just posed.

An attempt at broadening our perspective is indispensable, and a passage must be made—as Tafuri himself did—from the critical to the historical field.[28] It is precisely history that fully embodies an analogical but utterly independent condition with respect to architectural phenomena. Tafuri speaks of historical space—that is, how architecture is writing such that history occupies a place whose specificity is not that of establishing "improbable ties between different languages, between media that are distant from one another. Rather it explores what that very distance signifies; it sounds the depths of a void, and attempts to make the silence that inhabits that void speak."[29] Elsewhere Tafuri calls this space "the space of conflict."[30] Just as physical space is subjected to the torsions of the avant-garde, historical space must abandon the comfortable idea of perspectival vision. Far from being able to boast neutrality, history, as Tafuri warns us, has productive ends[31] and long-term objectives—it is the production of meaning(s). As he writes:

> History is viewed as a "production" . . . the production of meaning(s), beginning with the "meaningful traces" of events, an analytical construction that is never definitive and always provisional, a tool for the deconstruction of certifiable realities. As such, history is both determined

*and determining: it is determined by its own traditions,
the subjects it analyzes, the methods it adopts; it determines its own transformations and those of the reality
that it deconstructs. History's language therefore implies
and assumes the languages and techniques that act upon
and produce what is real: it "sullies" those languages
and techniques, and, in turn, is "sullied" by them.*[32]

Thus we arrive at a definition of that duplicity assumed to a
certain extent—albeit in different terms—in the affirmations of
Wittgenstein and Tafuri: historical language (like critical language, from which it hardly differs) is determined and determining, the acted upon and the agent, chained and free.

Earlier, in analyzing the relationship between the interpreted
and the interpretation as set forth in Tafuri's words, the almost
physical tension between them became clear. Here Tafuri confirms this impression: for him, it is "the constant battle between
the analysis and its subjects, their irreducible tension"[33] that
regulates the historical process. "History's subject is the analysis of this 'conflict'"[34] between "the 'many languages'"[35] and the
many dialects that make up the real.

And yet, "[more] precisely, such tension is 'productive': the
historical 'project' is always the 'project of a crisis.'"[36]

Herein lies both the crux of Tafuri's discourse and the focus of
this book. It is worth repeating: history's product is crisis, and
crisis—as we have already noted with regard to criticism—is ety-
mologically a break, a separation, a de-cision.

We must not forget here the general field within which the
idea of crisis was situated during the 1960s and 1970s: Giulio
Carlo Argan's *Progetto e destino*, for example, opens with the
concept of crisis. Its immediate reference is Edmund Husserl's
work on the crisis of European sciences,[37] which is Tafuri's fundamental reference point, more as a critical point of departure

than a goal. But above all we must not forget—nor in any way did Tafuri conceal—the influence of such a presupposition of his own discourse on history, so fraught with consequences, with considerations put forth by Massimo Cacciari in one of his first, most determining essays on Benjamin.[38] These considerations culminate in the role of technique in Benjaminian thought: "the discourse on technique,"[39] developed by the expressionist avant-garde and understood by Benjamin as the twofold embrace of works that only appear to be distant from one another, such as his *The Origin of German Tragic Drama* and "The Work of Art in the Age of Its Technological Reproducibility," entails, writes Cacciari, "the idea of *crisis*. . . . Technique is the expression of differences, of the crises that determine them."[40] Reread from this critical perspective, Benjamin's "Work of Art" "speaks of the impossibility of dialectically reconciling industrialization and rationalization . . . abandons the hypothesis of linear progress in the development of techniques, and instead grabs onto the historical-conflictual aspect—understands the being-sign as *difference and crisis*."[41] From this a more general consideration can be deduced, which functions as a cornerstone of Tafuri's historical framework. Cacciari writes: "An authentic discourse on technique(s) cannot be made unless one *theorizes* the structure of *crisis*: technique cannot occur unless based on a crisis. . . . Crisis is not a moment that the development of technique passes through, but rather is their immanent structure."[42]

Tafuri's assimilation of not only architectural language but also critical language into technique justifies the centrality of crisis within his historical project; it displaces the barycenter from an illusory external point, outside the system, to an absolutely intrinsic point within it. That is, crisis, as Cacciari writes, "cannot be applied speculatively . . . it must be produced. . . . Any intellectual position that doesn't posit itself as *productive* is reactionary. But *productive* means not only integrated into production, but also capable of transforming or launching into a crisis the technical-linguistic apparatus."[43]

Throughout Cacciari's analysis—and therefore the analysis Tafuri based upon it—is the fundamental question Benjamin poses in "The Author as Producer":

> *Instead of asking, "What is the attitude of a work to the relations of production of its time? Does it accept them, is it reactionary? Or does it aim at overthrowing them, is it revolutionary?"—instead of this question, or at any rate before it, I would like to propose another. Rather than asking, "What is the attitude of a work to the relations of production of its time?" I would like to ask, "What is its position in them?" This question directly concerns the function the work has within the literary relations of production of its time. It is concerned, in other words, directly with the literary technique of works.*[44]

Tafuri's *The Sphere and the Labyrinth* is highly affected by this displacement: from that which posits itself in relation to the means of production to that which attempts to act within it. Likewise, in his other writing, this displacement both foreshadows *The Sphere and the Labyrinth* and emanates from it, with all the consequences that this involves. As Tafuri writes, "Keeping the central question in mind—what is the position of a work within the modes of production?—many 'masterpieces' of modern architecture assume a secondary or marginal role, and a large part of the current debates will be relegated to a field of peripheral considerations."[45]

It is clear, then, how such a program expresses what Cacciari calls a "technique-crisis"[46] and needs to confront it productively. In this light, historical work, Tafuri writes, can present itself as an "operation that sinks into the interstices of techniques and languages"[47] toward the goal of "bringing out what is attested to at the confines of language(s)."[48] He concludes: "Historical work thus calls into question the problem of a limit: it confronts the division of work in general, tends to stray outside of its own boundaries, *it designs the crisis of the given techniques*."[49]

It is precisely from this point of view that history presents itself as a *project of crisis*. Naturally this position throws history's sacred principles off axis, from unambiguity and unequivocal objectivity to ambiguity and arbitrariness. In fact, in the game of alternating deconstruction and reconstruction within historical-critical writing, "the figures one can compose are theoretically more than one"[50] and the results are therefore consistently different. Even if it is true that the pieces, the meaningful traces, are useful as a guide, this does not free the construction from being never definitive and always provisional. One could say, paraphrasing Wittgenstein, that on its own the interpreted does not determine the meaning.

This is not a limitation, however; the richness of the historical-critical act renders it fundamental, makes it a *vital* phenomenon. This incompleteness—or, in the Freudian sense, interminability[51]—ties into all the other articulations of Tafuri's method: genealogy, beginnings, the interweaving of phenomena, relational meaning, "in lieu of one . . . multiple meanings."[52] With a precise methodological instruction: "To unwind a tangled clump of wires we must lay out in parallel many independent stories, [in order] to then recognize where they exist, the mutual interdependencies, or, more often, the conflicts."[53]

In light of these articulations we can now clarify what must be, for Tafuri, the correct relationship between the critical act and the given—and consequently, understood in a negative sense, the *bifurcation* of criticism, its projection into a *second* language. As it must be understood in a negative sense, if the latter is in fact reduced to the creation of pyrotechnical linguistic performances, of a "congeries of metaphors without depth"[54]—at most capable of charming, or pleasantly fooling, often having works of real or presumed masters at their origin[55]—then the task of history, as Tafuri sees it, is at the opposite pole from these phantasmagorias. The task of history is criticism capable of transforming and breaking into bits the material of its own analysis, transforming and breaking itself and its own language, "capable of continually inspiring a crisis in itself, provoking a crisis in all that is real."[56] It is a critique, then, of the complexity and stratification of the modes of production, where "an integrated analysis of linguistic production and material production should enter into a dialectic with the modes of distribution and consumption."[57]

From this it seems evident how the scenario of historical work assumes, for Tafuri, the connotations of a battleground rather than a salon. As on all battlefields, traumas, fractures, scars, and sutures abound. The same architecture in which such a conflict is carried out presents itself in the guise of an uncertain edifice.[58] In sum, the state of crisis dominates here, an uneasiness, against the pacifying false promise of an apologetic and anecdotal history. In this crisis and uneasiness history, according to Tafuri, is not passively limited to taking note, but to the contrary, with all possible means, it retraces, follows, and intends, if not directly solicits.

At this point it might seem necessary to ask ourselves (and, if possible, with more decisiveness and clarity than before): to what extent does this historical product—crisis—adhere to the data present in the field? And to what extent is it the fruit of interpretation? The question would be most reasonable within the context of a reconstructive history, where—in an auspicious way—the discovery of meaning is always at stake. In history as project, "interpretive knowledge . . . has a conventional character and is a production, a positing of meaning *in relation*."[59] In other words, if history is a project of crisis, nothing guarantees that the awareness of crisis that infuses Tafuri's writings from beginning to end is not an integral part of his own project. Tafuri's indication of this point is honest but not reassuring: "History is a 'project of crisis,' then. No guarantees on the absolute validity of such a project: no solution within it."[60]

All of the critical techniques (including his own—something of which Tafuri was well aware) "decipher only by hiding the traces of 'homicides' perpetrated more or less consciously."[61] In other words, historical analysis spreads its own denials as it unveils elements that have remained in shadow or been removed. It projects its own shadows on the field it illuminates—more through its own false certainties than through the things it voluntarily neglects or ignores.

That this corresponds precisely to a "criticism capable of continually setting itself in crisis by placing all that is real in crisis,"[62] now seems undeniable. But one may still wonder: is the crisis that moves the historical-critical analysis the same to which the real is subjected? Or is it, rather, a reflection? When all certainty regarding the ties between interpreted and interpretation decreases, the tools with which to evaluate whether a project of crisis has greater validity than the interpretation of the (architectural) world as the best of all possible worlds also decrease. Not because the project of crisis is less probable; simply put, it does not yet say anything about the effective state of all that is real, nor does it in any way decide anything about the reality of the crisis. Wittgenstein's suggestion to look to stable use or habit is not applicable in this specific case, since it would clash with the unacceptable paradox of judging the crisis against the meter of stability, of rendering crisis typical.

But neither should the result between the critical act and the subject of analysis be understood as a total disconnect. On this point Tafuri is extremely resolute. Deconstruction foresees construction; there is no disjunction. In order to avoid an endless dispersion of the traces and data used in Foucauldian and Derridian practices, the "plural historical space, as the *space of conflict*, must allow remaining traces to intersect and therefore must be able to depart from texts . . . as elements, albeit not transparent elements, of a real power exercised on things."[63] It is the intersection of traces as the residue of real conflicts that the project of crisis confronts (which is not a discourse on crisis in general, but rather the analysis of single, historically determined realities: the crisis of the architectural object, of the subject-architect, of ideology, of history, of critique, and of language; crisis provoked by the techniques that connect them and by the transformations caused by them). Beyond such intersections, interpretation for Tafuri remains a purely linguistic game, devoid of "rules that are verifiable in their social effects."[64]

On the other hand, Tafuri's name becomes strongly associated with the most potent critique launched against the historical project that presents itself as "projective." As he argues in *Theories and History of Architecture*:

> *What is normally meant by operative criticism is an analysis of architecture (or of the arts in general) that has as its objective not an abstract survey but the projection of a precise poetic direction, anticipated in its structures and derived from historical analyses, programmatically distorted and finalized.*

> *By this definition operative criticism represents the point of encounter between history and design. We could say, in fact, that operative criticism designs past history, projecting it toward the future. Its verifiability does not require abstractions of principle, it measures itself time after time against the results that are obtained. Its theo-*

retical horizon is the pragmatist and instrumentalist tradition.[65]

The critique of operative criticism is essential to analyzing Tafuri's historical project in its embryonic phase. Distancing himself from a methodology that tends to unify thought and action,[66] and thus transforms the former into the latter, Tafuri not only comes to terms with Bruno Zevi and Sigfried Giedion, but also establishes the basis for his *own* critique of architectural ideology:[67] "Operative criticism is an ideological critique (the term 'ideological' is used here, as elsewhere, in the Marxist sense): it substitutes analytical rigor with value judgments that are already formulated, ready for immediate use."[68]

The decisive difference between an ideological critique and a critique of ideology lies in this very substitution. Whereas the critique of ideology breaks value judgments, those "dead, petrified words"[69] around which knowledge (and therefore history) crystallizes, operative criticism, in an ideological critique, constructs "impenetrable monuments."[70] The construction of these monuments should in no way be confused with the design that the historical construction implies. If in the first case history is used exclusively for the objectives of the present, as a support or confirmation of the designs already outlined by it, in the second it is motivated by a desire to bring back to light what the past contains. In the majority of cases, more than a linear design, a complex intertwining of different signs occurs—a process, or several processes, in which a multiplicity of factors intervene, including the failures and dispersions that riddle history,[71] always and in any case with the knowledge that it is the present that selects, evaluates, and imposes its point of view, but without bending the past to its ends.

The distinction between the two historical procedures is in no way indifferent or captious. It is intrinsic to Tafuri's historical project, as its unavoidable presupposition: "The way I look at historical phenomena may be described as 'that of a designer,' although I still refuse any category of the operative type."[72]

The distancing from operative criticism (which elsewhere Tafuri calls normative or prescriptive)[73] at the end of the 1960s seems aimed at its effective surpassing, rather than simply re-proposing it on another level.[74] That Tafuri condemns what he considers an ideological critique with nonideological weapons, venturing into a historical critique of ideology that, in other periods, he maintained was an operative approach, is proof enough.

To comprehend where this surpassing leads, it is necessary to return to the texts that mark Tafuri's method (or, more precisely, his methodological eclecticism).[75] Otherwise one would risk reading the abandonment of operative criticism and its designing with history as a banal divorce of convenience "between historical writing and architectural design,"[76] to find accommodating refuge in a disciplinary, academic autonomy.

A testimony to how much Tafuri constructed in those years— and not just destroying or accumulating for himself—can be found in the very book in which he confronts the problem of operative criticism: *Theories and History*. The dominant theme (albeit often only implied or elusive) is once again that of crisis, observed in all the complexity of its articulations; crisis that, according to Tafuri, traverses architecture in the broadest sense, as an institution, and of which he not only identifies the multiform effects, but also analyzes the causes, the genesis. As much as the paths taken by such analyses appear discontinuous and at times even forced, there nevertheless emerges the initial profile of the character that Tafuri's later reflections fully come to reveal: the productivity of crisis. The experience of the artistic avantgardes, set at the center of the field so fully embraced by *Theories and History*, perfectly embodies this attempt at making crisis an agent. The "nihilism and totalitarianism of the avant-garde,"[77] the adoption of the tabula rasa as the only type of historicity still allowed after the consummation of any and every other relationship that was not autonomous of all commerce with the past—all this, together with the annulment of the object, the adoption of mass production and assembly-line techniques, and the acceptance of the destruction of the object's aura, shows the "courageous act of conscious realism"[78] that distinguishes avant-gardes at work. "Bringing back the tangled jumble of opposites, the grotesque, and the incongruousness of daily life, the apocalyptic sinking of the European rationalist tradition,"[79] on a par with "rendering institutional . . . the ambiguity of daily life, the already arrived prevalence of *things* over man, the clash of absurds," thus become some of the strategies used by the most radical movements of the twentieth century facing the disorder of the urban condition.

Clearly, in this reading of the relationship between the work of art and the new conditions created by technology, the fundamental guide for Tafuri is Benjamin's essay "The Work of Art in the Age of Its Technological Reproducibility."[80] Nevertheless Tafuri does not just passively follow Benjamin. The field of inquiry is moved to the deep disruptions that occur in architecture during the shift in its production and consumption during the age of reproduction (or late capitalism).[81] The plurality of positions identified by Tafuri attest not only to the various degrees of modification that architectural work confronting a revolutionary situation has undergone, but also to the necessary transformation of criticism that confronts it in the wake of such disruptions. If, then, *Theories and History* still presents more than a few ambiguities, obscurities, generalizations, and omissions,[82] it is nevertheless infused with the precise intention of providing "more than definitive answers . . . some provisional statements and solutions";[83] statements and solutions in which free rein is given to contradiction.[84]

Attributing a *positive* value to contradiction (or to that which constitutes the negative moment of the dialectic, as will later be clarified) theoretically plays the role of what in practice is represented by the unrestricted seesaw patterns of the dialectic form. Indeed, a veritable dialogue opens *Theories and History*. "The couplet [a reference to the quotation from Peter Weiss's *Marat-Sade*, with which Tafuri opens the book] struck me inasmuch as it is an example of open dialogue. I saw it as a way of bringing into relief the position that I had taken with the book, which didn't offer certainties. At the end of the book I recognized that my reflections were a sort of dialogue with myself."[85]

The point is that the historical-critical contribution is built like an internal dialogue—rather than a fictitious, literary dialogue, such as that between Didascalo and Protopiro in Piranesi's "Parere sull'architettura" ("Observation on Architecture"), in which Tafuri spots the "testimony of the discussion that Piranesi sets up with himself."[86] Tafuri sees dialogue as the *substance*—not simply the form—of the continuous oscillation and doubt to which he naturally falls prey, since it corresponds to the complexity and *contradictory nature* of (historical) reality.

It is precisely in this sense that, at the end of *Theories and History*, Tafuri clarifies the tasks of critique:

> *Because contradictions by now make up their own autonomous reality, any critique must know how to recognize its own particular and limited (yet indispensable) role within them.*
>
> *In this sense we can take for our own the affirmation that Weiss gives the "divine Marquis" at the end of his* Marat-Sade: *"in these dialogues our intention / to set some antitheses in opposition / and have them repeatedly clash / and in this way illuminate the doubts"; nor*

is it important that the critic—like Weiss's Sade—must declare that in the present situation he sees himself obligated to "desperately look to find the solution."

In history "solutions" do not exist. But you can always try to suppose that the only possible way is the exasperation of the antitheses, the head-on collision of positions, the accentuation of contradictions.[87]

This concept will return, either overtly or implicitly, in all of Tafuri's later books. Instead of marking the limits with which the historian-critic collides, for Tafuri, contradictions, "intimate tensions . . . lacerations,"[88] "divarications . . . cracks,"[89] the absence of certainties, all represent the *openings* of a territory within which he moves, the space of freedom that anyone who deals with history is obliged to respect and foster.

Thus configured, the relationship between historian and history determines an unforeseen subversion of the rules assigned to them by a Ranke-like conception: while history guards multiple, contrasting possibilities within itself, the historian, on the other hand, faces the task of not reducing them to overly linear and unequivocal current events. With this in mind it becomes clear how the traditional closed nature of history, its apparently deterministic nature (the *dead determinism* of historicism), is nothing other than the closure that is often imposed upon it by the historian, whose problem then becomes that of "singling out the rhythmic beats of the period under analysis. These are plural rhythms, to which . . . an equal or greater number of investigative methods, narrative styles, and philologies must be made to correspond, in the hope that what is questioned at a distance is then listened to in such a way that the distance is not lost, such that it can continue to question."[90]

Leaving behind for a moment the fundamental question of distance, to which we shall nevertheless have to return, it must be emphasized how Tafuri shows the subversion of the aforementioned relationships: here it is the past that questions. The historian is the one charged with giving adequate space to such questions, more than with giving answers, to reflect their full complexity. In Tafuri's words: "To give voice to a dialectic that doesn't take for granted the outcome of the battles described: with the result of keeping the verdicts open."[91]

In this way nothing is passed off as past.

Tafuri's profession of uncertainty does not function as *excusatio non petita* with regard to personal, subjective limits, nor as a legitimization of the intrinsic difficulties of historic practice. The *incertum* is instead completely innate to history. At the most, the only thing in the historian's power is to not go against the order (or perhaps disorder) within it.

Understanding to what extent and why this is closely tied to the productivity of crisis is not difficult at this point. If indeed crisis is the uncomfortable legacy left by the modern movement to the architectural culture of the 1950s and 1960s (an architectural culture on which Tafuri pronounces articulate diagnoses—attempts at "historicization of current contradictions"),[92] then critique itself becomes an absolutely open, as opposed to secret, agent of crisis. The critic, no longer reduced to executing the servile task of mere description, commentary, or support, no longer "prompter or proofreader,"[93] surgically intervenes in historical material,[94] penetrating its most intimate parts, but moving with the utmost care among its various organs. The objective, however, is not that of curing the patient of crisis, nor that of perpetuating crisis by taking on its trappings. A critique that can truly be called pure critique works on sections within the fabric of data (another Benjaminian phrase): it explains, precisely formulates diagnoses, and aims to "understand the intrinsic meanings,"[95] armed with maximal openness to accommodate the shapeless multiplicity of information that often appears with absolute incoherence.

The image of the historian's endeavor is—akin to the cinematographer that Benjamin compares to the surgeon—multiformly fragmented. This is the fruit of a work of *construction*, but this is not why it is completely operative. Just as this process differentiates itself from a straightforward archival-documentary collection, forcing the gathered materials to *speak*, to react each in its own way and in contact with one another, similarly "a critique that wishes to maintain a distance from the operative practice can only subject the latter to a constant demystification to surpass its contradictions, or at least to bring them to mind with exactitude."[96]

It could perhaps seem that an outline of this sort is much more suited to critique and the critic than to history and the historian. But no such separation is suggested in Tafuri's work. For Tafuri, the architecture critic—a "truffle-hound set on seeking the new and ridding himself of the old"[97]—can simply be traced back to a bad historian. Instead it is the problems, the intellectual contexts that must be sought and evaluated, that must occupy the mind of the critic as much as that of the historian. The difficulty common to both (which, in reality, is only that of the historian) is that of maintaining a precarious, hairline balance. Tafuri writes: "Historical critique must know how to play along the razor's edge that acts as a border between separation and participation. Therein lies the 'fruitful uncertainty' of the analysis itself, its indeterminability, its need to return, over and over again, to the examined material and, contemporaneously, to itself."[98]

There is perhaps no more pregnant image than that of the razor's edge that historical critique is forced, and not fleetingly, to touch upon, and with which it must even learn to play—always restless in this perilous condition, but at the same time still master of itself, always in full possession of the necessary cool detachment. This Tafurian razor cuts sharply, and runs the perennial risk of inflicting painful wounds on anyone who loses his balance while directed toward one of its two extremities: that of supreme detachment and that of immediate participation (literally without mediation). This is the precise problem of history (especially of contemporary history): knowing how to take the right position with respect to the phenomena it considers.

"Distance is fundamental to history,"[99] and more so for a history that, like Tafuri's, does not delude itself into thinking it is able to identify with the past and reconstruct events exactly as they happened. This distance is not only factual and temporal, but also essentially mental. This distance allows us not to confuse the voices of the period in question with the voices of the present day. In short, it guarantees against the irruption of the living past into the sphere of the historical present. It is this that creates the perspective with which the historian can establish positions and measure differences.

Nevertheless, that distance is not always-already a given; in some circumstances it must be taken. This is precisely the case with contemporary history. As Tafuri writes, "The historian who brings into question a contemporary work must create an artificial distance. . . . The way we have of distancing ourselves from our epoch, and thus giving ourselves a certain perspective, is by comparing the differences it has with respect to the past."[100]

Distancing oneself from one's time, creating a deviation with respect to the present, and turning to other periods, to a time objectively distant yet subjectively living, which according to Tafuri constitutes the past, does not represent two substantially different operations, but merely two different angles from which to observe the same problem (or rather, the sole angle from which to observe the various facets of the same problem). The insertion of distance, even if artificial, therefore presupposes a historical position in which the problem is removed from any simple manipulation—that is, any and all simple possibilities of solution. If indeed "it is the problem and not the subject that preoccupies the historian," the problems of history actually evade the logical siege to which problems are subject. Thinking coherently of a historical problem to its very end—if this were truly possible—would be tantamount to dissolving it, rather than resolving it.[101] If Tafuri's reflection on the foundations of contemporary architecture has often appeared to focus on their dissolution (a dissolution of the architectural object, but also of historic space), this dissolution nevertheless remains always and only thinkable or imaginable. This problem continued to obsess Tafuri even after he had dedicated all of his attention to it.

A capacity for dialogue, the act of doubting, the acceptance of contradictions, the insertion of distance, these are just some of the tools the historian must arm himself with in order to try and confront the difficult enterprise of constructing his role. Akin to historiographic work, presented by Tafuri as a "labyrinthine route . . . torturous and complex"[102]—a "waiting game" whose pieces are available only in part and could in theory make up more than one formation—even Tafuri's historical *construction* in relation to the contemporary becomes labyrinthine, torturous, and complex. It is a project whose configuration and composition call for a laborious waiting game. In this game, the various pieces, names, and voices that can be identified (and those that elude concrete identification) appear almost inextricably mixed up, not simplistically sorted out.

The only way to penetrate such a project of crisis is to try to put it into crisis—to analyze it, dissect it, deconstruct it—in order to come to an understanding of the true contribution it has made to the interpretation of the period in question. Doing so will mean abandoning all established orders of discourse, all reassuring chronology, giving up the production of systematic and didactic compendia of Tafuri's writings and instead striving to remix the documents to follow the traces scattered throughout.

This is a question, then, of working—*à la* Tafuri—toward an "analytical disassembly"[103] of the subject of research. The recomposition of its fragments, its "reassembly,"[104] will be the most delicate and potentially dangerous moment—that critical action which should remain in tension with the subject of the analysis, but whose concrete and continual risk is instead "being swallowed up by quicksand"[105] (even if it is Tafurian quicksand, perhaps even more treacherous than others). It is for this reason, ultimately, that we will proceed with this analysis: to have a parameter with which to test the attempted construction—without forgetting that even this has no pretext of being anything but one of what Tafuri would call the many possible "provisional constructions."

1
CRITIQUE OF UTOPIA

*I don't see it as a prophecy, but what I wrote fifteen years ago
in* Architecture and Utopia *has since become a rather normal
analysis. Utopias don't exist anymore. Engaged architecture, which
I tried to make politically and socially involved, is over. Now the only
thing one can do is empty architecture. Today, architects are forced
into either being a star or being a nobody. For me, this isn't really the
"failure of modern architecture"; instead, we have to look to what
architects could do when certain things weren't possible and when
they were.*[1]

Architecture and Utopia—the expanded and published book form
of Tafuri's long, 1969 essay "Toward a Critique of Architectural
Ideology," which first appeared in *Contropiano*[2]—is the cornerstone of any critical analysis of his historical construction as
applied to contemporary architecture.

The conclusion of *Architecture and Utopia* (and the section that
already distinguishes it from the various texts that comprise it)
focuses on what Tafuri considers "the 'drama' of architecture
today: that is, to see architecture obliged to return to pure architecture, to form without utopia; in the best cases, to sublime
uselessness."[3]

Such a categorical assertion, so weighty in its implications,
cannot help but question its original and fundamental reasoning.
Tafuri underlines the fact that many read "Toward a Critique of
Architectural Ideology" as a "homage to an apocalyptic attitude,

as a 'poetics of renunciation,' as the final pronouncement of the 'death of architecture.'"[4]

Yet for Tafuri it is fairly clear that this is not the correct interpretive framework.[5] How else, then, are we to understand *Architecture and Utopia*? Why was it that architecture lost the grace of being utopian over the course of its history? And who deprived it of such power?

In response to the last question, Tafuri offers a concise reply in the foreword: it is capitalist development that has robbed architecture of its utopian dimension. As Cacciari explains, "The science of capital assumes utopia as a foregone moment"[6]—and does so in the precise measure that architecture prefigures itself ideologically. This response opens the possibility of resolving the first question as well, provided that one assumes the implications and proceeds from a simple critique of architecture to a critique of architectural ideology. In fact, only in this last sense is it possible—through the liberation of ideology's incrustations (or rather, through its various constituent disciplinary ideologies)—to observe the reality of architecture and to understand the consequent reality of its role and tasks. If for Francesco Dal Co, in one of his earliest attempts at critiquing modern architecture's ideology, the moment when "reality becomes . . . the essential aspect of art and architecture" coincides with the Bauhaus,[7] for Tafuri a rethinking of the entire modern movement embraces a much broader period, and follows a much more convoluted and difficult path.

Yet before analyzing how a critique of utopia and an arrival at reality can be fully and positively understood, we must linger on the itinerary outlined by *Architecture and Utopia* and read it within the "theoretical context for which [*Contropiano*] spoke."[8] Outside of this context, most readers have failed to notice the organic insertion of Tafuri's essay amid the subjects that each issue of *Contropiano* tenaciously and insistently pursued.

As early as the first issue, which opens with an essay by Antonio Negri on Keynes's economic theories, followed by Mario Tronti, Alberto Asor Rosa, and an initial survey by Massimo Cacciari on dialectics,[9] it is clear that the magazine's core interests center on a rethinking of the historical conditions of the birth and development of capitalism, and the role of intellectual labor in political procedures and "class struggle." More generally, there was an attempt at analyzing and uncovering the shrewdness of ideology (understood in the way Karl Marx and Friedrich Engels used it in their *German Ideology*, as a structure of false intellectual conscience) and its consequential critique.[10] Within this landscape, utopia emerges in its full importance, beginning at the moment when "utopia, as the extreme limit of 'negative' thought, becomes an essential tool of capitalistic prefiguration."[11] Ultimately utopia paves the way for capital in the name of overcoming all contradictions. Yet in all these interventions, and the ones to follow, a lead role is reserved for contradiction and its unmasking, or its reworking whereby ideology becomes its herald. It is in light of this strategy of contradiction that we must understand Cacciari's essays on Hegelian dialectics and the genesis of negative thought.[12] These, in fact, are simply two sides of the same coin: romanticism on one side, Arthur Schopenhauer, Søren Kierkegaard, and Friedrich Nietzsche on the other, with Georg Wilhelm Friedrich Hegel and dialectics in the middle, as a divide. The problem lies precisely in such mediation: Cacciari writes, "The form of dialectics is the form of the negative asserting itself positively, of a productive contradiction."[13] To study dialectics, then, means to study the very form in which contradiction, or the negative, is reintegrated into the system, made useful in relation to it. This ongoing labor of synthesis, carried out by dialectics and then analyzed and criticized through the various solutions or oppositions, has historically developed over time. Such analyses comprehend the negative contradiction, or rather dialectics itself, within the structure of bourgeois capitalism as a necessary constituent element. Contradiction therefore is not a neutral but rather an ideological character of dialectics. It is from this point of view that dialectics, in turn, is also subject to critique.

But there is another figure reflected in *Contropiano* that Tafuri's essays in *Architecture and Utopia* fix upon in their specific architectural and urban planning facets: that of the disenchanted intellectual with respect to "the givens of reality, in all its ruthless conditionality."[14] This is the position Max Weber proposes in his methodological and political writings.[15] Weber suspends value judgments, creating a *freedom* from value: what results, Cacciari writes, is the "intellectual who recognizes the process of rationalization and specialization . . . the intellectual as an examiner of facts, necessary connections, objective meanings."[16]

The acceptance of this position—to "gaze relentlessly on the realities of life"[17] while taking it upon yourself to "destroy the myth of permanence and the meta-historical validity of values and institutions"[18]—and the attempt to make it one's own by accepting the world as it is, exposes the sheer tragedy inherent in this project. The disenchanted contemplation of contradiction is tragic indeed.[19] But solely from this, solely through the comprehension of the world's rationalization by industrial capitalism, does it become possible to establish (or reestablish) the old disciplines as the basis of a new, scientific plan. Once again, one must carry out a critique of the underlying ideology, liberate science from its suffocating grip, or, as Tafuri writes, radically reject "any and all compromises between science and ideology."[20]

"Anyone who cannot accept [the fate of our age] in a manly fashion," Weber writes, "must be told to remain silent and, without the customary public pronouncements of the renegade, simply return, without fuss, to the old churches, which will receive him back mercifully with open arms."[21] Tafuri heads toward this courageous acceptance of reality, of sober Weberian disenchantment (sober insofar as it bears its tragedy) in unison with the other intellectuals of the day united around *Contropiano*'s political project. From this multifaceted point of view it becomes clear why, according to Tafuri's preface to *Architecture and Utopia*: "We will always prefer the sincerity of him who has the courage to speak of that silent, untimely 'purity' over any mystifying attempts to dress architecture in ideological garb. Even if this 'purity' in and of itself hides yet another ideological motive, pathetic in its sheer anachronism."[22] As Tafuri well knows, the trap of ideology is all-enveloping and difficult to free oneself from. But the disenchanted "ought-to-be" (*dover-essere*) that he leans toward is due more to his unconscious naïveté than to an astute obfuscation. If "ideology is as useless for capitalist development as it is harmful from the laborer's point of view";[23] if utopia, as an operative reversal or opposite of ideology, as a "construction of destiny"[24] conceived "in the name of development"[25] (and therefore in its modern version of "capitalist-industrial utopia,"[26] in contrast with earlier bourgeois utopias) is, in turn, useless and harmful to both; then from an intellectual point of view, through the "tools of knowledge," we are consistently left with nothing but silence as an alternative to direct involvement in the political struggle. For Tafuri, acting out this disenchantment becomes a critical but not operative situation.

The essays Tafuri publishes in *Contropiano*, which are then reworked and elaborated for *Architecture and Utopia*,[27] create the argument for the antefact and analytical verification of his conclusion. The discontinuous and nonlinear course of reasoning indicates not classical utopias, but rather noteworthy centers of development in architecture and urban planning over the last two centuries, characterized by the contradictions generated by changed modes of production—that is, capitalist development—and various attempts to correspond with them, more often than not through utopian veilings or the denial of contradictions themselves. From the very start Tafuri points out this stumbling block: "To ward off distress, come to understand it, and assimilate its causes: this seems to be one of the main ethical imperatives of bourgeois art. It matters little if the conflicts, contradictions, and lacerations that generate this distress will be absorbed by some all-encompassing mechanism capable of temporarily reconciling those rifts, or if catharsis will ultimately be reached through contemplative sublimation."[28]

Bourgeois intellectuals (those more or less consciously allied with the capitalist system) aim to develop tools for contrast—tools that are as peaceful as possible, yet capable of canceling out the effects of such contradictions. Thus, Tafuri interprets the eighteenth-century tendency to view the city as natural as one of the first reactions against a growing awareness of its anti-organic nature. Assimilating the city into nature ideologically covers the existing, imminent clash between "urban capitalism in formation and economic structures based upon pre-capitalist exploitation and the use of fertile ground."[29]

For Tafuri this results in a myriad of architectural positions, from an autoptic approach to a scientific bent[30]—positions which, behind their apparent variety and differences, mask a substantial "Enlightenment realism."[31] This is precisely where eighteenth-century architectural culture reveals its ideology: "The process Enlightenment architecture carried out is a consequence of the new ideological role it assumed. Architecture must redimension itself while becoming part of the bourgeois city's structure, dissolving itself in the uniformity of preconceived typologies."[32]

According to Tafuri, it was Giovanni Battista Piranesi who initially and clamorously exposed Enlightenment ideology. Although Piranesi lies outside the time frame considered in this book, it is worth pausing briefly to examine his work in order to understand its underlying dynamics. It was Piranesi who drew the most consequential and piercing conclusions from the discourse on eighteenth-century realism, positing what Tafuri calls "the ideals of totality and universality"[33] that had until then been contained within architectural form, explicitly under the label of crisis. Tafuri's reading of Piranesi's famous plates from the *Campo Marzio* series aims to prove that typology as an element of order, of rationalization within the city, reveals itself to be the exact opposite. Piranesi's "discovery of contradiction as a pretext for salvation"[34] leads to his discovery that the "irrational and rational must stop being mutually exclusive."[35] (Within this critical framework we can discern Max Horkheimer and Theodor W. Adorno's *Dialectic of Enlightenment*, in particular the chapter "Juliette, or Enlightenment and Morality," dedicated to the Marquis de Sade, a figure Tafuri repeatedly returns to in relation to Piranesi and others.)[36]

In light of *Contropiano*'s core political project, which explores the genesis of negative thinking—the line of thinking that holds fast to contradiction[37]—Tafuri's intention is evident: he aims to set Piranesi within this history, or at least within its perspective. It is no coincidence that Tafuri openly speaks of negative utopia in relation to Piranesi's architecture.[38] He even goes so far as to interpret Piranesi's images and forms voluntarily, being conscious of the "silence of 'signs'"[39] that responds to the "silence of things,"[40] which Piranesi painfully exposed in his *Carceri*.

The first chapter of *The Sphere and the Labyrinth*, "The Wicked Architect: G. B. Piranesi, Heterotopia, and the Voyage," unifies Piranesi's *Carceri* and *Campo Marzio* in the historical mission to prefigure crisis by setting language itself into crisis.[41] Here subject and object—the subject's rights and the object's need to completely dominate[42] the former—are shown as coercively symbiotic protagonists of an endless clash. This is the world of capitalist production. Though it was historically still dawning, capitalism was already perfectly and effectively operating (as the "absolute alienation of the subject"[43] has proven). Tafuri explicitly evokes the effects: a world in which machines really do dominate; the mechanical universe—seen as a refined and endless succession of torture instruments—of the *Carceri*; "mechanical architecture,"[44] gear-driven machines or hermetic machines; homogeneous magnetic fields, jammed with foreign objects;[45] and the overall building complexes of the *Campo Marzio*. It is no coincidence that this is a *"typological negation . . .* an architectural banquet of nausea . . . a semantic void created by an excess of visual noise."[46]

Once again, the problem is already stated: Piranesi does not "adapt form and material"[47] and therefore does not hesitate to mask contradiction. Thus he does not so much set himself outside of the history of Civilization, as set himself on its negative side.[48] This is the substance of his negative utopia: a highly modern triumph of *principium individuationis*, which is simultaneously a negation of any overall order and every structure that transcends mere singularity; the "exceptions that do not confirm any rule . . . devoid of hierarchical organization";[49] and "prophecy of what will happen in the sphere of the bourgeois-capitalist administration of the city."[50]

As a negative utopia, *Campo Marzio*, like the *Carceri*, is at once a "project and a denunciation."[51] Tafuri's almost Weberian terms for such an ambiguous proposal are symptomatic: "Insofar as it is a disenchanted documentation of the impossibility of any univocal definition of language, [*Campo Marzio*]—projecting this situation into the past—sounds like a merciless satire on the infinite capacity of the late-baroque typology to reproduce itself metamorphically."[52]

Within Piranesi's "representation of an active decomposition,"[53] Tafuri also reveals the presence of its opposite: the "demand for language," a paradoxical revelation of its absence.[54] Once again "negation and affirmation cannot divide themselves. The 'naïve dialectics' of the Enlightenment are already surpassed."[55] Piranesi's dialectics lead us back, in the manner of Schopenhauer, to contradiction rather than synthesis. Or rather, the tragic nature of his representations responds romantically to the conflicting symbiosis of opposites. For Piranesi, opposites are the foundations of architectural language[56]—precarious, arbitrary, and yet unavoidable in their "relentless authority."[57]

To reassert—and, if possible, amplify—Tafuri's use of Piranesi, in *The Sphere and the Labyrinth* he parallels the discourse on negative utopia with that of a positive utopia that is present in Piranesi's *Prima parte di architetture e prospettive*, proposing thinkable yet unrealizable models: propositions as value, as positive anticipation, as the only adequate escape for an intellectual work that does not want to renounce and absolve a duty of prefiguration; imagination in all its ideological significance; a projection in the future of the "emergence of present contradictions."[58] If such affirmations expand the overall framework within which Piranesi is included, and constitute an in-depth analysis, they can also be included in the framework of Tafuri's more general construction.

It is precisely within this consequential logic that Tafuri posits Piranesi's diametrically opposed projection: "The Piranesian prophecy questions the functionality of intellectual work in the field of architecture, faced with the needs of the new bourgeois patronage. Insofar as it is a merely ideological, Piranesi's prefiguration . . . already posits, with incredible lucidity, the question of the dissolution of the professional architect . . . the extinction of architecture as intellectual work."[59] That this latter prophecy prevails over the former strengthens rather than disavows Tafuri's interpretive position. Where the principle of contradiction is already set into action, where the "discovery . . . of the negative, inherent contradiction to the real" occurs,[60] and where one "acknowledges the presence of contradiction as an absolute reality,"[61] contradiction will predominate. This is precisely what Tafuri sees as saving itself through "tragic Piranesian dis-enchantment."[62] He continues: "The greatness of his 'negative utopia' lies in his refusal to lay the foundation for, after such a discovery, alternative possibilities: in a state of crisis, Piranesi seems to want to prove, one is conflicted and true 'magnificence' lies in being able to freely accept such a fate."[63]

At this point, the dissolution of form and emptiness of mean-ing clearly reveal themselves as instruments of this "awareness ... accepted with such 'virility'"[64] (here the mutation of Weber's expression is obvious). Dissolution and emptiness "are, there-fore, the presentation of negativity as such."[65] This negative, however, cannot expect to act absolutely on its own negativity in any way: on the contrary, "the construction of a utopia of the dis-solved form ... constitutes a return to that negative, and the at-tempt to use it."[66] The dissolution of form is not equivalent to its complete disappearance, but rather its multiplicity of fragments, programmatic disorder, obtained through bricolage. Foucault's definition of heterotopia, which Tafuri applies to Piranesi's "discontinuous montage of forms, quotations, memories,"[67] only formally sidetracks the discourse from a negative utopia. In fact, for Tafuri, where positive utopia consoles, Foucault's heterotopia upsets, "destroying 'syntax' in advance, and not only the syntax with which we construct sentences but also that less apparent syntax which causes words and things ... to 'hold together.'"[68] Heterotopia for Tafuri is nothing but a negative utopia.[69] As he writes: "The Piranesian heterotopia consists precisely in making that contradiction speak out in an absolute and evident way."[70] "And no one wonders ... which contradiction. The tools of his trade exclude any such specification, reaching degrees of ab-straction that allow for multiple interpretations."[71]

The solid establishment of contradiction necessarily conflicts with the reduction of the "subject that recognizes the relativity of its own actions" to an "absolute 'solitude.'"[72] It is no coincidence that the Piranesian negative "will only reemerge, at intervals, within architecture during the Enlightenment as the sudden resurfacing of a suppressed guilt complex."[73] Nevertheless, the seed Piranesi sows will bear fruit. For Tafuri, it begins a voyage that will culminate amid infinite contradictions in the historical avant-gardes (which he came to call the "nihilism of negative utopia")[74] and the neo-avant-gardes of the later postwar period. The one consequence is that what was acceptable to Piranesi in a very early phase of capitalist development (including, paradoxically, his "transgressions") is for the architects of late capitalism transformed into complete impracticality, a desperate aphasia. Even transgression is denied, or at least reduced to the perfect indifference of gesture and to emptiness, the void, or the "deadly silence of the sign."[75]

This is not the best place to retrace, step by step, the entire development of Tafurian discourse. But it is worth noting that, from his point of view, "The end of utopianism and the dawn of realism are not merely mechanical moments in the ideological formation of the modern movement. Rather, beginning in the 1940s, realistic utopianism and utopian realism overlap and balance one another. The decline of social utopia leads ideology to surrender to the politics of things brought about by the law of profit. Architectural, artistic, and urban ideology are left only with the utopia of form, as a project for the recuperation of human totality in an ideal synthesis, the possession of disorder through order."[76]

The politics of things and the utopia of form thereby divide the architectural terrain, establishing an uncertain border. But, in turn, they also manage to find some hybrid, common ground. One is that of the avant-gardes, intent on exploding the many inherent *contradictions* in the system and enacting a reality in which older values are destroyed without being replaced by new ones.

Here it is worth considering the several pages Tafuri dedicates to such events, and to Dada in particular:

> *Dada goes right to the roots of Nietzschean thought. If the winds of global commodification have made all value anachronistic and every type of form ridiculous, then sinking into formlessness could end up being a way to "save one's soul." Subjected to the absolute rule of commodification, the city becomes anarchy: here, everything "familiar" is a lie; only the most unbridled forms of chance count for anything. With poetry composed of "words in liberty," pictures dictated by unthinking automatic gesture, or collages—photographic, like those of Raoul Hausmann, or of objects, like those of Kurt Schwitters—Dada exhibits not only the indifference with which courageous human beings look the reality of commodification in the face, but also the sheer emptiness that the end of all values (the Nietzschean "death of God") leaves in its wake. Jean Arp, Hausmann, and Schwitters annul the anguish that threatens to assail those aware of the fact that the signifier—the word—has lost all significance. The indifferent objects, which "float, suspended in the currents of the monetary economy," now become available: reduced to signs, they can be inserted into a process of continuous metamorphosis. This is Marcel Duchamp's ultimate aim when he mounts a bicycle wheel atop a stool, or lays a urinal on its back and calls it Fountain (1917). . . . Reality is "ready-made,'" already given. And yet this "yes" given to the real permits its transformation; makes it possible to act upon it.*
>
> *This is how the destructive work of the so-called negative avant-garde reveals its constructive side.*[77]

1.1
Kurt Schwitters, Merzbau
in Hanover, 1923–1927,
reconstruction 1983. ©
Artists Rights Society (ARS),
New York.

The centrality of the avant-gardes—starting from the loss of center they mirror—is thus reaffirmed not through a critique of form (or the formless) but rather through a critique of relationships that the avant-gardes establish with the productive system as a whole, which manifests itself as global commodification. The negative is not simply contemplated in its disarming inevitability; it is made active. Montage has a *passe-partout* for interpretation, and the small-scale reconstruction of an overall "universe-machine"[78] already recognized as such. But montage also exposes the "self-sufficiency of reality and the definitive repudiation of all representation by reality itself"[79]—a state that has certainly been achieved. The assumed domination of form thus absorbs the social function of utopia within personal, subjective experience. "The only utopia avant-garde art discovers it can offer is a *technological utopia*."[80] This utopia is of its own linguistic media, and is thus tautological.

Tafuri outlines the sum of this thinking in his analysis of the complex relationship between the avant-garde and the theater, or rather, in theater understood as a virtual city.[81] The attempts of the avant-garde theater to control the metropolis's formlessness by representing it scenographically—or translating it into various forms of building-theater—fail: "The 'total theater' as a form of counter-city was never realized, and not only for economic reasons: it was superfluous. The real city is already total theater."[82]

In the face of such a setback, and leaving reactionary positions aside, there is no other option but to overturn the previous discourse on irony, or retreat into hermetic silence. This points to new and unforeseen possibilities, but it also leaves an indelible sense of loss in its wake: "Utopia no longer lives in the city, nor does it live in the city's spectacular metaphor, unless merely as a game or a productive structure dressed up in the city's imaginary."[83]

But no univocal solution comes from this. An inexorable contradiction remains within advanced capitalism, amid equally present events and facts: forceful steps forward dictated by the transformation of economic functions into mechanisms of social control—increasingly all-encompassing, romantic, and regressive—slip backward in the direction of a utopia.

For Le Corbusier, architecture can still mediate between realism and utopia, between the rationalization of the home (the "house as a machine for living in") and the irrational hopes projected upon the salvation of the master plan (Plan Voisin or Ville Radieuse). For Ludwig Hilberseimer, however, only the single building cell and the urban organism remain. Those sole parts play a role in the architect's vision, where a "continuous chain of production,"[84] a continuous assembly line, connects the two levels—the identical gears of different scales that make up a "bona fide unity,"[85] a single enormous social machine.

This certainly saves Hilberseimer from "involving himself in the 'crisis of the object,'"[86] given that the organizational laws are the only things remaining to consider. One could object, however, that he is still entangled in the utopia of general and synthetic control, whose principal champion is invariably the architect himself. For Tafuri, Hilberseimer's resistance to any and all regressions compares with the interventions of Ernst May in Frankfurt, Martin Wagner in Berlin, Fritz Schumacher in Hamburg, and Cor van Eesteren in Amsterdam. Here in these "oases of order,"[87] in these islands of realized utopia, are the *Siedlungen*, which echo the profound nostalgia for the organic community Tönnies yearned for, against the cold and precise analyses of the metropolitan *Gesellschaft* accomplished by Simmel and Weber.

Nostalgia, which later reemerges as a privileged moment in Tafuri's critique of late postwar architects (from Kahn to the postmodernists), appears here for the first time within its most consonant framework, or rather, as a logically founded element.

1.2
Ludwig Karl Hilberseimer,
Hochhausstadt, Project for a
Highrise City, 1924. © The
Art Institute of Chicago.

In fact, it is only in light of the more general and structural critique of utopia that a critique of nostalgia (be it formal or social) can be fully understood. According to Tafuri, nostalgia is an unequivocal sign of a regression toward obstinacy and an equally useless refusal of the necessity of the intellectual and his role in contemporary society. Such a refusal manifests itself both as an inability to rationally read reality and as an incapacity to confront the irrationality ("improbability, multifunctionality, multiplicity, and lack of organic structure")[88] that lies within it, or rather, in the contradictory bosom of the modern metropolis.

There is no nostalgia, however, in Le Corbusier's Plan Obus for Algiers. On the one hand, "the urban structure as it is, in its physical unity and function, is a depository for a new scale of value."[89] Tafuri's insistence on the organic unit does not preclude him from seeing the positivity of contradictions, a reconciliation between the problematic and the rational, the heroic composition of violent tensions that emerge from the plan for the Algerian capital, where necessity finally merges with liberty.

Nevertheless, as Tafuri points out, the entire project assumes the character of a laboratory experiment: "And no possibility is given, for any laboratory model, to transform itself *tout-court* into a reality. But that is not enough. The generalizability of these hypotheses clashed with the backward structures they intended to stimulate. If the real need is to revolutionize architecture, in accord with the most advanced requirements of an economic and technological reality that is still incapable of coherent, organic form, it is no wonder that the realism of these hypotheses is assumed as utopia."[90] Localized settings, technologies, and patronage are all potentials, possible but not yet actual or realizable. In this way, utopia indicates a new point of balance (or imbalance). But this is quite a different utopia from that of the totality carried out through technology (insofar as it is conceived as a "continuous and perfect 'process of becoming'")[91] that still dominates the Plan Voisin and the Ville Radieuse. And it seems just as different from the utopia Kahn sought. Although, like Kahn, Le Corbusier makes a grandiose attempt at surpassing the modern tradition (at least in Algiers), overcoming this is still the equivalent of producing fissures within his well-ordered, highly rational *corpus*, just as for Kahn it is equivalent to enacting new (old) impossible syntheses.

It is significant that Tafuri titles the chapter in which he analyzes the plan for Algiers "The Crisis of Utopia: Le Corbusier at Algiers," because it is clear that crisis does not start here. In Algiers (to which Tafuri repeatedly returns in numerous writings to reiterate and emphasize its importance) Le Corbusier confronts the differences that inevitably comprise urban structure. The contradictions between technology and culture, architecture and nature, modernity and tradition are not mediated, but rather literally climbed over, like the bridge suspended over the casbah, between the residences in the hills and the corporate skyscrapers by the sea, thereby demonstrating the impossibility of reconciling one with the other. "It isn't a matter of canceling out all diversity, but rather ensuring that it can coexist and live together."[92] Furthermore, it is a matter of accentuating "the substantial 'difference' that secretly undermines the unity of the overall 'machine.'"[93]

Le Corbusier's Plan Obus is just the beginning. The Cité de Refuge, the Palace of Soviets, and the Unité d'Habitation in Marseilles all sanction a "break from fictive unity,"[94] and are posited as fragments of a thinkable yet unrealizable globality. This route, dotted with "discontinuities and fractures . . . interruptions, postponements, distortions,"[95] leads to Chandigarh, where urban planning limits itself to speaking "quotidian languages, the inevitably *conventional* jargon"[96] typical of planning and its attendant instruments. Meanwhile, three "'desiring' objects"[97]—the Capitol Building, the Parliament, and the Supreme

Court—inexpressible through such instruments, try out "a coded language, speaking in differences." An irreducible "tension informs the dialogue between symbols that have lost the codes that once gave them the value of names"[98] (and here one is implicitly left to take measure of what for Tafuri is the abyssal distance between Chandigarh and Dacca). This tension closes with the *main ouverte*, an ambiguous sign of human labor, of a "will to power" left temporarily suspended, "awaiting,"[99] but also arrested, the outer limit against which the will of the plan is shattered. "Thus the 'impassable utopias' of the 1920s and 1930s break apart; Le Corbusier's critique is now applied also to the disciplinary borders."[100]

The deterioration of utopia that Tafuri narrates does not end with disciplinary borders. In fact, many relapses lie ahead for architecture: "The proposals of the new urban ideology may be summed up as follows: architectural and super-technological utopianism; rediscovery of the game as a condition for involving the public; prophecies of 'aesthetic societies'; and invitations to institute a *championship of the imagination*."[101]

The *raison d'être* of such an "International [Academy] of Utopia"[102] can once again be found, according to Tafuri, in the failed confrontation with the "limits . . . imposed by the managing structures that oversee the various sector levels."[103] Utopia becomes the refuge for those who believe that here they can take cover from reality—from the reality of bureaucratic red tape or from real engagement and political intervention. This results, little by little, in a rediscovery of the avant-garde's traditional tools combined with a renewed "machinolatry" (machine idolatry) and an enthusiasm for the implicit potential of electronic calculators, spatial devices, disposable packaging of the electro-atomic age (Archigram); a complete faith in technology's capacity for climate control (Buckminster Fuller); an ironic attraction to the neometaphysical (Archizoom, Superstudio) and sci-fi (Kiyonori Kikutake, Metabolism); an earnest propensity for large-scale projects, which, not insignificantly, were termed a new dimension at the time (Kenzo Tange, Paul Rudolph, Jan Lubicz-Nycz);[104] research aimed at creating an improbable synthesis of prefabrication and informal aesthetics (Moshe Safdie); and a withdrawal into industrial design as a minor scale in which one can exercise complete control over the design process (the majority of 1960s Italian design).[105]

The problem is that through all these escape routes and evasive techniques, the real dimension of the "explosive contradictions of the metropolitan structures"[106] is carefully avoided—be it through sublimation into a cathartic irony, through imprisonment in the microenvironment of private life, or through aggravation to the point of losing any and all concrete outlines.

For the "'futurists' . . . 'separateness' [becomes] a sort of last shore upon which they band together to safeguard an unproductive autonomy."[107] It is unimportant, in this sense, that what now dominates them is basically a "nostalgia for the future"[108] rather than for the past, because both are rooted in the same terrain.[109]

So the fate, it seems, that the new urban ideologies have condemned themselves to—be they in the realm of architecture or industrial design—is, according to Tafuri, that of fighting a rearguard battle, deluding themselves while creating a tabula rasa. Sweeping away the mess with their presumed aesthetic rupture, whether alternative or radical, they deceive themselves by attempting to rid themselves of a system that, on the contrary, perfectly understands their attacks, reabsorbing them and, at most, marginalizing them. The result of the entire cycle of modern architecture (the ideology of the plan, including the ambiguous, contradictory, and utopian aspects lurking within it) is rejected by its heirs—and, on closer inspection, by its very protagonists as well—when faced with the "extreme consequences"[110] of the processes that the cycle helped trigger. As Tafuri concludes in

Architecture and Utopia, "Architecture as the ideology of the Plan is overcome by the reality of the plan once the latter, having surpassed the level of utopia, has become a working mechanism. The crisis of modern architecture began at the precise moment when its natural beneficiary—large industrial capital—overtook its fundamental ideology, setting superstructures aside. From then on, architectural ideology had exhausted all its tasks. Its obstinacy in wanting to see all of its hypotheses completed became either the impulse for surpassing outdated realities or an annoying disturbance."[111]

Tafuri's diagnosis could not be clearer: "The crisis of modern architecture is not the result of any particular 'tiredness' or 'dilapidation': rather, it is a crisis in the ideological function of architecture. . . . There is no 'salvation' to be found there anymore: not by running restlessly round the labyrinths of [architectural] images so multipurpose they are ultimately mute; nor by withdrawing into the surly silence of geometries satisfied by their own perfection."[112] Thus the critique of utopia intends to free the architectural discipline (in all its many articulations) from deceptive misunderstandings, false objectives, and, even more, anachronistic hopes. In this sense, it should be viewed as positive, as Tafuri sees it, rather than as apocalyptic, as its detractors do (this assertion nevertheless deprives them of the very ground on which they stand). All frivolous hopes of recharging architecture with symbolic or ideological value at this point—now that its functions and limits have been rigorously defined[113]—are pure nostalgia or, worse, regressively utopian attempts that refuse to come to terms with reality. "For this reason," Tafuri argues, "it is useless to propose purely architectural alternatives. The search for an alternative within the structures that condition the very character of architectural design is indeed an obvious contradiction of terms."[114]

Faced with an unfolding process of remote causes and close effects, Tafuri can only suggest proceeding in a direction that, in his view, is the only one left open to those who take a stand in relation to the reality of things: "Reflection on architecture, inasmuch as it is a criticism of the concrete 'realized' ideology of architecture itself, cannot but go beyond this and arrive at a specifically political dimension."[115]

This evidently cannot be understood as reopening the gates, yet again, to ideology's seductions: "From the critique of ideology we must move on to an analysis of planning techniques and the concrete ways in which they affect the modes of production: to an analysis, in other words, that now is only being attempted, with the necessary rigor and consistency, in the construction business."[116]

This leads to engagement, by which Tafuri does not intend to drag architects and intellectuals into foreign terrain, but rather to place them in the precise position into which capitalist development forces them: "To those who are anxiously looking to pin down the efficiency or output of critique, we can only answer by inviting them to become analysts of a precise economic sector, with eyes set on tying together capitalist development and the processes of reorganization and standardization of the working class."[117]

While for those who wish to actively work in those sectors "that hide behind the unifying categories termed art, architecture, [or] city,"[118] the only true alternative now is the scientific construction of a *contropiano*, or "counterplan." But this counterplan cannot be reduced to the mere distinction between good plans and bad. Once it has become a "new political institution"[119]—that is, once it abandons its old role as a "simple 'stage' of development"[120]—the plan, in order to be a counterplan, must embody the contradictions in which the real is interwoven. It must act on the imbalances, live up to them as swiftly as possible. To enact a dynamic development, an organized imbalance, through interventions that imply continuing structural revolutions—in other words, to go from the use of static models to the development of dynamic models—is to assume the fundamental directions gleaned from the critique of ideology and to turn them into political action.

The path Tafuri follows, however, is not that of direct political engagement. His historical construction of contemporary architecture nevertheless presents the critique of architectural ideology as an indispensable presupposition: an essential component of the "duty of awareness"[121] that inspires a conscious renunciation.

2
KAHN AS DESTROYER

The critique of architectural ideology that demystified the modern movement and its historical bases is perfectly explained by several factors: in the same years the critique was conducted, not only did the modern movement shift into a state of irreparable crisis, but Nikolaus Pevsner's presumed historiographic unity of the modern movement dissolved.[1] Tafuri counters the misleading certainties of this mythical construction with a historiographic operation aimed at systematically sectioning the vast field that falls under the modern movement, "in order to seek out, thread by thread, oblique line by oblique line, tangents and branches of the institutional world, that those multiple tendencies (contradictory in and of themselves) entail."[2] But if Tafuri's analysis of architecture after the modern movement appears methodically precise with respect to architecture—from his *Architecture and Utopia* to his sector- and subject-specific studies, that often assume an almost *choral*,[3] collaborative effect—his project of crisis, to the contrary, has a less systematic, more subjective structure. Nevertheless, his argument remains equally precise: "When we finally decide to objectively evaluate Louis Kahn's legacy within the international architectural debate, we'll realize, perhaps, that its effects have been much more destructive than constructive."[4] The beginning of the introductory essay to the catalog of the Italian exhibition of the New York Five is, in many ways (from a conceptual, though certainly not chronological, point of view), also the beginning of the construction of contemporary architecture as we know it; a construction whose final effects are now before our eyes.

This obviously does not mean that one can attribute the faults and merits of today's situation to Tafuri. Nor does it imply that he can be saddled with any direct affiliation to it (it would be improper and pointless to even consider such an idea!). Rather, it induces us to turn to his project of crisis (keeping in mind the impossibility of his ever being able to control and evaluate all its implications and developments), suspecting that this is precisely where we should seek the causes of present-day phenomena. My working hypothesis is that these phenomena seem to find in the project of crisis not only their best explanation, but the unmistakable imprints of their own genetic heritage, with all the uncertainty inherent in the genetic transmission to offspring of one or more hybridizations: the uncertainty factor that precisely such phenomena end up committing the worst betrayal of their presumed father.

Tafuri's first approach to Kahn's architecture aims entirely at teasing out the issues and contradictions, including those of previous critiques: "Kahn's oeuvre, in effect, lends itself to many interpretive ambiguities, and runs a rather noteworthy risk of repeatedly falling into an unwanted sort of paralysis. The quality of many of his works, the specific interest expressed in many of his proposals, and the clarity of some of his methodological propositions lead his critics to run the risk of making naïve interpretations, concentrating their analysis on those sole aspects that, in reality, are nothing more than a few details within a much broader and highly topical discourse."[5] In bringing the foundations of Kahn's architectural oeuvre into focus, however, Tafuri does not succumb to doubt or uncertainty. The clear, incontrovertible tone of his assertions (written before he turned thirty) foreshadows his later, more mature work: "Undoubtedly, within the realm of contemporary architecture, and not just American contemporary architecture, Kahn offers one of the most formidable examples of an attempt *to return to the expressive image*. . . . Furthermore, it is also clear that Kahn's entire line of investigation is a decisive turning point within the rather empty American formalism that recalls the pseudo-poetics of the *curtain-wall* and, in opposition to it, instead proposes a rigorous and often severe *intelligence of form*."[6] The analysis derived from this is less axiomatically peremptory, less final, yet because of this it is perhaps also more developed and open to nuance than his later analyses.

For Tafuri, what distinguishes Kahn from the already solidified tradition of the modern movement—and, in good measure, also helps to "launch not only . . . its marginal aspects . . . into a state of crisis"[7]—is Kahn's revision of the methodological and formal approach to architecture. Such a revision is supported by what Vincent Scully summed up in the poignant expression *the past as your friend*.[8]

And yet "a revisionist process, based upon a reconsideration of history, is by no means an unknown idea in postwar architecture."[9] In addition to J. J. P. Oud's Shell building, Tafuri cites as an example the large number of Italian architects responsible for bringing the relationship with tradition and history into the international debate, and thereby returning to some of the points ignored by the rationalist debate (the only name Tafuri explicitly and predictably mentions is Ernesto N. Rogers). But, rather than weakening Kahn's perceived criticality, this somewhat legitimate self-objection gives Tafuri the most penetrating and precise interpretive framework; if, in fact, Rogers and others sought "to gain a sense of the *general* relationship between the present-day operation and its historical background," as Tafuri writes, "for Kahn the problem is entirely different. . . . The past, before all else, is not a referential horizon, but rather a presence that, little by little, becomes increasingly concrete in [the form of] well-defined 'memories'; [the past] is a methodical support on par with direct 'quotation,' for a figurative expression that is often built around the original core that is in turn represented—depending upon the different needs of the contingent lines of investigation—by the memory of an ancient building, of an historic city, of an artistic period."[10]

The past is seen as a presence, then, as opposed to a straightforward horizon against which all contemporary phenomena are outlined. That the historical sources of Kahn's architecture lie in late Roman architecture (specifically that of Hadrian's reign) and in Piranesi's interpretation of it, though not necessarily original (even Scully, among others, has pointed this out), is useful to Tafuri at this point. It allows him to draw the conclusions that will ultimately become, with the exception of a few adjustments and rigidities to which we will return, his final judgment of Kahn's oeuvre.

If, for Tafuri, Kahn's choice of a Piranesian viewpoint already sounds "like a nostalgic yet measured appeal to some past order with a critical function toward the present,"[11] even more emblematic is his choice of a lineage reaching back to Hadrian: "An architecture . . . that is not a rigorous affirmation of a new way of seeing the world but that marks—even if reaching its own intrinsic and autonomous validity—the dissolution of an entire *Kunstwollen*, preparing the way for a different conception of artistic practice."[12] Basically, all that can be viewed as Hadrian-era detail in Kahn's work is the preventive acceptance of a few historical facts (in this specific case, the orders and methods of the modern movement), but only to critique them more deeply, from within. His attack on the late-modern world is therefore analogous to Hadrian's of late antiquity—analogous, but not exactly equal and in certain respects even opposite. For Tafuri, where Hadrian and his famous villa at Tivoli aim at "negating the univocal nature of

Form and the absoluteness of *Order*," Kahn searches for "a con-
cretization of the *Absolute*, of an *Order* that becomes *Design*."[13]

Here we come to the crux of the matter. Kahn's frantic quest
for an absolute order leads to an ongoing, irreconcilable contradiction. His architecture, in fact, represents a yearning for a "res-
pite against mobility, a fixed point of reference that summarizes
the many contrasting instances that coexist in a social and cultural order torn by growing contradictions, a *rootedness* and a *historicity*,"[14] that lies beyond the existing realm. In other words, it is
always possible to impose one's synthetic, creative will on form,
but it is more difficult, if not impossible, to transmit that desire
for total completion to society and those institutions whose architectural form represents their concrete faces.

Faced with such a clear contradiction, which he himself brings
to light, Tafuri nevertheless does not assume an intransigent
stance; rather than dismissing it as unrealistic, he penetrates the
heart of this contradiction and analyzes it. (This also casts a different light on his later, more marked position that seems to be
an a priori closure.) But then, the Tafuri of the early 1960s does
not yet seem conscious of the dangers of these Kahnian poetics.[15]
During these same years, Kahn had just begun to make his more
abstractly metaphysical work, to return for a moment to Tafurian categories—most notably the complexes at Ahmedabad and
Dacca.

The dialectic openness of Tafuri's critique—not broadly ab-
solving, but at least justifiable—thus ends up including and understanding this attempt at surpassing the intrinsic limits of
the capitalist system through architecture. Tafuri even ascribes
some of the more positive aspects of Kahn's work to them:

> *The creation of forms through a phenomenology of the
> real and the projection of this "real" onto a horizon that
> surpasses all limits imposed by present-day contingencies*

has its own highly significant function, even in a so-
ciety dominated by mobility, the rapid replacement of
structures, and the ongoing renewal and consumption
of forms in service of neo-capitalist myths. . . . The les-
son gleaned from Kahn proves that the disappearance of
the accentuated ideological stances that characterized
the heroic period of the modern movement can today be
substituted by an engagement that does not aim to revo-
lutionize the world through architecture, but rather takes
on its own space for exploration and investigation as
one of the many possible operative tools—and the more
rigorously these tools are analyzed, the more valid they
become.[16]

This almost political reading of Kahn's architecture (albeit a
politics stripped of its more movement-driven characteristics)
would seem paradoxical and contrived if the validated part of
Kahn's teachings were not accompanied by another, unacceptable part: "Beyond the continuous reference to history as a basis
for action—a reference we have criticized for the particular definition Kahn has generally given it—is the proposal of an objecti-
fication of architectural research and reference of architecture
to a meta-historical and definitively abstract realm that cannot
represent a sane methodology to pass on."[17]

In sum, a strategy that tends to divest itself of reality to focus
on forms already viewed as passé seems a potentially pernicious
approach. In fact, it is no coincidence, and even a bit too predictable, that the limits and perils of this method that Kahn privi-
leges fall onto the delicate and slightly less respectable shoulders
of his students and followers.

The Tafuri of 1968 still replies more decisively than does the
cautious Tafuri of 1964, who looks more toward possibilities
than anything else.[18] Within the broad—and in many respects

nonbinding—framework of *Theories and History of Architecture*, echoes of Kahn can be heard explicitly and implicitly throughout. And since the subject here is crisis (the crisis of architectural criticism, above all, but also of the architectural object, the project of critical attention, and history), Kahn's sheer omnipresence portends his active involvement, as a key protagonist in such processes. He can also be pointed to—as an ideal, and in his role as the noble father of less noble emulators—as the target of Tafuri's incisive observation (in the fourth edition foreword) on the ineffectual "brilliant gymnastics practiced in the prison yard of the model jail in which architects are allowed, temporarily, to roam freely about."[19]

But let us proceed in an orderly fashion. As early as the first few pages of *Theories and History*, we see Kahn's name grouped alongside those of an extravagant and seemingly dissimilar group: Claude Lévi-Strauss, Michel Foucault, and artists of American pop art. The relationship of such characters—from different places and with different interests—forms the crux of this new Tafurian interpretation. Lévi-Strauss's "ethnological structuralism,"[20] Foucault's "archaeology of human sciences," pop art's "antihumanist orgy," along with Kahn's search for a *"new objectivity,"* are, in fact, all positions that insist "upon one and the same ideal area . . . based upon an antihistorical knowledge and practice."[21]

Totally overturning—at least at first glance—his earlier reading, Tafuri now posits the issue of the antihistoricity at the very center of Kahn's oeuvre. But this is not the last of such surprises: the antihistoricity of Kahn's new objectivity, his "hermetic dive into the materials history has to offer in order to excessively dehistoricize architectural design,"[22] are nothing other than an updated extension of the traditional antihistoricism of the avant-garde. On the one hand, then, Kahn is seen as continuing the European avant-garde spirit, a provocative, even destructive sprit, with regard to canonical architectural language and form. On the other, paradoxically, this continuation is carried out—through a hermetic dive into the materials of history, as we have just seen—by using precisely the things and modes he intends to destroy. In short, Kahn arrives at antihistoricism carried forward through historicism.

This leads us to two levels of reflection. First, Kahn's historicist and antihistoricist definitions live side by side in *Theories and History* without irreconcilable contradictions. Second, more than a shift of interpretation, there is a radical shift in Tafuri's point of view from the position articulated in "Storicità di Louis Kahn." If in the 1964 text—as can already be intuited from the title—Tafuri was entirely focused on exploring the internal dialectic that lay within Kahn's reclamation of history and tradition, four years later he confronts the same problem in a completely different way. At this point, he argues for the failure of Kahn's univocal marriage to history and its consequences.

Thus, all manifestations of a fundamental (and not incidental) duplicity are of central importance to Kahn's oeuvre: namely, the subtle ambiguity inherent to Kahnian historicism[23] and the presumed guilt complex regarding history.

Why does Kahn betray the very thing he also espoused? And what could have caused such a guilt complex? These two questions are closely linked, since in reality—as seems clear in Tafuri's analysis—Kahn's guilt complex actually hides his betrayal. Above and beyond any other objective, the goal of what Tafuri calls Kahn's complex cultural operation is ultimately reduced to demonstrating the "ambiguous link that ties contemporary architecture to its historic sources."[24] Ambiguity as a programmatic limit is thus imposed on the relationship between history and design where history is exclusively used (or, better, exploited) for ends intrinsic to the project, and never with the aim of facilitating possible revivals or causing conflict with history.

If Kahn's betrayal lies in this underestimation of history and all its potential, then the reasons underlying his guilt complex become clear: everything he takes from history, limiting its realm of action, somehow seeks out reparatory compensation in an empty and excessive overexposure, which at times verges on abuse. In Tafuri's words: "In this sense, we can affirm that . . . for Kahn, history is nothing more than an *ingredient* to be manipulated. For him, it is useful only insofar as it justifies choices he has already made, or in order to semantically, allusively illuminate the discoveries of his references, values that aspire to [attain the level of] institutions and symbols, but at the same time want to make themselves felt and easily legible without betraying a code that refuses all permanent myths, symbols, and institutions."[25]

We will soon see what these considerations imply. But first we must emphasize that this attempt to bring Kahn's ambiguity to a level of greater involvement and rigor—the hypothesis that this could denounce the unresolved dilemma between the tradition and modernity of American architecture—is, admittedly, carried out by Tafuri and then essentially left on its own. The vehemence of this denouncement cannot be reconciled with indifferent display, with any kind of cover-up through evocative theoretical baggage—in short, with the detachment Kahn often flaunted. Rather, the new objectivity is relaunched and fortified by his detached demeanor. This objectivity was not formal or ideal in the least (basically, it has little or nothing in common with *Neue Sachlichkeit*), but, rather, procedural, and characterized by a high "capacity for rendering the path leading to architectural communication, in all extensions of its complex structures and articulations, both objective and verifiable." This task of imperturbable abstraction ends up, according to Tafuri, acting directly upon formal principles, rather than on the analysis of their genealogical roots. "The critical value of Kahn's work is not, then, aimed at historical material, but rather at the manipulation of form that the less advanced currents of the modern movement brought about."[26]

Here we return to the problems we recently put on hold. Kahn's aspiration to arrive at values that look to "institutions and symbols, and at the same time want to be felt and easily legible without betraying a code that refuses all permanent myths, symbols, and institutions,"[27] hints at an ambiguous approach. It simultaneously accepts and refuses a solidified, traditional realm of reference, and reduces historical criticism to an illusory, merely superficial game. Here, once again, we can recall the symbiotic coexistence of historicism and antihistoricism in Kahn's work, a point that Tafuri more or less openly emphasizes. As we have already seen, the question is not just an issue of terminology. If antihistoricism (or, perhaps more aptly, the surpassing of a concept of historicity)[28] was the only way the avant-garde could historically legitimize and situate itself within history, Kahn's antihistoricism stems from a rather different source: in his case, we have to speak instead of the antihistoricism of historicism. Any attempt to "purify the permanent, unrepeatable, even mythical values of architectural objects"[29]—which is on a par with yearning to reinsert such objects into a system of urban values, as occurred naturally in the historical city—is antihistorical in the development of architectural planning and urban reality during the twentieth century. In short, Kahn's historicism is basically antihistorical in relation to the antihistoricism of the modern movement.

To step out of Tafuri's labyrinth for a moment, we might wonder how everything traces back to the concreteness of Kahn's architecture. While the historical dialect, despite its internal contradictions, maintains a comparable design philosophy (from the Philadelphia Civic Center to the Laboratories of the Richards Medical Institute, to name two examples), Kahn's

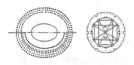

2.1
Louis Kahn, Philadelphia Civic
Center, 1956–1957. Aerial
perspective drawing.

second-order antihistoricism does not immediately assume a more concrete form in a design-oriented or architectural work.[30]

Here we must be extremely careful, for it is, in fact, through the aforementioned attempt to accentuate the value of form (and the value of geometry, materials, and spatial layouts) that Kahn opens his debate with the modern movement. This debate is precisely what the Ahmedabad, Dacca, and Islamabad building complexes bring into discussion, and, according to Tafuri, therein lurks Kahn's destructiveness. Tafuri chides Kahn not because his work represents the end of the modern movement (or at least the movement's definitive overtaking and ultimate obsolescence), but because the solutions he points toward signal the phantasmagorical return of long-worn, empty values. These values are an illusion, at least from Tafuri's point of view, of bringing to life a truly synthetic, expressive, communicative, speaking form, capable of reviving something long defunct. It is a "collective memory"[31] (or, perhaps more simply, a collectivity), indispensable to places of cult worship, such as major institutions, museums, universities, capital complexes. Their realization is Kahn's clear calling. "To find new public symbols"[32] is the hubris to which he perilously exposes himself; for those who still count on a new beginning, Kahn's oeuvre seems lethal.[33]

A rereading of this passage by Tafuri and Dal Co in *Modern Architecture* is worthwhile:

> *This closes [down] any and all space left for the myth of the eternal return of the sacred principles of the tradition of the new, and opens up the ineffable space of the narrative of nostalgia. This is a nostalgia for a sign that runs throughout its history, in search of the moment, lost in the labyrinth of an unspeakable history, in which it has lost even its own referent; a nostalgia for the multiple universes of discourse that architecture can no longer*

explore without giving up its own presence in the world;
a nostalgia for the reassuring relationship between the
rules and [their] transgression, capable of unleashing
from the alembic, through which ruptures and lacera-
tions are distilled, a circularity of the word, a fullness of
the word, a globality stemming from an awareness of its
own limits. Nostalgia *is what differentiates Kahn's view*
on institutions from the celebratory acts carried out by
his contemporaries. [34]

When we compare this to the first text on Kahn, the tone—even more than the content—changes quite a bit. The "nostalgic but also measured evocation of a past order"[35] has now become an unfulfillable yearning, steeped in nostalgia for the "myth of Or-der"[36] that Tafuri presents in *Theories and History*. But, above all, it is Kahn's rebellion against what Tafuri views as the unavoid-able destiny of modernity that rouses his disdain: "Kahn's oeu-vre explicitly lashes out against the logical impasse that lies at the very center of modern architecture, against the reduction of architecture itself to a 'minor subject.' But this would mean subtracting all values from history's process of becoming, morph-ing them into symbols, trying to recover everything arcane within it."[37] Challenging the course of history (armed with his-tory's weapons, even), battling "against the 'loss of the center,'"[38] attempting a "desperate recovery of the mythic"[39]—these are the chief accusations Tafuri launches, with merciless precision and relentless insistence, from *Theories and History* to *The Sphere and the Labyrinth* to *Modern Archtiecture*, with "Les bijoux indiscrets" in between.

Again it is necessary to distinguish and listen closely to the tones and accents of Tafuri's progressive critique if we are to understand its true nature—and with it, perhaps, the true, un-derlying reasons and logic. Architecture as a minor subject takes shape as a theme in *Theories and History*, in which it is a central, albeit occasionally fleeting, benchmark. In comparison to the rather dry, even scolding lecture in *Modern Architecture* (taken up once again—with a few significant variations—in *The Sphere and the Labyrinth* and "Les bijoux indiscrets"), the debate on Kahn's opposition to the minor, dismissible nature of architecture in *Theories and History* has much richer motives and nuances. It begins closer to the root of the issue, with the problem of distinct perception,[40] to which Kahn, along with Boullée, Le Corbusier, the constructivists, and many others repeatedly returned, as opposed to confused perception, which was followed by the romantics and the expressionists. Ultimately, after a convoluted journey, it considers Benjamin's "detached observation."[41] It is only when faced with this problem that Kahn's architecture retreats into a backward march—but does so in order to exercise an uncommon right to freedom: "Their assault—with all the weight and allusiveness of images and structures—upon the common rhythms of daily existence, their emphatic allusions to a space different from, if not entirely in opposition to, that of shared everyday life, their having closed themselves within the realm of their own forms, [all] express a desire for self-protection against any and all actions of the outside world, enclosing themselves within the *hortus conclusus* of a self-sufficient mechanics of form."[42] This seemingly aggressive (or at least off-putting) behavior is triggered, as Tafuri points out, by a fear of participating in a process that is resolved entirely through use and consumption. In light of this intuition, many other points are easily explained—not least of which are the many, even second-rate, antihistoricist historicist strategies that Kahn brings onto the scene. Kahn's position is not, therefore, a choice made in favor of tradition or against the modern movement as such, but rather a choice made to distance his architecture as much as possible from dreaded consumability. "These, then, are architectures that do not want to be consumed, that want to impede the realization of a careless use, and that, in consequence, do not allow themselves to disappear as 'objects,' as 'things.' They want, instead, to reconstruct an 'aura' around themselves."[43]

Brought back into these terms (which are entirely apt and pertinent in this case), Tafuri's analysis grasps the distinction between Kahn's investigation and those of his predecessors and contemporaries. Tafuri's final verdict is equally succinct: "And yet, regardless of his intent, [Kahn's architecture] never manages to reestablish a condition of gathering with regard to the complex dynamics of their images: they never manage to sink into the viewer, to use Benjamin's words."[44]

If all this seems complete and final, then the evolution of this analysis (which circles around the same main arguments) is not immediately explicable. Its evolution toward a critical harshness has no clear motive. What really happens, between one moment and the next? More than an adjusted critical judgment of Kahn's work, one might hypothesize that this is instead a different way of considering its effects. What is really at stake is the role Kahn is given (more than the role he actually played). In a way, Tafuri projects his expectations of Kahn's possibilities as a way out from the impasse of the modern movement. The hopes Tafuri places in the salvation of Kahn's architecture progressively shrink. Whereas *Theories and History* already signaled, with respect to "Storicità di Louis Kahn," a partial darkening of those hopes, Tafuri's later writing clearly signals an almost angered disillusionment. Kahn's failure therefore seems that much more searing, precisely because Tafuri believed so deeply in his work, and had supported it. (Perhaps Tafuri himself had held onto some expectation of a new beginning?) The disillusionment, in this sense, resounds bleakly. Kahn does not represent a missed opportunity so much as a single-handed destroyer of any possible positive redemption of the modern movement. That makes him even more guilty, in Tafuri's view. In fact, Tafuri increasingly sees a growing concentration of the most fatal symptoms around Kahn and his work: from wanting to transform utopia into reality, thanks to the contemporary city's welcoming of any and all things, including contradiction, as part of itself; to promoting an "architectural 'refoundation' . . . just as artificial as the myths and institutions it relies upon";[45] to, finally and most damning, "selling out to the highest bidder" the entire heritage of myths and institutions so miraculously rediscovered at the height of the modern crisis—myths and institutions in which Kahn even claims to believe: "His message masks, behind the façade of an uncommon formal sureness, readily available ideas: his values and his forms are at the mercy of any and all possible exploitation, they can serve any and every end."[46]

To return to the central argument of Tafuri's critique: if, from the moment consumability embodies the triumph of capitalist ideology, it is an enemy to be fought (a common enemy, theoretically speaking, of both Kahn and Tafuri), then Kahn's fault lies precisely in his betrayal of this common cause, if not (more extremely) in his becoming a veritable traitor and joining the enemy's side—transforming the architectural project into a consumer good, or, in other words, into merchandise. Kahn's unkept promise, then, is the unmasking of capitalist ideology and a critique of the architectural ideology that necessarily comes along with it. For Tafuri, Kahn could operatively have produced as much as Tafuri did on a theoretical (or even historical) level. But faced with such a supreme task, Kahn ends up being fatally naïve, or at least deplorably disinterested, disengaged. Kahn ultimately surpasses and consequently criticizes the modern movement's ideological rigor, but merely in order to empty it of any ideal significance or influence. He substitutes it instead with manipulable forms and messages, realizable utopias.

Kahn certainly is not held solely responsible for the causes of this crisis, but he is considered the most responsible, insofar as he was the most talented among his generation of architects and the closest to fulfilling Tafuri's hopes. It is precisely because of this that Kahn's wasted opportunities and failed objectives are seen as the most destructive.

3
THE PULL OF THE VOID

Tafuri's analysis of Kahn's work in *Modern Architecture* varies only slightly from that in *The Sphere and the Labyrinth* (and "Les bijoux indiscrets"). While these variations might appear insignificant, they are nevertheless essential in understanding the problems presented here.

Between his vehement denouncement of the nostalgia in Kahn's architecture and his attack on the unimportance of architecture as the main aporia of modernity,[1] Tafuri inserts another, rather different order of considerations:

> And yet the search for the lost word ended up, inevitably, in another loss. What European observers have almost always undervalued in Kahn's work is the profound Americanness of his desperate attempt at salvaging [architecture's] mythic realm. The fact that the underlying myth lacked any shared foundations is just one of many disquieting aspects of Kahn's project. His work, as if part of some sort of compensatory rite, proceeded, paradoxically, to closely connect the regeneration of the architectural word to the artificial creation of a myth of the institution. It once again proposed (in absolute discretion and wholly unchecked by any external references) a new oath in blood between the architectural word and institutions. Kahn believed—despite himself—that he could make sense of the cornerstone of radical architecture's

> *poetics. From the Yale [University Art Gallery] to the National Assembly at Dacca, we witness a reiteration of his quest for an architecture of analogy.* [2]

The clarification of Kahn's yearning for the unfounded myth of institutions is accompanied by two other themes: Americanness and analogy. Not coincidentally, both correlate to postmodernism. Tafuri does not use the term Americanness here merely as a neutral geographic or cultural indicator. Rather, he deploys it as a synonym for an impractical, superficial attitude, lacking any substantial roots and credibility (an attitude that could be detected in the peculiar mixture of pomposity and irony unique to postmodern American architecture). His reference to analogy leads in the same direction. The analogical criteria recall a universe of nexus points implying true or (more frequently) presumed affinities, resemblances, and correspondences between material forms and abstract, symbolic meanings; or they create a striking short circuit between different, incompatible levels of communication and language. Essentially, Kahn's argumentation follows the same path, albeit via a less noble and more elaborate route—via postmodern architecture.

The suspicion that, over time, Tafuri's reading of Kahn gradually approaches an assimilation of the nascent, yet already detectable, postmodern experience [3] is borne out by a second, significant and explicit assimilation of Kahn and Venturi. For Tafuri, juxtaposing their names is not tantamount to confusing their roles and specificities, nor does it diminish their differences. Rather, it allows Tafuri to focus on both in greater detail, and realize the radical contrasts between the two. Nevertheless, in his view, they both share certain conditions ("two opposing hypotheses for reestablishing modern architecture"), [4] just as they share the similar effects of their respective work—to such a degree that, in *Sphere and Labyrinth*, Tafuri references them both when condemning Kahn's architecture: "both Kahn and Venturi acted in a way that was much more destructive than it was constructive."[5]

To understand the implications of this critical stance (as it clearly is, since Kahn and Venturi cannot be grouped together stylistically or generationally, nor does the master-pupil relationship justify panning them both), we will again have to return to the origins of Tafuri's thought—this time, his ideas as they specifically relate to Venturi.

The space reserved for Venturi in *Theories and History of Architecture* is much narrower than the in-depth treatment given to Kahn (which is also quite logical, given their respective biographies). Despite this, its content is in many ways more emblematic. Before touching upon (and quickly concluding) Venturi's case, Tafuri lingers on the emergence (or reemergence) of significant form as an issue in architecture in the 1950s and 1960s, an expression used "to describe a search for a new density in the architectural image."[6] This type of critical yet operative approach questions the significant value of the image. The ambiguity, Tafuri notes, lies "in the attempt at establishing an artistic language beginning with research aimed at bringing certain reading techniques into focus."[7] It clearly confuses roles, but it is also outrageously tempting, in his view, to play with meaning by simply being distracted with form. This is precisely where Venturi steps onto the stage:

> *A more recent example of this kind of misunderstanding is the sort an in-vogue architect like Robert Venturi fell into in* Complexity and Contradiction in Architecture.
>
> *Venturi exalts ambiguity in a way that at first glance might seem stimulating. Only later, after observing that the tensions, contradictions, and complexities in his*

historical analyses become all-purpose critical param-
eters—adapted to explain Blenheim Palace by John Van-
brugh and the double churches by Ferdinando Fuga in
Calvi dell'Umbria, as well as the works of Frank Furness,
Edwin Lutyens, Francesco di Giorgio, Louis Sullivan,
and Alvar Aalto—does one discover that this adoption
of the concept of "ambiguity" in works of art (taken and
mutated from William Empson's and T. S. Eliot's analyt-
ical texts) aims to justify personal design decisions that
are more equivocal than ambiguous.

Naturally, over the course of his treatment of the
subject, Venturi has the chance to make many timely
observations on the structures of complex architectural
organisms, uncovering the more or less evident cultural
matrices that helped shape them. What I am criticizing
is, on the one hand, the mechanical historicization of
architectural ambiguity, which becomes an a priori cat-
egory devoid of any meaning that is not entirely generic;
and on the other, the finalization of its investigation,
which—through a historiographic leveling and confusion
between the analysis and methods of architectural de-
sign—is bent to justify personal, figurative choices. Apart,
of course, from the great modesty of Venturi's designs and
realizations. . . . Venturi's book adopts "fashionable"
analytical methods and transforms them, without any
mediation, into "compositional" methods. Thus the val-
ues of ambiguity and contradiction lose their historical
consistency and are repurposed as the "principles" of a
certain type of poetics.[8]

The charges here, as in Kahn's case, are quite weighty. First, Tafuri accuses Venturi of using a critical approach conceived and

utilized for his own end. Additionally, he is found guilty of riding the wave of fashion, if not overtly contributing to launching the fad himself. Later we will see how this association of architecture and fashion (the latter is understood as certain rapidly spreading behaviors and styles that fall out of favor just as quickly as they rise) is a cornerstone of architecture's recent evolution. But now it is important to see how Tafuri's perception of the innate danger of this relation is proof of his early intuition of the role and fate of the current architecture, especially when the tendency to reduce architecture to mass consumption is connected with Tafuri's interpretation of Venturi's poetics. This is why Tafuri views Venturi's contradiction as suspiciously unfounded. None of contradiction's devastating character—beginning with its heated critique of ideology—survives in the apparently neutral, ahistorical, and "multitasking" category Venturi outlines. In this neutralization and inflated usage Tafuri glimpses—barely masked behind the outlines of cultural discourse—the mystifying action of capitalist ideology.

Tafuri also attacks Venturi on ambiguity. Here one cannot forget that this same topic was also part of Tafuri's critique of Kahn. It is a topic that, aided by such flexible usage,[9] for Tafuri connotes an effective uncertainty and confusion, rather than a controlled rule over design complexities and contradictions. But if Kahn's ambiguity is inherent to his historicism, then Venturi's ambiguity is entirely suprahistoric. Yet in this antithetical relationship, Tafuri identifies a possible parallelism. After all, Venturi's approach to architecture is equally antithetical to Kahn's: in Venturi, "there are no longer any fanciful communicative ambitions; architecture has dissolved into a de-structured system of ephemeral signals."[10] The distance between Venturi and Kahn could not be vaster: "In lieu of *communication* comes a flow of *information*; in lieu of architecture as language comes an attempt to reduce it to a mass-medium, without any ideological residue;

in lieu of an anxious effort to restructure urban systems comes a disenchanted acceptance of the real, to the point of cynicism."[11]

This is the key Tafuri uses to unlock an understanding of Venturi's work. At the same time he also uses it to counter its demands. According to Tafuri, behind the apparently unequivocal, evident formula of Venturi's message—"a disenchanted acceptance of the real, to the point of cynicism"[12]—lie hidden traps that must be carefully untangled and disarmed, to use the formula without risking misunderstanding or false expectation. If, in fact, one were to read it literally, the formula would not only represent present-day architecture in its entirety, or at least its latest victors, but it would consequently and directly link Venturi and his architecture to the present, making him a perfect contemporary of our time. Instead, everything separating present-day architecture from Venturi's architecture precisely measures the distance between a disenchanted acceptance of the real and a *mise en scène* (accurate and credible as it might be) of the real.

The problem lies entirely in how one understands the real. Going back to Tafuri: "Kahn's promise—communication is possible if the institutions are given a voice—was answered by Bob Venturi's statement that the only institution that exists is *the real, and that's what's speaking.*"[13] At first glance, the abandon, as Tafuri represents it, with which Venturi greets "the idea of America *just as it is*, of objects *just as they speak*, of goods *just as they govern [us]*,"[14] effectively approaches immediate actuality. But such a flamboyantly pop idea (as would become clear in the 1980s, through Venturi and other postmodern works) is still a mediation; one must not be deluded or confused here. Venturi's reality is Edward Hopper's, Andy Warhol's, and Walt Disney's reality. It is the reality of Las Vegas; in other words, it is more a hyperreality or surreality than a *bona fide* reality.

Tafuri clearly understands this, since he writes of "Bob Venturi's affected, purposeful irony."[15] On the other hand, the

3.1
Venturi, Scott Brown and
Associates, Inc., Monument
in Marconi Plaza, Philadelphia,
1985. Courtesy Venturi, Scott
Brown and Associates, Inc.

alliance between Venturi's "new architectural realism"[16] and pop art (though in decline) would be inexplicable if not for a hint of something greater than straightforward reality—"subtle games of split personalities with the masks of the real."[17]

With this it is clear that architecture's course of development is in fact the one indicated—at least conjecturally—by Tafuri. From Kahn's feasible utopias to Venturi's "sanctification of the banal,"[18] architecture's drift between the 1960s and 1970s seems clear: a progressive yet inexorable shift from the pompous discourse of shattered ideological bits left over from the modern movement, to the increasingly improbable scripts written within the huge warehouse of triumphant capitalism. The distance from dream to reality may be small (and the reawakening all the more brusque), but it is never as small as the space separating Kahn from Venturi. In other words, if one's dream is crudely realistic, then the other's reality looks astoundingly like a dream.

Yet again, the most useful clues come from the dialectical relationship Tafuri establishes between Kahn and Venturi. By acknowledging that both operate within what he terms an "exclusively linguistic problem,"[19] Tafuri reveals the radical depreciation of language in Venturi's work: "The meaning of the advertising world must not be looked for in external reference points. Thus Venturi obtains a result that is the polar opposite of the result reached by those more rigorous about composition. The latter [sought] a metaphysical recovery of the 'being' of architecture as extracted from the flow of existence; in Venturi's work, the nonuse of language—once its inherent ambiguity has been discovered and come into contact with reality—renders any and all pretenses of autonomy illusory."[20] This does not mean, however, that there is an unbridgeable gap between Kahn and Venturi. Venturi's nonuse of language, the fact that he lets things have a voice just as they are (although only after carefully selecting and screening them, to the point where nothing is left to real-world chance), parallels Kahn's hypermannerist use of language. Tafuri's tone as he makes this discovery approaches an involuntary irony: "For someone who wanted to overturn Kahn's rigorousness, Venturi sure understood many of its underlying motives."[21] Yet Tafuri's conclusions are anything but ironic: "Kahn could have produced a school of mystics without any religion to defend, and Venturi could have produced a school of the disenchanted with no values to violate. But both take part in the same ideology of self-reflection. That is, both go beyond their own histories to embody an attitude that was widespread among the fringes of lost intellectuals who made their homeland in exile. . . . They turned their eyeballs inward, facing the eye sockets, in order not to be blinded by a universe in which one's gaze risks being extinguished."[22] This flight toward the interior, toward the ideology of self-reflection—on which Tafuri sees both Kahn and Venturi, architecture's protagonists who move beyond the Americanness of the modern movement, agreeing—evidently could not occur in these terms if Venturi were a straightforward mirror of reality. It would be even less possible if, with a merciless sense of security, he were to overcome the ideology of reality. (The same would hold true for Kahn, if he were to turn to the grand forms of utopia rather than to their emptied simulacra.)

Yet these limits only define the outlines of Venturi and Kahn's operations. They do not change their substance in the slightest. For Tafuri, this substance shows its true colors only after a well-played masquerade—in a morality lacking any sense of ethics: "In the reversal carried out by Kahn and Venturi, it is fairly insignificant that the material of their new imaginary consists entirely of the dreams of nonexistent institutions or nightmares dominated by masses of transient icons of cosmic commodification. Both pursue a type of work on a par with that of the exorcists of the Inquisition. The architect-inquisitor is always on familiar terms with evil: that is precisely where Kahn's order without any center and Venturi's overly ambiguous ambiguity come to a fluctuating point of convergence."[23] Everything we have seen thus far allows us to look more closely at "the basic given that . . . characterizes the deep-seated matrix"[24] of such investigations otherwise marked by clear differences: "a reversal of architecture, which legitimizes the idea of diving into the bottomless pit of formal autonomy."[25] The fact that this reversal, or rather ideology of self-reflection, reaches a supposed formal autonomy eloquently expresses how Tafuri situates Kahn and Venturi on the edge of an abyss: a void that swallows up not only the misunderstood assumptions of the modern movement,[26] but all hopes of critically surpassing those misunderstandings. This is essentially the same void Foucault speaks of,[27] although Tafuri sketches it as simply the process of reducing architecture to the easily neglected object. Curiously, this process (or trend) occurs at exactly the same time that the architectural object—in all its physical, material, and perceptive aspects—is growing ever more garish, and is literally impossible to overlook. Instead of being an internal contradiction within Tafuri's discourse, however, this trend actually reinforces it.

But what does this reduction of architecture to an easily neglected object really mean for Tafuri? When he uses this expression for the first time in *Theories and History of Architecture*, he does not explicitly specify what he means. In the second chapter, dedicated to architecture as an easily neglected object and the state of crisis that has befallen critical attention, he immediately notes an "oscillation between a type of communication aimed at absorbing the field of criticism into its artistic structures, and figurative formulations that are increasingly aimed at substituting a rigorous 'construction of form' with pure images":[28] the characteristic aporia of contemporary art.

The trajectory of art and architecture—from the Renaissance to today, which, Tafuri claims, passes through a decisive avant-garde period—has gradually led to an increased consumability and ambiguity of the object, to the point of its complete destruction.[29] This crisis of the object coincides with architecture's transformation over the course of the 1960s into a happening, an event (one cannot help thinking of the experimental British, Japanese, and Italian neo-avant-garde groups: Archigram, the Metabolists, Archizoom, and Superstudio). Yet it is also evident that their work represents little more than the final act of a more complex development that reaches its height in Piranesi, Étienne-Louis Boullée, Antonio Sant'Elia, Bruno Taut, and Ivan Ilich Leonidov, to name just a few.

This progression of event-based architecture—architecture made of a unique, unrepeatable here and now, of a singularity in which formal and objective outlines tend to paradoxically dissolve into pure potentiality (in which, curiously, there is virtual symbiosis embodied in the fictional realm of graphic representation)—is therefore easily overlooked due to the very characteristics it connotes. "From the drawings of the neo-avant-garde, . . . from the attempts at integrating the mass media with playful and cybernetic utopias, from vitalistic neo-Romanticism . . . we get only 'demands.' Hence," Tafuri deduces, "we are left solely with ideas destined to remain on paper."[30] Even while the architectural object is becoming more easily neglected because of its reduction to pure image, another equally important phenomenon is taking place: the architectural object becomes more easily overlooked because of its reduction "to a mere typology."[31]

These two phenomena, which initially seem antithetical, may actually intersect to become a single, unique object. The alternative Tafuri points out (a work "so open that it self-destructs as a finished, recognizable structure" or a work "so closed that it is reduced to a totally empty object")[32] ends up looking compatible, if not overtly composed of temporally different, alternate states of the selfsame work. In both cases, a void (a close relative of the aforementioned type) results that dominates in formally indefinite periods (of self-destruction) as well as in periods of claustrophobic closure (or self-referentiality).

Tafuri sees Kahn's work as a rebellion against this void. But it is not surprising that it is precisely Kahn's failure to fill this void that has the opposite effect of bursting it open wider. Remember Tafuri's warning that "this quest for the lost word necessarily ends up creating an additional loss."[33] Kahn's implicit, parallel critique of the serialization of the International Style and the showy utopianism of the neo-avant-gardes leads to nothing more than this. As a result, his architecture echoes equally vacuously, perpetually undetermined between the large, memorable gesture and the quest for solutions that, over time, can neither avoid repetitiveness nor steer clear of the standard. It must be noted that the emptiness, the void that emanates from his work, is "built" with arms of massive concrete. Indeed, as Tafuri quotes Gerhard Kallmann, "in its physical concreteness, in the solidity of 'the built,' Kahn's work strains to confirm its own identity and existence in order to counter the very real terror of nothingness."[34]

This result—despite appearances—is not so different from that of Venturi's work. To be sure, "whereas Kahn dreamt of an earthly resurrection, Venturi championed a wary sense of abandon."[35] But, no less than Kahn's pseudomonuments, Venturi's snobbish antimonuments elevated to the status of "American kitsch"[36] show all the shortcomings of seeking to "reduce the contradictions of present-day America to a problem of taste."[37] In Venturi's work the void is not obscured—on the contrary, it is flaunted, but a massive dose of irony is certainly not enough to fill it with any degree of content. In fact, Tafuri diagnoses the situation years later: "Venturi thought he was ironic, but in reality he ended up more like Mickey Mouse than anything else."[38]

In other words, Venturi ends up not so much as unreal, but as having the depth of a cartoon.

The same degree of depth characterizes Las Vegas. Here Venturi finds not only the field to which he applies his timely urban analysis,[39] but also the foundations of his own architecture. The first person to learn from Las Vegas is Venturi himself. The lesson it teaches him translates into an utterly casual, uninhibited use of the "most [widely] consumed emblems of mass culture" and an "intentionally childish phantasmagoria of light."[40] The decoration of Philadelphia for the American bicentennial, which Venturi designed alongside Denise Scott Brown, was in this sense a timely application of Las Vegas principles. The extension of the project to a citywide scale is one implication of its influence, and by no means secondary. This is the real, actual scale at which the lessons of Las Vegas exercise their power—at city scale. The stratification of signs, their haphazard and aggressive clashing, and mutual multiplication and canceling, assume their full value. In other words, by making all value relative, these signs effectively nullify and liquidate any and all meaning that is not strictly tied to a pure, freely fluctuating, perfectly rootless evocation. Only when a project reaches a sufficiently contradictory, complex, critical mass can it bring to fruition everything learned from Las Vegas. Once again, Tafuri captures with great exactitude the design rules that govern Las Vegas: on the one hand, they require "domination of all visible space"; on the other, they call for a conception of space "solely as a network of superstructures."[41]

These two fundamentally antithetical aspects (one is an extension, the other a restriction of the field into which architecture can intervene) confirm the intrinsically contradictory nature of Venturi's project, and the substantial unity and complexity (not an effective complication but a multiform nature) that lay at its core—a core supremely occupied by a void. At this point, it would be useless to clarify this void—the same void one senses along the Las Vegas strip—and not point out how it betrays itself in two ways: through dominating all visible space (an omnipresent system of signs unregulated by the usual hierarchies) and through a super-dense network of superstructures (nothing, that is, that involves or modifies the structural aspects of a building). In other words, the same two ways that Tafuri articulates self-betrayal in Venturi's work.

The void, or the sheer emptiness of Venturi's architecture, which reproduces the empty architecture of Las Vegas, thus willingly participates in a much broader phenomenon. The city of Las Vegas is the most spectacular (albeit neither the first nor the only) material incarnation of the absence of any predetermined plan for contemporary urban growth. This certainly does not lead to a chance, lawless chaos; quite the contrary: nothing escapes the ironclad laws of the capitalist economy. It leaves its mark on everything, and everything conforms to its dictates. It is a chaos whose every part is well structured but by no means controllable or disciplined within the broader whole. It is precisely this image of the void chockfull of contradictory signs—each in force per se—that characterizes the American city once urban planning becomes an easily neglected discipline.[42] Tafuri describes this as a city where the "petitions of principle"[43] that have essentially become superstructural "remain inoperative"[44]—a city where real-world economic processes expel any urban planning tradition. Thus it results in a "city without qualities"[45] (if not the sole qualities of history rendered irreparably banal, a banality elevated to the level of a new value) "that builds itself as a direct expression of the real-world forces that govern it."[46]

For Tafuri, architecture as an easily neglected object and urban planning as an easily neglected discipline both meld into one project which affects all levels of discourse. Despite their different modes of expression, both share the same strategy: the call for an emptying of all ideal content and a return to reality.

Such competition between outcomes appears to split into two paths only when one attempts to locate its origins, just as Tafuri only appears to identify different effects stemming from Venturi or Kahn: "On the one hand, there's the city as a field of images, as a system of superstructures, as an alogical sequence of surreal, chance forms to be salvaged in an asyntactic visual reorganization. On the other, there's the city as structure, as container of 'value' interconnected by urban history—even more than by a perceptual continuity—as the permanence of 'places' involved in constant conversation with one another."[47] Tafuri thus shows that only by "schematically reasoning"[48]—via abstract formal arguments—is it possible to "recognize, in the first ideal model, the result of the continuing 'destruction of the aura,' and in the second, an attempt to bring back the permanent, unrepeatable, even mythic values of architectural *objects*."[49] On an urban, city-wide level, "the problem is, in reality, much more complex. . . . The dissolution of *attention* into immediate fruition reduces all structures to superstructures. The city, having absorbed every architectural object into the informality at its core, covers itself up as a structure, and presents itself to the distracted perception [of its observers] as an asyntactic, alogical field of pure images to be consumed on a daily basis, [thereby] establishing a new realm of collective behavior."[50]

The crisis of critical attention thus not only contributes to but is the very *cause* of the ease with which it is overlooked. This applies to individual architectural objects just as it does to urban planning. Faced with the threat of being overlooked, the differences between what overtly presents itself as superstructure and what looks instead like an actual structure tend to grow more and more limited, if not to disappear altogether. If, paradoxically, under this lack of attention Kahn's architecture morphologically ends up being equivalent to Venturi's, the same thing happens typologically to their respective models of the city. Between

Dacca and Las Vegas there is not as much distance as one might reasonably expect. If, for Tafuri, in Las Vegas, "the symbolic values connected to typology . . . are [effectively] destroyed after being covered up by the vast sea of overlapping, piled-up, dominant images, to the point of dominating the formal clarification of the typology itself," at Dacca, "the schematic identification of the type with the form's structure . . . is not substituted with a return to the unique, but rather with the increasing rhetorical vanity of typological structures."[51]

Beyond these differences and shortcomings, the argument in favor, albeit no less critical, of Tafuri's thesis identifies a movement that is more generally valid within the aforementioned, deeply American realm: the "absorption of critical attention of the observer in a pure game, a diversion, an *imagerie* of sorts. . . . The city [becomes] a dysfunctional amusement park, rich in persuasive images and redundant signs, and ever more emptied of meaning."[52] The symbolic monuments of this trend are not, according to Tafuri, or as one might otherwise suppose, Las Vegas or Los Angeles, but rather Philip Johnson, Wallace Harrison, and Max Abramovitz's Lincoln Center and the World's Fair New York pavilion in Queens. The Scandinavian new towns of the 1950s (where "urban space mimics itself, becoming a permanent theater and an open field for 'pleasurable' formal diversions")[53] and the designs for the restructuring of 1960s Paris are also symbolic monuments. Tafuri links all these monuments to a common factor: "an emphasis on the void as the recurring structure of this new urban rhetoric."[54] This *kenosis* (emptying out) is in Tafuri's view the most valid key for understanding a vast array of degenerate phenomena in architecture and the city. It may not be vast enough to include the whole of modern architecture without leaving any outliers, but it is broad enough to coincide with the modern movement, the "central aporia" of which is precisely the reduction of architecture to an easily neglected object.

At this point, limiting this aporia solely to the modern movement must be read as an intention to save at least a part of the modern experience from falling into the fated void. But what should have been a turning point with respect to the twofold ease with which the modern movement could be overlooked marks instead—any way Tafuri looks at it—a new defeat:

> *Language has reached the point where it is talking about its own isolation—whether it aims to retread the path of rigorousness, staring at the mechanisms of its own writing, or whether it aims to explode toward the Other, toward the problematic space of existence. But does not such a path, which was, historically speaking, already trodden in the period from the late 1950s to today, simply repeat an experience that has already been lived? Is not Mallarmé's answer regarding the subject at hand— "it is the word itself that now speaks"— . . . perhaps the complement of a tragic, consolatory acknowledgement of Kraus and Loos. "Facts, actions have the word, and what is merely thought has become inexpressible"? Was not the fate of the historic avant-gardes that of dissolving into a project—a historically frustrated project—of intellectual governance of Everything? Language's return home ensues from an open observation of failure.*[55]

The repetition of the great adventure of the avant-garde's language (alongside that of the modern movement)—once it was stripped away from its conditions—cannot but end by repeating its same results, results that nevertheless saw tragedy substituted by farce. If the attempt at controlling everything created a dissolution, repeating it would mean—grotesquely—dissolving a void. Thus the fate of modern architecture (no longer a movement) and urban planning proved to be supremely *kenotic*.

4
LES BIJOUX DANS LE BOUDOIR

Those who seek confirmation of the direction Tafuri's historical-critical discourse took with regard to contemporary architecture need only read some of its new, significant chapters.

Once again, we must begin with Louis Kahn and the analytical, critical rigor of his school ("at least . . . before this, too, became a phenomenon of consumption").[1] Tafuri writes in 1968: "The historicism of the Kahn school is a throwback to the European myth of reason: at that rate it is an opposition to the American pragmatist tradition, which hangs in the balance between a feisty irrationality and a guilty cynicism."[2]

Binding oneself to the European myth of reason means rooting oneself in a tradition that arcts from Claude Nicolas Ledoux (or, better yet, Étienne-Louis Boullée) to Le Corbusier. For Tafuri, this means aligning against the "sleep of reason"—the semi-unconscious state "of those who act . . . in a limbo of sleep-walking"[3]—that is the loss of the subject. In this sense, one could say that the myth of reason is the myth of the thinking, planning, designing subject itself: the Cartesian *cogito* conjugated into the various modes and tenses of architecture. Although upon closer inspection, it is precisely "action without a subject" that is "the sole real, de-alienated action that can be reconciled with the world,"[4] exemplified, for Tafuri, by Walter Gropius's Pan Am Building and the other works he realized alongside The Architects' Collaborative.[5]

"Turning architecture back upon itself," like turning one's eye toward its own interior,[6] thus becomes the practice that—in its "flight in the face of the 'big *Yes*'" that George Grosz spoke of[7] (or rather, before the acceptance of desubjectification that the world imposes upon anyone who would ally themselves with such an idea)—yet again unites different lines of research, even polar opposites like Kahn and Robert Venturi. Its scope, in any case, remains that of reaching a "formal autonomy,"[8] albeit one anchored to a presumed foundation of myths.

That it is a matter of the European myth of reason in Kahn's case, or the American myth of opportunities in Venturi's case, is not particularly important, nor is there much difference, as we have already seen. Yet in order to retrace their original paths—back to where their "two proposed extremes of regenerating impossible orders and playing subtle games of splitting the masks of the real"[9] become clear—to "shatter the ambiguous relationship between myth and language,"[10] one must have a secondary language. Such a language must be capable of speaking about itself, its own absolute autonomy, without resorting to myths. This would be a language of things with no sovereign subject, in which, as Tafuri quotes Foucault, any "unity of discourse . . . continually falls to bits."[11]

Not by chance, such considerations of a secondary language immediately precede the discourse about the Five Architects exhibition mounted in Naples in 1976.[12]

Tafuri is careful to dismantle the group's apparent unity, redefining the limits and peculiarities of each of its participants while acknowledging that "forming a group is necessary, in the American professional jungle, if for no other reason than to create a tool by which one can be identified. It is a sort of temporary lifeline, even if, as with every lifeline, this one, too, is destined to either sink or allow for a more solid embarkation."[13] Between them he finds few common elements, yet they share a clear distinction between the pragmatism of an unscrupulous American professionalism and a not insignificant opposition to large corporate architecture. "The five are," however, "well aware of the artificiality of their own fame, tied as it is to the formula of the 'Five.'"[14]

With these comments Tafuri introduces us to the conceptual universe within which Peter Eisenman, John Hejduk, Michael Graves, Charles Gwathmey (with, in Tafuri's essay, Robert Siegel), and Richard Meier move. For Tafuri, the construction of the Five was very strategic, and was supported by an equally striking critical unfolding.[15] For, since they are "the new knights of purity,"[16] there is more than one element that seems to tarnish their innocence. But let us not get ahead of ourselves.

Employing similar apophatic terms to those Arthur Drexler uses in his preface to *Five Architects*, published in 1972, Tafuri, in 1980, introduces the New York Five: "Negation of any and every neo-brutalism, as well as every reductive or content-based interpretation of architecture, in order to arrive at an absolute purity, a rigorous semantic specificity [is evident in them]."[17]

Since their debut as a group, the Five seem to Tafuri to be driven by a strong determination to distinguish themselves from their immediate predecessors—above all, the "mysticism of the Kahn school"[18] and "Venturian exasperations";[19] the "eclectic mannerism"[20] of Paul Rudolph and I. M. Pei; the "'young Californians' artificial vitalism";[21] the "rarefied reminiscences of Philip Johnson"; the commercialization of typological research in John Portman and Kevin Roche; and the various survival movements emerging in the United States. Distancing became the group's catchword, at least as important as their aim of pursuing a merciless selection of linguistic tools. How important this differentiation was—and at what point the phase of selection is reduced to an ultimate instance in and of itself—can be fully understood only when one realizes how it diminishes everything that lies outside the rigorous legacy of the historic avant-gardes: Amédée Ozenfant and Charles Édouard Jeanneret's cubism, Le Corbusier

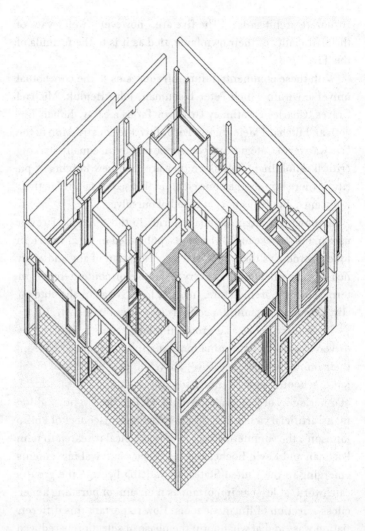

4.1
Peter Eisenman, House II,
Hardwick, Vermont, 1969–1970.
Courtesy Eisenman Architects.

and Giuseppe Terragni's purist rationalism, De Stijl's neoplasticism, Soviet constructivism, and more or less everything that remains after all the rest has been cleared away. These avantgardes are precisely what Eisenman, Hejduk, Graves, Gwathmey, and Meier draw from, having cleansed their sources of all ideological content.

Liberating signs from their traditional meanings, reducing—or, better still, returning—the semantic to the syntactic: this seems to be the Five's program, and their challenge. In this regard, Mario Gandelsonas's analysis of Eisenman's early works, appropriated by Tafuri, is illuminating: "By 'paralyzing' the semantic dimension, the syntactic dimension is seen in a new light. In this way both the syntactic and semantic dimensions of architecture stand uncovered, thus permitting not only new access to their makeup but also a potential point of departure for the development of a nonideological theory."[22] The relationship between pure signs (even purified of the utopian-apocalyptic incrustations of the avant-garde) leads to a linguistic absolutism[23] that speaks only of architecture's conditions of buildability, completely trimmed of any potential value. That this buildability translates into an effective construction, or remains merely thinkable, does not really matter: the concreteness of the Five's houses (with the necessary distinction made between them, as Tafuri underlines) has something in common with that of abstract, nonobjective art, from which it also borrows. This concreteness coincides with the planar, flat surface of the canvas and the material pigments of (primary) colors, in the case of neoplastic painting; with the planar volume of paper and cardboard walls, in the case of Eisenman's cardboard architecture; and with the planar colors of the volumetric walls, in the case of Hejduk's Wall Houses. In each case, it is not the material aspect that matters. The dematerialization of architecture is not the equivalent of the complete resetting of its physical aspect:

what is experienced, rather, is the abolition of any plan, or plane, of becoming, the perfect asymptote between the abstract reality and the possible experience of these project-buildings.[24] The latter does not modify the former (if not destroying its "suspended tonality"),[25] nor does it actualize it. As Tafuri points out, it is not an accident that in Eisenman's houses "the presence of people causes a scandal: . . . The syntactical laboratory suggested by objects that are perfectly circumscribed in the dialogue of signs amongst themselves *does not allow for any intruders*."[26]

Rationalism's sign-based paraphernalia is hereby completely split (one might be tempted to say, abstracted) from the discourse of functions it should inspire. The language of modern art and architecture speaks—but only about itself—self-referentially and tautologically.

What Cacciari identifies as the "suspension of all subjective considerations of language" and the "surpassing of the natural *religio* that gravitationally binds us to language"[27]—aspects taken straight from the art of Mondrian—seem to take place. Tafuri's "Perfectly autonomous objects, enveloped in an exploration of the transformational possibilities of elementary geometric figures," and "subtle mind games that subjugate the absoluteness of forms,"[28] are terms that might best be used to describe Theo van Doesburg's work, just as they can be used to describe Eisenman's early works.

That Tafuri establishes relationships for the other Five with other figures—whether they can be traced back to the avant-garde or not—does not limit to Eisenman alone the validity of his discourse on the interrupted semantic and syntactic relationship, or the silence that stems from it. In fact, it adds precision; thus, Hejduk's houses are brought into dialogue with Mondrian's paintings, Hans Richter and Viking Eggeling's experimental films, and Konstantin Melnikov's projects; Graves's houses are brought into dialogue with cubism, purism, and, again,

Melnikov; Gwathmey and Siegel's Whig Hall at Princeton with purism; Meier's residences with Adolf Loos's Tzara House, Walter Gropius's Kallenbach House, the Luckhardt Brothers' expressionist designs, and Fritz Kaldenbach's anthroposophic designs. Evidently in these parallels, engagement disappoints, and the commitment that originally characterized such evocative phenomena leaves room for only formal references.

Here one finds an autonomy without any myths to pass on, which is exactly what all Five (this time, all of them together) aspire to. This language, "taken up in the most abstract of dimensions, independent of the meanings it imposes upon itself,"[29] Tafuri identifies as their second language. (Eisenman further inflects this second language as a mute critique or self-interpretation of design, via complex grids and diagrams illustrating the compositional process, just as he analyzes and takes up Terragni's myth of reason in his own work as a logical schema without content.)[30]

Adopting the syntax of the avant-garde (or significant parts of it), freed from semantic and historical implications,[31] would seem to set the work of Eisenman, Hejduk, Graves, Gwathmey (with Siegel), and Meier on the other side—or rather, on this side—of the crisis of the modern movement and its illustrious attempts to move forward. Or rather: it would set their work in continuity with it, but at the same time in a position detached from its failure.

This is why the Five—like Kahn before them—seem to represent for Tafuri, at least for a certain, albeit brief, period, a possible future for contemporary architecture. Tafuri's closeness to the New York scene led to two short trips to the United States in the early 1970s and a collaboration with the Institute for Architecture and Urban Studies (IAUS) as well as the magazine *Oppositions*, which were both under the direction of Eisenman.[32] Biographically, both trips attest to more involvement—specifically in Tafuri's investment in crediting their attempt at exiting the checkmate in which architecture culture found itself—than a critic normally would have with several promising architects. The conference held at Princeton in April 1974 and the resulting text, "L'Architecture dans le boudoir," reveal just how scathing, and not at all academic, Tafuri's bet was:

> Today, he who is willing to make architecture speak is forced to rely on materials empty of any and all meaning: he is forced to reduce to degree zero all architectonic ideology, all dreams of social function, and any utopian residues. In his hands, the elements of the modern architectural tradition come suddenly to be reduced to enigmatic fragments, to mute signals of a language whose code has been lost, stuffed away casually in the desert of history. In their own way, those architects who from the late 1950s until today have tried to reconstruct a common discourse for their discipline, have felt the need to make a new morality of content. Their purism or their rigorism is that of someone driven to a desperate action that cannot be justified except from within itself. The words of their vocabulary, gathered from the desolate lunar landscape remaining after the sudden conflagration of their grand illusions, lie perilously on that sloping plane which separates the world of reality from the magic circle of language.[33]

An emptying of sense (here again the void—or, more accurately, the evacuation of original content—returns), abandoning all ideology, all social function, and all utopia—these are now the conditions architecture must confront, the conditions within which it must operate, following the fall of all illusions about its tasks and possibilities in the contemporary period of late capitalism.

Architecture's maneuvering space is thus restricted, rigorously delimited; it is the space of marginality, of separateness, if not of outright constriction, yet gilded, as one might imagine, in effect, a *boudoir* space. It is a boudoir in which the Weberian acceptance of one's need to be seems to survive—stripped of its virile features—solely in the dimension of the frivolous.

Among the architects whose work willingly borders on this boudoir space, the Five—Eisenman, Graves, and Hejduk, in particular—position themselves on the front line, a position that simultaneously opens the sole apparent path to salvation. The duplicity and critical implication of the movement they carry out does not escape Joan Ockman, who notes: "Tafuri took the works of James Stirling, Aldo Rossi, and the New York Five as the paradigm of contemporary architects' retreat from the 'sphere of reality' into the 'universe of signs,' the latest symptoms of a 'widespread attitude that is intent on repossessing the unique character of the object by removing it from its economic and functional concepts . . . by placing it in parentheses with the flux of objects generated by the productive system.'"[34]

From the sphere of reality into the universe of signs—the nature of this retreat they set into operation does not, therefore, pass from one state of reality to another, as one might pass from the openness of a street to the enclosed space of a room, or from one room to another. Rather, it passes from a state of reality to one of unreality. That is, it is a derealizing movement, where what is at stake is the very survival of what initially appears to be the inalienable foundation of architecture. But architecture does not lose its reality by diving into the universe of signs; on the contrary, it is by plunging into the universe of signs that architecture safeguards itself within the sole condition for continued existence. The boudoir of architecture is not a space of reality; rather, it is that dimension wherein signs—like sex in the Marquis de Sade, to which Tafuri explicitly refers—establish relationships exclusively among themselves, and take up a closed discourse that they, and they alone, comprehend. The boudoir is a virtual space of extreme subsistence of sex and signs that have undergone the ultimate reification, the pornographic reduction of their finality to themselves.

As a path to salvation, or as an escape route for architecture, this boudoir might seem to offer too few outlets: it is, after all, as technically sterile as the sex in de Sade. And yet there is still hope that Tafuri will follow this path, as the only one that is still practical now that the modern movement has—in light of all that happened during the war and immediate postwar years—exposed its own weaknesses and transience. Nevertheless, the signs and symptoms of a perilous crack that threatens the conceptual foundations built (or even just planned) by the Five are clear to Tafuri from the start; all that is achieved by the rigorously controlled, almost frozen use of the (opportunely lobotomized) avant-gardes is in fact syntax and semantics and, contradictorily, a "poetics of nostalgia."[35] And with this we are, once again, back to Kahn.

In Tafuri's view, the Five clearly have "an intention to occupy, without any mysticism, the 'space of nostalgia' ambiguously opened by Kahn."[36] As with their works in which "linguistic structures are exposed, . . . they are asked to be rigorous only in their absolute ahistoricity,"[37] since "only in this way can their nostalgic surrenders be neutralized, to recognize the necessity of their alienation from all those punctilious analyses."[38] But such a nostalgia is not without consequences. It is no accident that the adjective Tafuri resorts to most in defining the lines of research taken up by the Five—the adjective that, therefore, unites them— is "magical."[39] It is an unpredictable adjective, to say the least, after designating their virtual place of action as the boudoir, and radically impossible when viewed from the correct Sadeian outlook. The term magical, which Tafuri reiterates numerous times, nevertheless indicates early on the suspension of judgment regarding the Five. This suspension is not to be confused with abstention; rather, it is to be understood as the reflection of a suspended situation in which, according to Tafuri, the Five's works can be found. To say that they are enshrined in a magical aura—to reveal their suspended tonalities—projects them into a region protected from the brutal intrusions of the everyday and its unquestionable judgment. To suspend reality, from Tafuri's point of view, therefore, means to see a positive *epoché*[40] at work—one which does not immediately lead to a utopian position.

Yet if it is from retouches and *pentimenti* (repentances) that one can estimate the true, secret relationship of maker to work, then it is from an affirmation present in "Les bijoux indiscrets" and absent from "European Graffiti" that one can fully comprehend Tafuri's thinking regarding Eisenman and the Five: "Eisenman pursues the utopia of a syntax freed from informative values."[41] So what may have seemed like an exit from reality without any collateral effects thus now reveals itself as a regression toward nostalgic utopias—the utopia, that is, of perfect fracture between sign and meaning, the residue-free liberation of this from that. It is the same nostalgic bent—which Tafuri more than once attributes to the Five—that is, in the final analysis, an *ou-topic* bent. Indeed, nostalgia is a tension toward something that no longer takes place, and perhaps never did take place. In this sense, nostalgia of utopia can always be traced back to a utopia of nostalgia.

In "Toward a Critique of Architecture Ideology" and *Architecture and Utopia*, Tafuri demonstrates the ineradicable aporias inherent in utopia as it progressively ventures into modern terrain. Speculatively, one can now observe how, for him, contradiction is present in the work of the Five from the beginning, or, in other words, how the assumptions of their work generate such contradiction. In particular, Tafuri notes in Eisenman's work an ambiguity that makes the vices of Kahn and Venturi's legacies resurface: "The reduction to syntax carries with it . . . an 'involuntary semantics.' The 'suppressed meaning' reintroduces a degree of ambiguity into the emptied sign, and allows a further semantic dimension to penetrate the chain mail of rigorous conceptual interpenetrations—a semantic dimension that is antithetical to the original theoretical assumptions: a 'magical' semantics."[42] The objection to Eisenman's suspended discourse (and to Hejduk, Graves, Gwathmey, and Meier's as well) and evasion of the real world—architecture that takes refuge in an ideal, neutral space of pure signs—is thus already entirely inscribed in the magical character that unites the work of the *six* Five in Tafuri's critique.

But while magic clarifies the terms of their suspension, it still does not fully illustrate its reasons. What would be enough (and is, in effect, really enough) to condemn Kahn and Venturi without appeal does not suffice to close the discourse on the Five.

It is true that the Five speak the language of the dead (that is, of the avant-garde),[43] although they do so "with their eyes wide open to see the sinking ship . . . of [their] prime motivations."[44] Additionally, they have undertaken a "desperate search for a language independent of the by-now 'comical' subjective intervention."[45] It is not that their interventions lack individual (or individualistic) components. But their liberation from the myths—and the perfect autonomy such liberation offers—demands the liberation of the subject as a precondition (despite all the risks—extensively calculated risks, in the case of the Five—of commercial depersonalization that such liberation entails). Regardless of subjective intervention, the language itself is left to speak. Like Stéphane Mallarmé before him, Tafuri emphasizes that: "what speaks is the word itself."[46] This simultaneously safeguards the Five from potential relapses into the temptation of meaning,[47] as well as from the involuntary comedy that would result from the assumption of meaning. It does not, however, safeguard them from frivolity, whose generative mechanism lies in the "separation of the sign from its referents."[48] The intellectual ostentation of the Five is inexorably frivolous; they are perfectly conscious of their role, and just as perfectly well connected in the elite circles of affluent New York society. Frivolity is "freed from ideology,"[49] which also constitutes the strength of Eisenman and the others.

Tafuri continuously vacillates between approval and liquidation. Or, better still: his inexhaustible insistence upon the will to understand, practiced while leaving judgment to drift, hovering in more or less broad circles above its prey—another way of describing the suspension recalled earlier—attests to a possible misunderstanding, or an impossible illusion. The phantom of restless Miesian silence might metamorphose—in spite of it all—into the frivolous muteness of the Five.[50]

Tafuri is fully aware of what, exactly, is really in question in Mies's language of emptiness and silence.[51] Cacciari perhaps expresses it best: "The sign must remain *sign*, and speak only of its refusal to be *value*—only by way of this refusal will it be able to understand its own functions and its own fate: the only language that can work is one that is enlightened about its own limits."[52]

This highly serious emptying-out of language carried out by the Five inevitably resembles a caricature, a simulation, a conjurer's comic little joke, that could rightfully claim to be magic. Naturally, this does not mean that Tafuri is uncritically prepared to believe it. Nor would it make any sense critically to juxtapose "Eisenman's formal terrorism, Graves's polysemy, and Meier's rigor,"[53] nor—in the same passage, which appears again in the final chapter of *The Sphere and the Labyrinth*—the "linguistic cruelty of Gandelsonas and Diana Agrest, the metaphysical games of Rodolfo Machado and Jorge Silvetti, Giurgola's constructivism, Robert Stern's naïve aphorisms, or Rem Koolhaas's jokes,"[54] if

their common denominator were not to be found in a truly decisive (and, according to Tafuri, negatively decisive) aspect of
contemporary architecture: the "fear of reality"[55] that all such
behaviors display. This fear appropriates the languages of battle
of the 1920s and 1930s—transformed today into languages of
pleasure—as arms with which it might defend itself.

Fear and pleasure: their apparent contrast must not cause
confusion. It is no accident that, in the texts analyzed here, Tafuri resorts with unsettling frequency to the *Sadist* realm. Fear
and pleasure, in this sense, both express an attempt to bracket
reality by imprisoning oneself in the boudoir where, sadistically,
both are taken at full value.[56] Under the sign of fear and pleasure, architecture is banished from the field of social experience.
"The war is over,"[57] for sure, in Tafuri's view, but only to make way
for private cruelties, personal terrors, or egoistic pleasures. As
Roland Barthes—to whom Tafuri turns on this subject—reminds
him, along with everything else that is "overcome, split, is the
moral unity that society demands of every human product."[58]
Even this prospect seems better, in the view of these protagonists, than the idea of abandoning oneself to reality's uncurbed,
unchecked rule. For Tafuri, it is "too easy to conclude that such
architecture constitutes a 'betrayal' of the ethical ideals of the
modern movement."[59] Too easy indeed, to such a degree that it is
less difficult to affirm the exact opposite: "Such architecture re-
cords, rather, the mood *of those who feel betrayed*, and essentially
reveals the condition into which those who still want to make
'Architecture' find themselves forced."[60]

What exactly "saves itself" in this way, it is not easy to say.
Certainly not architecture, since it distrusts the wicked charm
of products coming from the new laboratories of the imaginary.[61]
Nor is it the "disenchanted avant-garde,"[62] those "new knights of
purity"[63] who brandish "the fragments of utopia as their distinguishing marks, fragments they do not observe head on."[64]

Perhaps, then, Tafuri's analysis must be considered by the same standards as a dream, yet with the awareness that "upon awakening, the world of facts and things will see to restabilize the merciless wall built up between the idea of alienation and the reality of its laws."[65]

5
FRAGMENT AND SILENCE

Tafuri's historical construction of contemporary architecture cannot be considered complete without a few figures who, in his estimation, stand out in the field, attaining prominence precisely because of their significant isolation. If this isolation reflects the special place Tafuri reserves for them, it also captures the particular character that distinguishes "the work of those who sought refuge from the surrounding commotion in isolation."[1] In fact, it is in these "golden, isolated individuals that one finds the highest level of formal [linguistic] coherence."

It is symptomatic, for Tafuri, that only four architects of the twentieth century stand out in distinct relief, and that they are not, any more than others, exempt from the stark conflicts and the vacuum of such isolation: Ludwig Mies van der Rohe, James Stirling, Carlo Scarpa, and Aldo Rossi.[2] According to Tafuri, these architects are the main proponents of the only two possible approaches to the crisis of modernity: the reduction of form and meaning to pure fragment, and the eloquent silence that surrounds it.

Let us look at the first approach. Stirling and Scarpa are, for quite different reasons, the key exemplars. Stirling's work constitutes a "bona fide 'archaeology of the present.'"[3] It is a collection, return, and rewriting of words of modern architecture without the intention or illusion of reviving a tradition. If anything, it is a complete rethinking of tradition as language, a language whose words generate a new text.[4] The echoes that reverberate thus make us recall, but only to clarify a sense of distance. We find ourselves at the center of the problematic relationship between architecture and language. Stirling's work refracts the bright light of this problematic, which makes it seem exemplary for Tafuri: "In this way, tradition becomes an unreachable, arcane mystery: what we love . . . is separated from us by a distance that can be measured solely by analyzing the depth of the sediments accumulated atop archaeological finds. From excavation sites no meanings emerge, just sounds. The sounds can be manipulated, they don't bind [their finder] to any [specific] content, they 'speak' only to the degree that they are composed according to new rules."[5]

Stirling employed rules "of contrast and opposition: the rotation of axes, the use of antithetical structures, technological distortions."[6] To begin with such techniques configured an entirely paradoxical symbolism that eludes the rhetorical ambushes looming in the nostalgia of symbolic fullness: "Stirling's symbolism . . . is built through exhaustions of form: exhaustions that, in his later works, disfigure language, to the point of wearing it down. But it is always an attrition that doesn't cross the line of breaking to bits."[7]

Stirling's bits give rise to combinations from which "a complete poetics of the *objet trouvé*"[8] can be inferred, although the result is more a metaphysical than an intellectual game. This game does not complacently aspire to transcendence or presumed universal values. Rather, irony[9] and self-irony deeply inform Stirling's work, showing that rewriting through textual fragments requires the use of hieroglyphs, which are "indecipherable unless viewed as subjective chains of association." In other words, the aggregations remain unfounded, or founded temporarily and subjectively, following a path of uncertainty: "This explains, for the most part, why many of Stirling's formal machines seem crystallized at the moment of their collapse . . . fixed in a photographic lens just a second before they explode."[10]

5.1
James Stirling, Engineering Faculty
Building, Leicester, 1959–1963.

Beyond Stirling's linguistic research and his capacity for distortion,[11] one element is absolutely clear for Tafuri: "Stirling's [works] are 'texts,' not explosions from some utopian imaginary."[12] This elucidates one fundamental point: as much as Stirling may excessively fragment, and thereby quote, the materials of the modern movement's laboratories (which have fallen into disuse), his operation halts before falling into complete dissolution, or reducing his own work to a mere pretext. In other words, for Stirling an architectural work is not an occasion for nostalgic forays into utopia; even the imaginary brings him back to the real, as does utopia itself: "Social utopia can be discussed only as a literary document, it comes into architecture only as an element, or, better, as a pretext."[13] And, even more clearly: "There is no utopian nostalgia, no 'tending toward something else.' Utopia is valuable only as a pretext, it is nothing more than an *occasion*."[14] By making utopia a simple pretext, Stirling avoids making architecture itself a pretext.

But on this ground, Stirling's strategy, according to Tafuri, goes further. It does not limit itself to demonstrating the unbridgeable distance from utopia by showing fragments that are now unusable for their original purpose; rather, it puts all residual desire for utopia in checkmate by unveiling its designs: "The operation Stirling carries out is exemplary: it denounces the utopia inherent in any attempt at salvaging architecture as a 'discourse.'"[15]

The poetics of the *objet trouvé*, of the fragment, now reveals its real interests: the renunciation of meaning through signs and of communicating with language. "[Stirling's] architecture does not pave any new paths, does not point to any destinations, does not entrust its fate to anyone outside of itself. Stirling frees architectural language from the duty of alluding, speaking, expressing: he condemns it to meditate and reflect upon itself, to being, in the very act of its appearing, a[n archaeological] 'find.'"[16] Thus it is easy to see how, for Tafuri, Stirling's work of quotation—in the extraction of withered roots from original contexts—lies just one step away from the abyss of the "mortal silence of the sign."[17]

Before understanding the broader context of this interpretation, however, one must analyze the other cases. Scarpa's work, though very different from Stirling's, also revolves around fragmentation. It is so different, in fact, that it is difficult to decipher Tafuri's readings on the two without stumbling across some systemic contradictions.

Tafuri maintains that "Scarpa outlines a bona fide poetics based on the accumulation of signs, the multiplication of formal hints, the indetermination of the organisms [buildings]";[18] nevertheless, "the pluralism of the innovations and the seething of each individual element introduce tensions resolved in favor of the detail, the exception, and the unique."[19] Tafuri thus temporarily concludes that Scarpa's work is a "game of formal skill played with fragments," an "open organization of interrupted sentences."[20] But—and here Tafuri's discourse takes an unexpected turn—that way of working with fragmentation could lead one to maintain that Scarpa's work is imbued with melancholy. Indeed, "a fragment, properly understood, always speaks of an irredeemably lost whole . . . it is, in and of itself, a 'tragic event.'"[21] In Stirling's case, fragments echo a distance, an impossibility of reactivating a discourse on the meaning of architecture; in Scarpa's, they instead convey an ineluctable feeling of nostalgia.

Confronted with this prospect, Tafuri turns toward understanding the fragment differently—apart from the tragic. From this point of view he invokes Maurice Blanchot, who writes: "We must try to recognize in this 'shattering' or 'dislocation' a value that is not one of negation. It would be neither privative nor simply positive; as though the alternative and the obligation to begin by affirming being if one wished to deny it had here been finally, mysteriously broken. . . . The fragmented poem, therefore, is not a poem that remains unaccomplished, *but it opens another manner of accomplishment—the one at stake in writing, in questioning, or in an affirmation irreducible to unity.*"[22]

Moreover, by following this different idea of the fragmentary in response to Scarpa, Tafuri discovers that "breaking all formal compactness, just 'letting' forms that are laid out like the residue of a broken, scattered labyrinth 'float around,' is not an end in itself. It lets recurring ideas emerge, ideally connected to one another, which obliges a reconnection—a process of restoration that is as patient as the architect's task—of those ideas in their transmigration, variation, and deformation from work to work."[23]

What might have passed for "fragmented exasperations"[24] are now reconsidered in light of a well-articulated and binary dialectic between the part and the whole. It is in the entirety, in the plurality of works, that one can find a broader, more articulate design, marred as it might be by voids and contradictions. "So in order to avoid contradictions perhaps it would be more correct to speak not of a poetics of the 'fragment,' for Scarpa, but rather of a poetics made up of 'figures.'"[25]

The term *figure* is used by Franco Rella to allude to an "'intermediate realm' between the abstraction of the concept and the fullness of the myth, the analogy, and the image."[26] For Tafuri, however, the term connotes a secret iconology that unites otherwise different and distant places and functions in Scarpa's buildings into an "uninterrupted dialogue."[27] But take note: the closer relation of such materials does not deny the dispersion of the now recurring, varied, and deformed figures; on the contrary, continuity and discontinuity cease to be mutually exclusive. Instead they live alongside one another in a continual state of contradiction. According to Tafuri, Scarpa's open universe of copresent possibilities, coagulated into polyvalent forms,

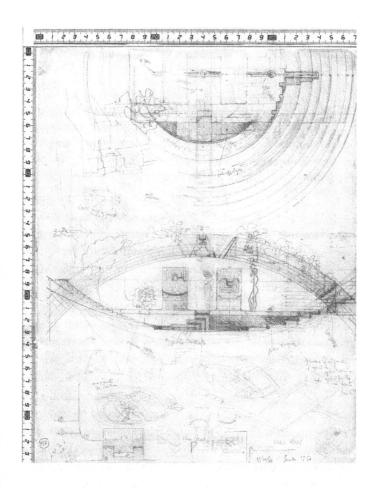

5.2
Carlo Scarpa, preliminary study
for the Brion's Tomb arcosolium,
San Vito d'Altivole, 1969. Image
courtesy Carlo Scarpa Archives,
Architectural collection, MAXXI
Museum, Rome.

signals new ways of making. In particular, Scarpa's museum installations result in an "alienation"[28] from spatial and temporal generality and a suspension in the specific tempo of his works so that they "appear *freed*: free from traditional links, and open to innovative readings, freed from the problematic of meaning."[29]

In this liberation of meaning (the opposite of the usual practices of the architect-demiurge, who is deluded in thinking that he confers meaning onto things, and in such a way as to deny it) we find the nucleus of the positive aspects that Tafuri sees in Scarpa's fragments and figures. Far from contemporary nihilism, it is content to reflect in its own disillusion and disenchantment, something that in Scarpa's art instead indicates a "possible happiness, even in a 'time of crisis.'"[30] It is certainly no coincidence that against this background of possible happiness—almost as its unavoidable matrix—Tafuri sees Scarpa's work as "foreign to all ideological trauma . . . cleansed of all utopianism."[31]

Tafuri's care in verifying the data and rarity of this liberation from the twofold stranglehold of ideology and utopia makes one appreciate the exceptional quality of Scarpa's work, which maintains a clarity not found in the work of other supposed masters. For Tafuri, the very idea of master—a rating of excellence rather casually conferred by the historiography of the modern movement—is far from being unthought. It does not equate to beatifying those who receive it, to shelter them from shadow or doubt. A paradigmatic example of this is Giuseppe Samonà. The space and attention Tafuri grants him in *History of Italian Architecture*[32] immediately follows the section on Scarpa. The premises are similar. Like Scarpa, Samonà is an "isolated master"[33] whose work likewise proceeds "through paradoxes . . . subjugating fragments"[34] and composition inextricably intertwined with decomposition. As Tafuri feared with Scarpa, the fragments of Samonà's "cultural autobiography"[35] evoke lost totalities in a climate devoid of nostalgia (without any real need for redemption from potential ambiguity, nor recourse to a different idea of fragmentation, totality, or accomplishment). And thus, from Tafuri's outline of the masterful Samonà, an implicit recognition emerges: that contradictions—historicism and antihistoricism, materiality and immateriality, desire for form and syntactic disintegration[36]—do not confer any radical imbalance. Alien to the "sad tones"[37] of Quaroni's work, and to Scarpa's disengagement, Samonà reveals himself as the master of limits.

The "'case' of Aldo Rossi"[38] presents rather different problems, and they are not problems that his architecture easily resolves. It is no coincidence that Tafuri's discourse on Rossi forces him to turn, once again, to the question of language in the terms he has already confronted theoretically in his historical project.[39] Tafuri re-posits the problem of the "'splitting in two' carried out by critique."

> *The simple linguistic analysis of an architecture that speaks solely of its being a language stripped bare would end up as pure description. It would not be able to escape the magic circle outlined by the work around it, it could not but manipulate the constitutive process of the text itself, repeating its axiomatic nature. The only external referent of such an "internal" reading within the subject of analysis would be identified in the cracks, in the interstices of the linguistic object/subject. The "splitting in two" carried out by critique, then, must be something other than the construction of a "second language," set afloat above the original text, first coined by Barthes and carried out by Stirling.[40]*

What happens when critique turns to "architectural proposals folded back onto themselves," to the point where the nonlinguistic residues—the world of the real unresolved in form—of the architecture of Stirling and Kahn are eliminated? "Where the absolute presence of *form* makes the presence of *chance* 'scandalous?'"[41] Here the magic circle does not offer any cracks or interstices, such that the language of critique (the critique of language) must oscillate between two false solutions—mere description on the one hand, and free invention on the other—without ever finding its own position. In short, the problem is yet again, as Tafuri points out, the naïve nonmanipulation of the work. Given this, Tafuri summons Rossi's work to the rescue: "To the poetics of ambiguity, of John Johansen, Charles Moore, and Robert Venturi, Rossi responds by freeing the architectural discourse from any leakage toward the real, from all intrusions of chance or empiricism in the fully structured system of signs."[42]

Rossi therefore suppresses the scandal of reality's chance nature in his own architecture, particularly the "chance comportment *par excellence*, human comportment,"[43] disoriented and lost in other contemporary architecture by contradictory messages, "shaken by an 'interrupted rhetoric.'"[44] Rossi's "invocation of form," on the contrary, "exists irrespective of any and all external justification." Tafuri continues:

> *Architecture's specificity lies in a universe of rigorously selected signs, wherein the law of exclusion dominates. . . . Rossi elaborates an alphabet that repels all facile articulation: as the abstract representation of the inflexibility of its own arbitrary law, it makes its entire realm of artifice. In this [artifice], such architecture returns to the structure of language itself. Presenting a syntax of emptied signs, of programmed exclusions, and rigorous limitations, it reveals the inflexibility of discretion, the false dialectic between freedom and the norm that is peculiar to the linguistic order.*[45]

There could be no better example of such abstention from reality—of nonmanipulation, or rather nonconfusion, of the work with reality. Yet Tafuri sees more distant roots of this retreat: with modernity all order of discourse was shattered; therefore, "only the ghost of this lost order can be shaken."[46] This is precisely how Rossi acts. There is no illusion of refounding the discipline on such fragile bases, just as there is no illusion of recuperating that loss with consolatory, formal islands. Herein lies Rossi's iron-willed "refusal of a naïve manipulation of forms"[47]—a refusal that, for Tafuri, converges with the work of Karl Kraus, the great interpreter, from a linguistic point of view, of such a refusal.

The juxtaposition of Kraus and Rossi might at first appear forced. And, in effect, it would be impossible to find a greater distance between Rossi's emptied signs, the "immutable, and eternal return of geometric emblems reduced to specters,"[48] and Kraus's all but "immutable and silent" invective .[49] Here we must be careful not to confuse the two different faces of this discourse—and ultimately the discourses of Rossi and Kraus. For Tafuri, Rossi defends the "original source,"[50] that "central point from which communication arises"—language—continuously circling it and thereby mutely showing the inability to draw anything from it. Kraus, on the other hand, defends language with sharpened polemics, a critique that mercilessly exposes the impossibility of reproduction, keeping its "tempters" away and making sure to avoid contemporary talk. Both Rossi and Kraus are conscious that "only the 'limit' of being is sayable"[51]—not being in and of itself. The fundamental difference that occurs is between those who try to *embody* that limit and those who try to *say* it. This difference is intrinsic to the difference between the architect and the critic. The guarded "object" is one and the same; it is the means that differ.[52]

5.3
Aldo Rossi, *L'architecture
assassinée*, 1974.

In this light, the long quotation from Kraus that Tafuri adopts for rereading Rossi must be considered. Kraus wrote, in 1914:

> *In these great times, which I knew when they were small, which will become small again provided they have time left for it . . . in these loud times, which boom with the horrible symphony of deeds that produce reports, and of reports that bear the blame for deeds; in these unspeakable times . . . you can expect no word of my own from me. Nor should I be capable of saying anything new; for in the room where someone writes, the noise is so great, and whether it comes from animals, from children, or merely from mortars shall not be decided now. He who addresses deeds violates both word and deed, and is twice despicable. This profession is not extinct.* Those who now have nothing to say because it is the turn of deeds to speak, talk on. Let him who has something to say step forward and be silent![53]

If Kraus's position gives voice to that which Rossi cannot say— evoking such a position through the silent world of forms and images—then such a voice speaks for Tafuri as well. This position and voice do not substitute Tafuri's, but rather anticipate them, providing a canonical and infinitely variable precedent. Tafuri's conclusion is, therefore, valid well beyond Rossi: "If fact and act have the word, then there is nothing left but to let them speak and to preserve, in silence, the great values about them—and Kraus, Loos, and Tessenow all agree on this point—'one cannot speak,' at least not without contaminating them."[54] Mirrored in this sentence, in addition to those authors already mentioned, Tafuri also sees a reflection of Mies: "'Fatti'—'facts and acts'— possess the language of existence with which the language of signs must not be confused, for fear of declining into a 'betrayal' of both 'facts and acts,' and 'values.'"[55]

In the work of Mies, there is a maximum separation between the language of signs and the language of existence, a maximum assumption of absence having-to-be, which the contemporary world imposes upon the language of form. If this is not a renunciation of form, it nevertheless renounces the possibility of opening any dialogue through it. Form exclusively communicates its own emptiness and silence—thus the order that is the negative of metropolitan chaos can only withdraw when exposed to it. With the Seagram Building (and again, with Kraus) "*Mies takes a step back and remains silent.*"[56] The semantic voids of his forms "speak the hallucinated language of nothingness, of silence," of "supreme indifference."[57] "Alienation, once absolute, attests solely to its own presence, separating itself from the world in order to denounce the world's incurable illness."[58]

Rossi is mirrored in the same observation—just slightly deformed by a greater ambiguity: "Because the fact and the act have the word, form can remain silent"[59] or withdraw into a "dignified reserve,"[60] in an "excited silence,"[61] or, more, into a mute telling of its own loss. In any case, Tafuri sees the "lingering on the void that Rossi proposes"[62] to be highly Krausian. Yet Rossi's silence is both similar to and different from Mies's. Like Mies, for Rossi "it is necessary to ignore the 'noises of the world' to contemplate the places of a sacred alienation,"[63] albeit "tellable."[64] Contrary to Mies, however (and again in accordance with Kahn), Rossi possesses a "desire to represent nostalgia."[65] Nevertheless, as Tarufi writes, "he does not express any regret for a condition preceding that transformation, but rather a nostalgia for an ancestral linguistic order. Like Kahn, Rossi, too, fights to exorcize the 'loss of the center,' but he does not nourish any hopes of getting help from the outside. Logic will be able to affirm itself only to the extent that language will be born of a continually varying aggregation of a few words brought back to their original semantic value."[66]

For Rossi, therein lies the role of representation: if representation is to open the door for nostalgia, then its realm coincides with a sayable limit that says nothing outside of itself. "Representation was everything," as Tafuri writes, "it was useless to worry about secondary meanings in inaccessible realms."[67] The fact that any "search for a primordial essence is always frustrated"[68] constitutes the true core of Rossi's work. Language becomes a "system of exclusions"[69] rather than inclusions, possible experimentation, confrontations with reality (such exclusions unified Rossi and Stirling, whose work was "oppositional yet complementary"). Here even nostalgia is simply shown, there is no discourse on it: "One can participate in subjective nostalgia only by forcing himself to communicate in a hermetic silence."[70]

Tafuri's judgment of Rossi's architecture cannot be correctly understood outside a complex twenty-year personal relationship of mutual respect and uninterrupted criticism. Given their ambivalent relationship, as evidenced in a letter to Rossi, Tafuri begins to push Rossi's work toward a hermetic silence in the early 1970s: "Your objects without objectivity, alluding to meanings that are suddenly emptied out, that refuse the world, are exact instances of acts of 'private poetry'; the more they remain enclosed in their hermetic silence, and the more they stray from the competition for that ambiguous 'neue Welt'—the new world for which the bad conscience of the 'engaged' intellectual is ready to play its worst cards—the less mystifying they are."[71]

Tafuri complains about the fundamentally consolatory character that draws parallels between Rossi's personal history and his architecture. Even Rossi's *La città analoga*, a panel he presented at the 1976 Venice Biennial, seems to be a composite form. Tafuri writes: "As a recording of disenchanted voyages into memory, Aldo Rossi's montages renew the desire for an ecumenical embrace with a dream-like reality. And yet this desire to understand the real in its entirety—object and subject, history and memory, city as structure and city as myth—in and of itself, expresses the mood Michelstaedter called 'the anxiety of the persecuted beast.'"[72]

This is the same anxiety that dominates the ambiguous *neue Welt*, wherein everyone, as Michelstaedter writes, "rushes about, meets one another, bumps into and bruises one another, gets on one another's nerves, and does business."[73] In view of this, Michelstaedter suggests, there is little left but the practice of steadiness, a capacity for consisting in the "eternal flowing and clashing of things that are and are not."[74] Rossi, on the contrary, "in his allegory of *La città analoga*, attempts a magical operation: to unite a desiccated nostalgia with the declaration of his own 'consisting.'" For Tafuri, this is incoherent and evidences weakness:

> Rossi's consisting is, contradictorily, in desperate search of a "place" in which to deposit its own "steadiness." That this place is the labyrinth of "many beauties" collected into an ideal montage has an equally contradictory meaning: it indicates the need for a public that "asks something," from which answers "can be expected." It is necessary to put these reciprocal roles back into their right places: to those who seek a conscious "steadiness," yet want to obtain approval at all costs, no reply should be given. The silence of criticism signifies, in such a case, the refusal of the fragility of the poet who announces, coram populo, his own desire to stretch out, in front of "his" public, on a consolatory Freudian couch.[75]

In the end, it is absolute separateness that Tafuri desires for Rossi. In a famous footnote in *The Sphere and the Labyrinth*, Tafuri writes that "Rossi must be advised not to teach architecture: not because of any hysterical or conformist ostracism, but rather to help him be more coherent with his fascinating and superficial silence."[76]

Those who try to resist, who aim to truly exist in the contemplation of pain, must know how to face a different reality. Tafuri sums up this difficult secret act as proof of a principle that is, in reality, a highly demanding *télos*: "The path of the real is not changeable, but in that accepted suffering, in that negation of utopian alternatives, therein lies *the duty of awareness*."[77]

Significantly, within the architecture of his century, Tafuri sees Mies—"Mies, who turns silence into a mirror"[78]—as embodying such a supreme duty. The Miesian ethos preserves those silent values while continuing to work with form. It aims to express the intangibility of the values through the deafening silence that hangs around them. These points correspond exactly to Tafuri's ethos, provided that in the above sentence the term *word* is substituted for the term *form*. The stylistically different architectures of Stirling, Scarpa, and Rossi can be grouped around this ethos as well. But this difficult, demanding ethos should not be confused with a current moral sense. Nothing could be further from a humanistic interpretation of the world. The models of this ethos are, instead, those rare destructive characters, the exemplars of what Benjamin calls "a humanity that proves itself by destruction."[79] Kraus is one of its members (although Kahn, a destroyer despite himself, is obviously not, in Tafuri's view). Tafuri was cast from the same mold. Tafuri's ethos, like Kraus's, is the ethos of civilization's critic—he who unveils ideologies, destroys overly tread paths, analyzes that which is broken to bits, and protects that which he can never possess. For these reasons, more than Rossi (as many American critics maintained),[80] Kraus—or, better still, Kraus as reread by Benjamin[81]—is Tafuri's authentic double. Kraus made himself the guardian of fundamental values, and dedicated his life to exposing inauthenticity.[82] He was nourished by a vital (rather than lethal) hatred of the interminable, swarming producers of public opinion. He made the discovery of new enemies a profession, and could not help but see himself as deformed by narcissistic reflection.

In Kraus, Tafuri finds the terrifying herald of the apocalypse (that is, of crisis) of his time, the penetrating analysis of the essayist, the inexhaustible polemical verve of a detractor and critic, the scathingly biting ways of the aphorist. In each of Kraus's pages, Tafuri finds a demand for absoluteness, that ultimate character (not dissociated from a highly human sense of pity) that has been called the "Krausian character."[83] By looking at Kraus, the Tafurian character is illuminated by the Krausian "splendor of a law that, in its ardor, burns and destroys."[84] No less than Kraus, Tafuri is a guardian of this law. Thus it is no surprise that both men set themselves well above justice, at the level of a judge who pronounces verdicts. There, where the word is authoritative, it is neither rare nor difficult to consider it the last word.[85]

Almost all that Benjamin affirms of Kraus can also be said of Tafuri. This does not reduce Tafuri's originality—rather, it simply defines its limits, the field from which it emanates, or, better, in which it becomes full, conscious. The secret game of this association[86] can be taken to the letter. The name Tafuri can easily be substituted for Kraus in Benjamin's description of him:

> Kraus has never offered an argument that did not engage his whole person. Thus, he embodies the secret of authority: never to disappoint. Authority has no other end than this: it dies or it disappoints. It is not in the least undermined by what others must avoid: its own despotism, injustice, inconsistency. . . . "Many will be right one day. But it will be a rightness resulting from my wrongness today." This is the language of true authority. . . .

> *Insight into [his work's] operations can reveal only one thing: that it is binding, mercilessly binding, toward titself in the same degree as toward others; that it does not tire of trembling before itself, though never before others; that it never does enough to satisfy itself, to fulfill its responsibility toward itself.*[87]

Beside such an incorruptible, aggressive, and seasoned sureness, there is a perceptible sense of guilt, often evidenced in Tafuri's first-person involvement in his pronounced condemnation. As the Krausian "grumbler," Tafuri also participates—at least to some extent—in what he criticizes and denounces.[88] All that can be delineated with obscure clarity is the tragic nature—the complex, polar opposites that exist in one being, which truly summarize Tafuri's modus operandi.[89]

Some aspects of Tafuri that seem character-based, particularly in light of Benjamin's portrait of Kraus, now appear completely different, revealed in the economy of Tafuri's critical construction. For example, we might not otherwise suspect Tafuri's tendency toward anthropophagy, which in the Benjaminian-Krausian looking glass reveals an otherwise unsuspected satirical vein. Satire, Benjamin writes, "consists in the devouring of the adversary. The satirist is the figure in whom the cannibal was received into civilization."[90]

However, it is those pages dedicated to Kraus as an inhuman "messenger of a more real humanism"[91] that most deeply resonate with Tafuri. Here every sentence and word is fitting. Briefly stated, it is the inhuman Tafuri who, in a Benjaminian sense, allows us to reread his destructive work as supremely purifying. It is precisely because Tafuri destructively intervenes in material, wears out what has been done, critiques its conditions,[92] that his work is masterful. This clarifies something that, said in any other way, would run the risk of being inexplicable: Tafuri as master is at one with his destructive character; the master lives alongside the destroyer, in spite of himself. This also clarifies the few other masters whom Tafuri's historical construct isolates and endows with an almost desperate importance. Masters such as Mies, Stirling, Scarpa, and Rossi must not be separated from their destructive character. Their fragmentation of their overly vast disciplinary terrain—their extraction of pieces, parts, possibilities, conjectures, and bits—and their final, yet effective fall into silence represent perhaps the most extraordinary forms produced in architecture in the twentieth century. For Tafuri, they are masters because they know how to destroy in such a way as to preserve, to save. Only thus could the sign be guarded in its mortal silence.

By now it is clear how the master's secret lies in his capacity to renounce. It is this, more than anything else, that more or less binds together Rossi and Kraus, as well as Tafuri and Kraus. The act of renunciation unites them in an uncomfortable operation of "freeing" them from the ideological projections of which they have been victims—an uncomfortable freeing, since it denies rather than creatively gives. All told, the condition of possible redemption is somehow inherent to the preemptive acceptance of an uncomfortable position. In this sense, Tafuri's self-imposed exile from creativity and purity, while it may not be his distinguishing mark, is at least his characteristic trait. Even a transparent glimpse of it indicates something in and of itself. Perhaps it would not have been visible, nor even imaginable, if Benjamin's "messenger in the old engravings"[93] had not pointed it out first.

6
POLITICS OF REALITY

In his essay on Karl Kraus, Walter Benjamin writes: "Work as a supervised task—its model being political and technical work—is attended by dirt and detritus,"[1] which, in his view, does not cheapen it in the least, but rather affirms its positive destructiveness. However, a creative person, he writes, avoids all assignments and checks.

As I have tried to demonstrate in the previous chapters, if Tafuri's historical construct denounces the ideological confusion of architecture and urban planning, from Giovanni Battista Piranesi to the 1970s (and beyond), then it also focuses on those figures who significantly abstain from or renounce the utopia of full linguistic communication. Yet Tafuri also considers a third, fundamental category: that of "engaged" architects. Strictly speaking, this type of engagement is not a political one such as active participation in a party, trade union, or other social organization, since—especially in postwar Italy—this would sketch the profile of an architect that recurs all too frequently, and would not provide a safeguard against the pitfall of such architects' ideological relapses.[2] Nor does engagement coincide with Tafuri's conception of an architect's assumed responsibility within the "new roles of the technician, building organizer, and *planner*":[3] he places those pursuing technical-intellectual work squarely within new forms of capitalist development, to be confronted through a specifically political preventive analysis.

Rather, engagement refers to an awareness both of the reality of things and of the self. This type of behavior stems from a close consideration of reality—of the conditions it prefigures, and the tasks and position the architect assumes within it. It is an approach of sensible realism. In this light we can detect in Tafuri's historical-critical work a special inclination for the interaction between architecture and reality—for those moments, that is, in which architecture explicitly posits itself as part of the politics of reality.

Of all the texts in Tafuri's vast bibliography, there is one that, more than others, is enlightening in this sense: "Architettura e realismo."[4] The kind of realism (or, better still, Realism) to which he alludes—though it cannot precisely be labeled "a fad that was lived as such by its protagonists"[5] and is tinged with multiple contradictions—is, upon consideration, more accurately called a populist stance. "Realism's set of reference points inevitably assume populist semblances,"[6] and thus have a particular propensity for communicating and diffusing the broadly shared values of similar cultures.

There are many supporting examples of this position: the digressions into traditional rural life by Russian architecture, even after the Soviet Revolution and in the hands of those considered more "engaged" than most—Konstantin Melnikov, the Vesnin brothers, Ilya Golosov;[7] the *Höfe* period in Red Vienna,[8] which was brief but extraordinarily intense in terms of participation and productivity; the planning work of the Regional Planning Association of America and the Tennessee Valley Authority during the 1920s and 1930s;[9] and, finally, the affordable housing and public building institutes in Italy between the 1930s and 1950s, with a recurring "exaltation of a middle-class domesticity for the masses."[10] This last facet found its best, albeit most contradictory, outcome in the neorealist "movement," and architects who perhaps shared only a few of its assumptions: Mario Ridolfi, Mario Fiorentino, and, above all, Ludovico Quaroni.

On the one hand, Tafuri's realism is in part influenced by György Lukács's epic view, albeit a nationalist-populist type of epic;[11] on the other, it is more richly nuanced. This is seen in the case of Quaroni, whom Tafuri repeatedly describes as a realist, in almost polemical opposition to his inclusion in the neorealist architectural current.

Tafuri wrote his first book on Quaroni[12] in 1964, and later returned to Quaroni's work in various historiographic analyses of Italian architecture.[13] It is not just for reasons of endearment that Quaroni occupies a relevant position in Tafuri's historical construct; this relevance seems specifically linked to Quaroni's interpretation of his own relationship to reality. If, in fact, many of the intellectuals (not just architects) affiliated with neorealism show, according to Tafuri, "a desire for 'engagement in the real'"[14]—which implies a decidedly antirhetorical will—Quaroni's engagement in the real appears in an extraordinarily complex, critical (and self-critical) way. In a word, it is *problematic*. In Tafuri's monograph on Quaroni, it is immediately evident how the "return to a verification of reality and a morality in their becoming"[15] constitutes for Quaroni "the very foundation of living"; but it is also clear how "reality, be it positive or negative, exerts an 'enormous weight' upon Quaroni himself"—a reality "against which, one might say, he is continually fighting, in order not to be dragged along or glorified by it."[16] Quaroni's relationship to reality is firmly and intrinsically contradictory, so it is no coincidence that, in the introduction to his text, Tafuri dedicates a full page to this theme:

> *One of Quaroni's most important teachings is the recognition of the* reality *of contradiction, of the meaning and value of each and every contradictory situation.*

Assuming contradiction for oneself—a contradiction inherent to the world and society, a characteristic and tragedy of the historical moment we are currently in— basically means: forcing oneself to be persistently aware of the present; not allowing oneself any idealization, in action or in thought; never entrusting one's societal hopes or struggles to be postponed to a more or less idealistic notion of an imprecise and cathartic future.

Likewise, assuming contradiction does not necessarily mean remaining caught up in it, there is a way—a profoundly moral way—of compromising with history. It lies in using an undeniably contradictory situation while not wallowing in the shallows of a sterile idealism; discovering its positive traits and bringing them to light; revealing the valid aspects that lie hidden, by definition, in every contradiction; and simultaneously finding the tools that enable one to exploit those traits and transform what reality has offered as a negative into a positive.

I cannot guarantee a priori the success of such an operation; rather, I can only verify it a posteriori—and therefore I must recognize the multiple errors committed and the setbacks suffered. I may well end up with dirty hands, perhaps in the most frequent cases; and then the story of my personal actions may well be the story of a series of failures. Let us not think we are being ungenerous toward Quaroni by recognizing these aspects of his actions, given that—since he initially abandoned [pursuing] a process realized in the positivity of a single work—the value or lack thereof can be verified only in the sum of his actions, in the same way as his being a human in relationships with other humans, with social structures, with social fetishes, with society's myths and hypocrisies. Requesting such a verification—and Quaroni is well aware of this—also means accepting a tragic way of being; it means accepting deep down seeing yourself in those very contradictions, which are combating one another while you are simultaneously immersing yourself in them, in order to combat them. It means not refusing—accepting, once again—to participate in that negativity, even if only to overcome it; but accepting its experience day by day, from one situation to the next. Herein we can see yet another aspect of acting as participation that we will repeatedly recognize as an essential characteristic of Quaroni.[17]

Reading this page, one cannot help but notice the degree to which it indubitably reverberates, allowing us to glimpse more than an objective, detached view of the positive value of a relatively unesteemed architect's practice. Instead, we see young Tafuri's impassioned analysis, which risks self-identification (even if the sudden switch from an impersonal tone to the first person is motivated by rhetorical ends, it is nevertheless a highly significant clue). Quaroni's conception—and, even more, perception—of the contradiction of reality (and of the reality of contradiction) is more or less reflected in Tafuri's thinking, which develops during the same period and in subsequent years. One might even suspect that Tafuri's thinking is significantly indebted to Quaroni, the man and the work. One could even read Tafuri's definition of reality in relation to the Italian situation during the late postwar period, when reality meant, as he writes, "not the reality of the indifferent technician who accepts any situation, any program—who poses as someone who resolves and rationalizes societal problems while confusing society with the monopolizing classes that are in power. Rather, reality referred to its historical meaning, that of an unstable, contradictory situation in which choice is inevitable, if often tragic."[18]

But let us proceed with the analysis we have just begun. According to Tafuri, the cultural climate to which Quaroni "spontaneously adhered" is marked by a "distrust of all preexisting interpretive schemas," such that, for those who belong to it, "the thrust into reality and the battle to transform that selfsame reality are values to be conquered with ever new methods, methods that should be questioned each and every minute."[19] A similar—fundamentally anti-ideological—attitude allows Quaroni to escape mere assimilation into the neorealist style and to overcome the stasis of his own realism. It is this capacity to critically surpass himself—and to carry out a historical interpretation of reality—that Tafuri sees in Quaroni (and, to a certain extent, in himself):

> From the phase of standardizing realism to the phase of fixing it into formal and formalistic schemas, Quaroni moved on . . . to a critical realism that without doubt has many points of correspondence in various sectors of contemporary Italian culture: from the exhaustion of the many pictorial, literary, cinematographic "neorealisms" to a surpassing of a whole series of misunderstandings that those movements brought along with them. Between 1956 and 1959 a new artistic awareness arose, one that recognized—as Cesare Luporini, among others, has observed—"that realism cannot be reduced to any one typology," since, in addition to including the demystified movement of phenomena, it "expresses and interprets this movement in its real sense, and at the same time anticipates it and aids its debut," and consequently refuses "any predetermined content or mode of expression."
>
> Here, then, we have a definition of realism as an experimental tendency in which it is not difficult to spot obvious analogies with Quaroni's life and work in those

years of increasing "demystification" of the misunder-
standings of the naïve realism of 1947–1952.[20]

Tafuri has no trouble seeing that this is still far from prefigur-
ing a safe, secure path along a univocal route. Perhaps his own
personal experiences enlighten him. He writes: "Those who . . .
stop themselves from making recourse to ideology—who deem
the inclination toward a codified utopia as being out of step with
the present-day human condition—have no other resource than
to trust a methodology that punctually reverses the dangers they
intended to overcome. It is just that, in such a way, the sole remaining moral support, the only test that can be proved, is that
of life itself—which means, once again, accepting the idea of
ethically experiencing every act of life, giving each act the same
quantitative value."[21]

Like Quaroni, those who propose through a critical rereading of reality to accept "reality as a structure for action"[22] face the
problem of subtly balancing between different, and sometimes
even opposing, factors. Otherwise, the "intellectual's task . . .
of demystification"[23] is unthinkable, except for methodologi-
cally refracting each facile evasion, each reductive solution, and
substantiating "an autonomy in the scientific development of
technical instruments that translate decisions into operative
reality."[24] For Tafuri, the degree to which all this inclines Quaroni toward "active doubt"[25]—which mirrors his meticulously developed aptitude—becomes clearer when one turns to *History of
Italian Architecture.* Here Quaroni is presented as "the most tormented and problematic of the protagonists of Italian postwar
architecture and a master of self-doubt and self-criticism."[26] To
be clear, he is not a master of an intimate torment, doubt, and
self-criticism, which would remain marginal (if not an obstacle)
to his design work. No, Quaroni's criticism is an "incessant criticism,"[27] perfectly capable of self-analysis and translation into

an equally "tormented line of research,"[28] an anguished reflection on the instruments of a design's configuration.

For Tafuri, the lesson of Quaroni's realism is not a unique instance to be contemplated in abstract isolation; on the contrary, his legacy is intertwined with two of his contemporaries, Mario Ridolfi and Mario Fiorentino—as well as, later, the thematically (but not stylistically) analogous legacy of Vittorio Gregotti.[29] But that is another strand.

Ridolfi and Fiorentino, alongside Quaroni, embody the turning point, the "passage from neorealism to realism."[30] But in what forms does this passage take place? Tafuri does not give a univocal response; instead, he offers many partial replies that are relatively valid with respect to this particular case. Quaroni moves beyond his neorealist residential designs for the Tiburtino neighborhood in Rome as they unfold, "while they are being built: without poetics, without 'languages'"[31]—that is, without fixing the results in place in any definitive way. As for Ridolfi, Tafuri sees several of his motives and approaches as tributaries that flow into realism. Various projects support this: in the towers along viale Etiopia in Rome, purged of "all sentimentality and every hint of nostalgia" and exposing "the isolation to which high-end artisanal work condemns itself";[32] then "the density of allusions taken up in the interweaving of materials and the dryness of architectural volumes" in the INA (Istituto Nazionale delle Assicurazioni) neighborhood in Cerignola, Apulia; and even in the "slap in the face of public taste" evoked by his building on via De Rossi in Rome, which makes a merciless "'portrait' of the project's sponsorship—divided, uselessly anxious, and ultimately quite vulgar."[33] According to Tafuri, Ridolfi's realism lacks any hint of an obliging or accommodating approach. It makes no easy concessions to what we would now call its audience. Ridolfi's ability to grasp the many different faces of reality confirms this. Tafuri writes: "The building on via De Rossi and

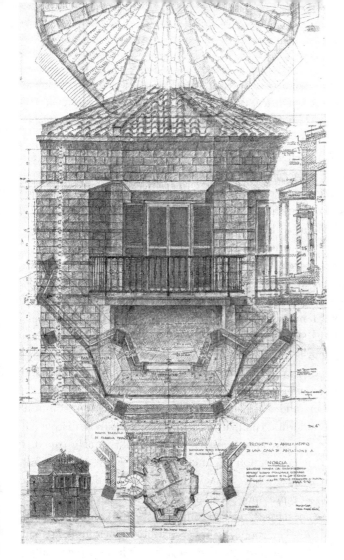

6.1
Mario Ridolfi, renovation and
extension of Casa Ottaviani in
Norcia, 1976–1981. First-floor plan,
elevation, section. Courtesy Modern
and Contemporary Archives, Fondo
Ridolfi-Frankl-Malagricci, National
Academy of San Luca, Rome.

the residential complexes on viale Etiopia: two languages for two copresent realities, the exception and the rule. Even if the former does not tarnish the reality out of whose chains it wriggles, and the latter is obliged to simply 'comment.'"[34]

With each new example it becomes increasingly clear that, for Tafuri, the term *reality* and the realistic attitude that stems from it are not rigid entities with a unique orientation that schematically counters an equally rigid utopian sphere. On the contrary, reality and realism oscillate to the point of spilling over into an only apparent other. Fiorentino's case seems emblematic in this regard: his project for the Unrra-Casas (United Nations Relief and Rehabilitation Administration–Committee to Aid the Homeless) development in the San Basilio neighborhood of Rome denounces—albeit unintentionally—"the dose of utopia that 'realism' contained";[35] while his project in Rome's Corviale neighborhood—done at a time when attitudes that were more pragmatic, even opportunistic, than realistic were becoming more widespread—"overturns utopia into realism."[36]

Reality and utopia cease to occupy fixed, antagonistic positions. And while a utopian temptation could easily be discovered behind even the most realistic intentions, it is equally true that a realistic proposition might end up being entirely chimerical. This is precisely what happens (albeit with the due exceptions, which Tafuri promptly points out) throughout Italy in the 1950s.[37]

In the best cases, realism continuously checks up on and verifies reality. The common thread that, for Tafuri, unites Italian architects of the reconstruction years (what he calls the architecture of reality, or the school of reality),[38] as well as a few sporadic figures in the 1970s, is precisely this approach—a way that is not ideological (at least, not in its solutions) and learns from experience, while simultaneously not being steamrollered into conformity by their needs and demands. Basically, what they share is an ability to read and interpret reality without being subjected to it, without simply repeating and amplifying it.

The architect who manages better than all others to transport this realistic praxis beyond the shallows and pitfalls of the period of reconstruction is Vittorio Gregotti. For Tafuri, the "fertile anxiety"[39] in Gregotti's work directly descends from "Ridolfi's anxieties, severely restrained and ironically expressed,"[40] as well as "Quaroni's systematic doubt."[41] Just reading Gregotti's chapter on the 1950s in his *New Directions in Italian Architecture*[42]—titled "Striving for Reality"—is enough to pick up the same thread of this discourse, wound around the same architects. This includes the many contradictions with which they must work and their positive approach: in other words, the approach that, amid all its instruments, looks to self-reflection and self-monitoring, and thus dialectically distances itself from its own openly predictable position. As Gregotti succinctly states, "Precisely because this realism was nothing more than the projection of the idea of reality, what was produced was an image, a protest and a demonstration of error, rather than an optimistic proposal; it was an extreme attempt to consider architecture as a protest."[43]

The detachment of realism—even from itself (from all illusory points of confusion and petty collaborations with reality)—is thus recognized as the impetus behind the development of an architecture that, beyond any discussion of possible style, aims to problematically face the tasks set for it. In Gregotti's case, this is also a good self-description: it describes him and his work in Tafuri's view.

Tafuri appreciates Gregotti's "disenchantment . . . raised up as a levee against the optimism of the 'city-territory' theorists and the utopianism of the inventors of facile megastructures,"[44] as well as the fact that his work proceeds "without leading to arbitrary meanderings."[45] He also appreciates the architect's "distancing of any temptation to turn the architectural project into a 'carnival of the intellect.'"[46] Thus, as the masking and apparent arbitrariness of reality become dominant, the sober, measured, and nonarbitrary end up becoming values. The problem Gregotti seems to solve, according to Tafuri, is the positive coincidence, the overlapping of the real and the necessary. That this aspect assumes the form of a "suspension of judgment"[47] with regard to technique, or a "return to rigor in composition,"[48] is not particularly important. The key lies in abandoning any ideology pursued through architectural means.[49] The fact that Gregotti excludes "utopia from his cultural baggage"[50]—and that his most successful projects stem "exactly from such an anti-utopian line of investigation"—is yet another coincidence between the views of the architect and the critic. It is one of the fundamental reasons they converge.

Tafuri's cherished discourse centers upon unveiling operative ideologies that conceal in more or less conciliatory forms "old fences between friend and foe [that] have begun to collapse."[51] This is confirmed by his adherence to Bernardo Secchi's extension of this analysis to the urban context.[52] Here, once again, the absence of ready-made, prefabricated solutions and the capacity to "accept the new hypotheses experimentally, judging them by their degree of realism . . . and not by the stories they tell about themselves,"[53] become a value, safeguarding against any and all a priori models. "Anti-utopian realism"[54] is perhaps "the result of a slow yet progressive consumption of myths and ideologies," but above all, a merciless tool of articulation and testing—a means and not an end.

All this leads to a point that—advanced and positively real as it might seem—is nevertheless a stopping point, a no-trespassing boundary of Tafuri's discourse:

> *The explosion of architecture outward toward the real*
> *contains within it a comprehensive project that becomes*

evident once we take into consideration that the tradition
of this sector of research is based on the activity of such
figures as Raymond Unwin, Barry Parker, Clarence Stein,
Henry Wright, and Martin Wagner. There is, nevertheless,
a certain undercurrent in such a shifting of the discipline
of architecture from form *to* reform *that might lead to*
a possible overcoming of its own equivocations. In fact,
at least the start of a trend is discernible in this body of
attempts: the premise for a "new technique," submerged
within the organizations that determine the capitalistic
management of building and regional planning.[55]

From form to reform: in this formula, there is much more than
just an adherence to a tranquilizing reformism; there is also the
detection of a program, a comprehensive project, that promises
to lastingly liberate architecture from the closed space of its own
linguistic games, using it as a technique for intervention. Tafuri
writes: "But this forces us to abandon almost entirely the paraphernalia of the traditional categories of judgment. Since an individual work is no longer at stake, but rather an entire cycle of
production, critical analysis has to operate on the material plane
that determines that cycle of production. In other words, to shift
the focus from what architecture wishes to be, or wishes to say,
toward what building production represents in the economic
game means that we must establish parameters of reading capable of penetrating to the heart of the role played by architecture
within the capitalist system."[56]

The significance of this passage must not escape us: reality
forces us to positively expand our vision from the single object to
a broader context: to the urban fabric, to urban-planning interventions, to the cycle of production. Just as significant, however,
is that there is almost no trace in *The Sphere and the Labyrinth*
of the aforementioned people, nor traces left by the creators

of form.[57] If the final effects of operative realism constitute a noteworthy jump in scale and depth of commitment within real modes of production, then an equally coherent, critical realism should inevitably provoke an "overturning of common values": a critique of reform, a critique of the technique architecture has become. How much of this critique stems from ideas formulated by Benjamin during his writing of "The Author as Producer" (a critique that, in fact, "will have to ask architecture . . . in what way it, as an organized institution, manages or does not manage to influence the modes of production")[58] is evident, although the reasons Tafuri limits himself to merely pointing out the development of such a critique must still be clarified.

Let us return to the problem that is increasingly the central issue: the critique of ideology. Realism can certainly be an effective drug against utopianism; but neither realism nor utopia can elevate itself to be an absolute remedy used with an abstract coherence and consistency. Once again: that which becomes ideological becomes an end in itself.[59]

In fact, where ideology dominates, it is not so much a problem of utopia or reality: both are perfectly capable of producing monsters, if guided by an ideological approach. And the monster is nothing but an illusory projection. "The illusion comes from an ideologically distorted reading of the real,"[60] just as it does from the equally ideologically distorted use of utopia. But if the conditions for surpassing utopia are—as we have seen—consubstantial to capitalist development (which, naturally, does not insure it against sudden relapses into utopianism), then the dialectics of reality are even more complex. On the one hand, the ever-shifting equilibrium that necessarily characterizes any realism capable of closely corresponding to a live reality that, in turn, is ever changing, easily ends up broken, or becomes rigid and friable; on the other, the hoped-for disappointment of all (apparent) ideological engagement exposes heavy limitations.

According to Tafuri, "The disenchantment with which the Italian intelligentsia faced this competition was the sign of an ideological indifference that had become widespread, as a consequence of the new climate, and whose roots were barely covered by disciplined commitment."[61]

In a more general sense (and without any twists, despite the jump backward in time), he writes:

> *Art and society, politics and culture, technology and democracy: from 1945 to today, these great problems have witnessed the fading of theoretical debate, as interest in concrete operations increasingly grew. And this interest in praxis had two simultaneous aspects: on the one hand, it was proof, in reality, of what was sought; on the other, we witnessed reality itself slowly and progressively absorb all energies—a reality that all too often lost all connections with a solid, clearly intentioned methodology.*
>
> *From the end of World War I to today . . . we have followed a trajectory that marks a constant loss of interest in a discussion on an ideological level, [which is] increasingly substituted by struggles over things, over immediate problems. The habit of discussing things, however—and this can easily be seen in [contemporary] architectural and urban-planning debates—also led people to become less accustomed to recognizing the expression of an ideal world in things themselves, nor can it be said that ideology has been substituted by any complete, coherent methodology.*
>
> *So, from the* difficulty of believing in precise ideologies, *to the* difficulty of developing precise methodologies: *this seems to be the path trodden by a large*

> *part of the various sectors of Italian culture, which in*
> *turn is certainly no particular exception seen within the*
> *general crisis of international culture.*[62]

It is not entirely clear from this passage just how the crisis of ideology can redeem itself through any complete, coherent methodologies—even less so if it is not yet fully conscious of itself. This would lead to a distinction between ideology's falling into crisis and something foisting it into crisis—or rather, the critique of ideology Tafuri himself pursues. This finally foists ideology into crisis with an ideology of crisis: reducing the crisis to nothing more than the crisis of that ideology (remember: "The crisis of modern architecture is . . . the crisis of architecture's ideological function"),[63] whose end has been prognosticated, if not explicitly desired and determined.

Here as elsewhere, one must resist—when faced with the complexity and intrinsic aporeticity of Tafuri's thought—the temptation to retrace it by taking easy shortcuts or, worse, attributing to it resolutely prohibited thoughts. It is vital that one should be able to observe the phenomena through Tafuri's own disenchantment. It is from such a position, capable of continuously placing itself in a state of crisis, that one must contemplate the crisis of ideology as one of the many faces that embodies the crisis of reality—thereby having one reflected in and by the other. As Tafuri writes, "It is useless to cry over a given: ideology has mutated into reality; even if the romantic dream of the intellectuals who offered to guide the destiny of the productive realm remains, logically, in the superstructure of utopia."[64] The critique of ideology's demystifying role is thereby transferred entirely to reality. Tafuri continues: "As historians, our task is to lucidly reconstruct the path taken by intellectual work, recognizing the contingent tasks to which a new organization of work could respond."[65]

The strong appeal of the "ought-to-be" (*dover-essere*) of the historian intellectual excludes any rear-guard positions: the intellectual's work is not impeded by following or analyzing the task society's evolution imposes upon him, however contingent they may seem. Once ideology has mutated into reality, the intellectual is left to concentrate on the field of reality, transforming the critique of ideology into a critique of reality (the latter being a total critique, or self-critique, since, as in the case of the former, nothing can be deemed external, foreign, to the system within which it acts—including critique itself). To adapt the critique of ideology to the new conditions of reality—to the point of rejecting those same forms of intellectual work upon which it is founded (strictly speaking, those identified by Karl Marx and Friedrich Engels, who in turn were subjected to the critique of Marxist critics)—thereby becomes the program of those who want to push that critique forward without disregarding (and prescribing) its ends.

For a closer approximation of Tafuri's multifaceted conception of reality, one must reread the final pages of *History of Italian Architecture*, wherein he declares—taking up Cacciari's discourse—that "any approach aimed at indefinitely prolonging the 'state of crisis'"[66] is ineffectual; including—implicitly—approaches that ride the crisis, transforming it into a point of departure that is not superseded nor completed, but simply used. For Tafuri, as for Cacciari, the problem is central: "How to *radically* interrogate, without useless illusions of being able to fix what is broken or resynthesize what is manifold, in a time that no longer allows for any accord between fullness and multiplicity, yet does not require solidarity with the latest victors."[67] Translated into the terms previously used, the question is how to be a realist without turning reality into an ideology, and while maintaining one's self-awareness, unease, questioning, and problematizing; and to also offer, from that reality, not just prefabricated responses, but plausible interpretive hypotheses without being pushed into a darker, more cynical opportunism, into the shrewdest pragmatism. This balance between adherence and detachment, empiricism and ideality, is undoubtedly difficult. Indeed, Tafuri writes, "It should not be difficult to understand that the era of nihilism can be surpassed not with further subjective inventions,"[68] but rather with forms of interrogation, which nevertheless have "the strength to *point out the problem*, not resolve it."[69]

There is an additional passage where Tafuri significantly develops these themes. His return to a meditation on the Renaissance not only reopens the discourse on utopia, but also profoundly rethinks the discourse on reality. In any case, and in light of all that has been said in the previous pages, the two aspects are closely associated, and Tafuri's later reflections head in the direction of this historical-philosophical foundation.

At the beginning of *Interpreting the Renaissance* is Tafuri's analysis of the *Novella del Grasso legnaiuolo* (*The Tale of Grasso the Carpenter*), a literally tragicomic description of a "derealization"[70] designed to mock the carver Manetto Ammannatini. What Tafuri demonstrates through this tale—and then reasserts through numerous other examples not linked solely to architecture—is the inherent contradictoriness of reality upon which the Renaissance casts full light. Reality—as can be deduced from Tafuri's analysis—also contains irreality, just as, in the Renaissance period, "linguistic pluralism lives alongside the *rule*."[71] The exception, in this sense, does not survive *despite* the rule; rather, exception itself (or, better still, an infinite series of exceptions)[72] makes the rule, sets the foundation of a code. In the same way, irreality is an essential part, a truly conformist part, of reality, and not just a parasitic function of it.

General considerations that stem from this are highly important in Tafuri's thinking as outlined thus far: "Architecture and culture of the humanist period attempt to keep the two opposing poles solidly united: the one based on stable foundations, the other related to subjective will. As has been noted, this is a matter of a *complexio oppositorum*, a *culture of contradiction*."[73]

So the problem of contradiction returns yet again, but this time from a theoretical point of view, and within a very different framework with respect to Quaroni and a few other key figures of Italian architecture. If, in the latter case, contradiction appears weakly structured around a series of empirical, personal experiences, in the case of the Renaissance it assumes the status of a bona fide culture. In this culture each aspect is consonant (or, more accurately, dissonant) with contradictory tones,[74] to the point where carrying out deeply serious, realistic (re)search on the Renaissance can only be equivalent to "articulating the forms of contradiction"[75] that lie within it.

What Tafuri searches for in the Renaissance is therefore the wealth of interwoven connections between utopia and reality (the utopicity—and even irreality—of the real, but also the realism of utopia). It is these connections that the Renaissance safeguards and embodies—contrary to all contemporary culture, where there is no *complexio oppositorum*, but rather a mere sum of simple pluralities, deformed multiplicities, within which each constantly aspires to prevail over the other, to differentiate and identify itself, to take everything on, to represent the sole synthesis, the solution. If contradiction (or rather, a startling quantity of contradictions) can be identified with relative ease in contemporary architectural culture (and Tafuri follows its developments through the names and events that I have at least partially tried to touch upon here), only humanistic-Renaissance culture opens up contradiction as an essential form of culture, and therefore—more generally—of reality itself.

Dedicating oneself to (re)searching the Renaissance—far from constituting a retreat from the contemporary realm, a sign of "boredom" or "irritation"[76] or the launch of a new career with respect to his previous one[77]—means, for Tafuri, dedicating himself to a search for, and research on, the *complexio* of contradictions that belong to reality as such. (From this point of view, research and project are equivalents in his mind;[78] each term always stands for the research—and the project—of crisis.) If the historical construct does not consist of unveiling a truth, but rather lies in shedding light upon a "constellation of events" or "nodes in which events, times, and mentalities intersect,"[79] the historian's task is to keep these nodes in tension among themselves. If, for example, the node of the Renaissance is in a productive, significant tension with the node of philology,[80] the latter is also in tension with the node of the critique of ideology,[81] which is in turn in tension with the node of contemporaneity. Both epochs are in a productive—albeit different—tension with the nodes of utopia and reality. Hence the necessity (the urgency, the strategy) of Tafuri's turn to the Renaissance is not to stop confronting problems that run through the contemporary—in which he never ceased to be interested, even in his last years and at the heart of his humanistic studies—but, rather, a different way of contemplating these selfsame problems. This method is comparative rather than mechanical, and functions by means of the differences and distances among the answers that can be gathered from it and broadened to more extensive, current contexts. It is certainly no coincidence, in this sense, that the central problem previously left on hold (but, upon closer inspection, left in suspense by Tafuri himself)—a problem that concerns the possibility of questioning reality without unacceptably betraying it—finds a partial and programmatically dynamic denouement in the Renaissance concept of reality as *complexio*. (It is no coincidence that historical research, understood in the aforementioned sense,[82] provides and represents the outcome of this denouement.) A passage in *Interpreting the Renaissance* addresses this question: "It is not the historian's task to 'recombine fragments.' Nor is it legitimate for the historian to identify with the victors—a vice that complements the apologia for present-day conditions that is, lamentably, still quite active. On the contrary: it is possible for history to lend its voice to a dialectical process that does not take the outcome of the struggles it narrates for granted. Hence it must suspend its judgments if it is to proceed at all. Nothing is given as past. Historical time is, by its constitution, hybrid."[83]

Suspension does not constitute a minor or transitory condition but is, rather, a paradoxical and fundamental condition of historical research that effectively aims to correspond to reality. The denouement therefore recalls the node; the instruments through which we come to know the real (and to understand the project as well) become forms of interrogation.[84] The constitutively hybrid character of historical time is configured, at this point, like the perfect double, the mirror image of the space of reality—and therefore also as the only feasible way of describing and even penetrating it. The space of reality is also a hybrid space, but it has significant differences from the various realities. In the case of Renaissance reality it is a space composed of fractures, cracks, and contradictions, "oscillating between a need for certainty and a bent toward the unfounded" (embodied best, in Tafuri's view, by Leon Battista Alberti, who was capable of casting an ironic smile to oppose the "tragic awareness of the irrepressibility of contradiction"[85]—a smile that is only one of the masks, one of the "modes of expression that render the *as if* of the disenchanted subject sayable"[86]). In the case of contemporary reality, its space is a literally critical space, an expression of crisis that no longer manages to hold the *complexio oppositorum* together. It is precisely in our contemporary reality that crisis, already revealed as a product of history, now reveals itself as the form of reality.

7

GAMES, JOKES, MASKED BALLS

Let us return to the critical point where we left Tafuri's project of crisis: the point, that is, where it closes all accounts of "architectural research of the past decade."[1] Tafuri saves a few yet significant words for the work of one of the youngest, least established architects at the time: Rem Koolhaas.

Tafuri's unflattering judgments, such as "Koolhaas's cynical game" and "Koolhaas's jokes"[2]—seem initially to write the architect off, along with the other members of what he considers the disenchanted avant-garde, be they "Whites," "Grays," or "Hypermoderns."[3] From Kahn to Koolhaas, contemporary architectural ideology covers a vast territory: from the selling off of its inheritance to the highest bidder to Koolhaas's bringing it fully into play. Given the span of conspicuous differences, however, we must not lose sight of the substantial crisis that, for Tafuri, runs throughout contemporary experience.

What is Tafuri alluding to when he speaks of Koolhaas's cynical game and jokes? In the absence of any explicit explanation, one must deduce a possible answer. The only image concerning Koolhaas that appears in *The Sphere and the Labyrinth* is Madelon Vriesendorp's painting *Flagrant délit*, which appeared on the cover of Koolhaas's 1978 *Delirious New York*. Curiously, the two sources Tafuri cites regarding architectural research during the 1970s do not reference Koolhaas, although he counts Koolhaas's presumed jokes.[4] In 1980—the year *Sphere and Labyrinth* was published in Italy—Tafuri could have known only a few Koolhaas projects: Exodus, or the Voluntary Prisoners of Architecture (1972, with Madelon Vriesendorp, Elia Zenghelis, and Zoe Zenghelis), published in 1973 in *Casabella*,[5] and the projects shown in the appendix of *Delirious New York* (The City of the Captive Globe, Hotel Sphinx, New Welfare Island, Welfare Palace Hotel, and the pool in Story of the Pool), all developed between 1972 and 1977. They were a conscious revival of Manhattanism and the use of New York strategies: the grid, congestion, the technology of the fantastic, the disconnect between interior and exterior, and the multiplicity of architectural programs. It would have been difficult for Tafuri to have known about Koolhaas's 1978 competition proposal for the extension of the Dutch Parliament in The Hague; the design for the renovation and extension of the Arnhem prison, also done in 1978; or the 1979 competition proposal for the Irish Prime Minister's Residence in Dublin, because they were first published in magazines only in 1980.

On the basis of this chronology, one can hypothesize that Tafuri's criticism of Koolhaas for playing a cynical game refers, in particular, to Exodus. Exodus was provocatively and ironically based on the Berlin Wall, conceived as a megastructure transferred to London and adapted to the idea of voluntary self-marginalization within the city. The rethinking of the structure of the wall, in this sense, contains a hefty dose of sarcastic disenchantment. It signals the total erasure of any ideology or ideal that does not belong to a reality of extreme regulation: it no longer carries the original, dramatic value of a political-military border, a cruel expression of the Cold War. Rather, the wall becomes a continuous monument of sorts, in the tradition of Superstudio, open to making concessions of hedonism, luxury, and well-being to those who cross through the checkpoint— significantly renamed a reception area. Exodus was simply too much, even for those who, like Tafuri, had tried to turn their

7.1
Rem Koolhaas and Elia Zenghelis,
Exodus, or the Voluntary Prisoners
of Architecture, 1972. © OMA

own disenchantment into an intellectual weapon, and who took on the critique of ideology as their own battle.

Koolhaas's American proposals, on the other hand, can be seen as veritable jokes. Above all, The City of the Captive Globe, which transforms the regular modules of Manhattan's grid into marble bases supporting parades of paradoxical constructions, evokes more or less well-known episodes of modern experience, from the cruciform skyscrapers of Le Corbusier's Plan Voisin to El Lissitzky's Lenin Tribune, even stopping by Salvador Dalí's corrupted revision of Millet's *Angelus*. The interventions for New Welfare Island propose "formally, programmatically and ideo-logically competing architectures,"[6] literally mirroring modern experience: the surrounding extant buildings (a counter-UN, facing the original United Nations across the river); "buildings that were once proposed for New York, but were for some reason abandoned" (including a suprematist *Architecton* by Malevich); and allegorical buildings and pictorial subjects transposed into plastic sculptures (Géricault's *Raft of the Medusa*). In each case, Koolhaas is plainly having fun, playing with the characters of Manhattan's architecture and modern mythologies, casting them beside yet other characters and mythologies in deliberate contrast.

Despite this, Koolhaas intends such proposals as anything but simple jokes or games: unlike Venturi's ironies, which essen-tially feed on the realm of play, Koolhaas aspires instead to give an image (if not real body) to a conceptually paradoxical yet seri-ous world. His floating pool with Soviet andro-propulsion from The Story of the Pool[7] is emblematic: at first glance it looks like the simple, chance subject of a brilliant, openly humorous liter-ary tale (and in part, it is precisely that). But it also aspires to something more: to grasp the programmatic lesson of Manhat-tan, subtracting it from its own grid and rendering it as unbind-ing and usable as possible.

There is even more, as Koolhaas explained in 1985: "The floating pool project was a reply to all the dilemmas New York and Leonidov posed, the purest demonstration of what I wanted to do with architecture: a project that was pure program and almost no form, that could coexist quite well with any other type of architecture . . . that countered Leonidov's intelligence with Tafuri's intimidation."[8]

Coming across Tafuri's name—precisely where Koolhaas outlines the concept of the architectural project after Manhattan—could at first seem surprising. What does Tafuri have to do with any of this? In Koolhaas's opinion, Tafuri represents the limit against which the project pushes—the *Raft of the Medusa* versus the raft of the constructivists, or pessimism versus optimism.[9] In Koolhaas's terms, countering Leonidov's intelligence with Tafuri's intimidation means recognizing Leonidov as a rich mine of unexplored possibilities and the unfolding of an unexpected freedom for modern architecture—a freedom that has been imagined neither before nor after him.[10] It also means recognizing, in Tafuri, the imposition of a severe, almost tyrannical rigor that somehow one has to resist. For the moment, it is not important to establish whether such a comparison has solid motives: what counts is that it fully depicts the other side of what Tafuri calls Koolhaas's jokes. And if, for Tafuri, Koolhaas really is joking, then Tafuri cannot but seem truly intimidating to Koolhaas.

Yet something even more problematic underlies the antagonism that divides them. Certainly, setting themselves at opposite poles can perfectly explain the distance, but it still does not clarify its existence. In order to grasp that, we need a few additional clues.

In *The Sphere and the Labyrinth*, Koolhaas's name appears a third time—but this time not just to stigmatize his games and jokes. Instead, it appears on the occasion of the architects' annual Beaux Arts Costume Ball, held on January 23, 1931, at the

Hotel Astor in New York. The ball is indelibly inscribed in architects' collective memory because of the photograph that captured seven very serious men lined up in front of a dark velvet curtain, dressed in a most unusual fashion. Six of them wear identical patent-leather shoes, shiny black pants, and jackets comprising a flared, white vest patterned with dark rectangles ("windows") and dark, shiny sleeves. But their headgear is what really distinguishes them: each, to varying degrees of accuracy, reproduces a building, or part of a building, that the six distinguished gentlemen had built. The photograph shows A. Stewart Walker as the Fuller Building; Leonard Schultze as the new Waldorf Astoria Hotel; Ely Jacques Kahn as the Squibb Building; Ralph Thomas Walker as One Wall Street; D. E. Ward as the Metropolitan Tower; and Joseph H. Freedlander as the Museum of the City of New York. The seventh gentleman, at the very center, is set apart from the rest by the even greater eccentricity of his garb. He is none other than William Van Alen, and his suit reproduces, literally from head to toe, the Chrysler Building.

In 1974 Koolhaas wrote an essay[11] about this photograph and the event it documented. In the entire history of twentieth-century architecture, this was destined to be one of the most resonant events. Tafuri cited this essay in a footnote of his own, with no further comment.[12] Nevertheless, in the same note, he paused briefly to focus on the ball, formulating an entirely different interpretation.

Koolhaas's interpretation (which four years later he took up again, with a few variations, in *Delirious New York*)[13] centers on the event's operative, strategic character. For him, it was an architects' congress masked as an architects' masked ball: "This ceremony [was] Manhattan's counterpart of the CIAM Congress on the other side of the Atlantic."[14] To emphasize this reading, in the version published in *Oppositions*, Koolhaas began with a

A Journal for Ideas and
Criticism in Architecture

Published by The Institute for
Architecture and Urban Studies

May 1974

OPPOSITIONS 3

7.2
Cover, *Oppositions* 3, 1974.

statement by Charles Joseph Prince de Ligne: "Le congrès ne marche pas, il danse . . ."[15]

More generally, Koolhaas used the evening of January 23, 1931, to reconsider the entire phenomenon of New York skyscrapers:

> *In retrospect, it is clear that the laws of a costume ball have shaped Manhattan's architecture, and that this is the secret of its continuing metropolitan suspense. Only in New York, architecture had become the design of tectonic costumes, which did not even wish to reflect or reveal the true nature of its repetitive interiors, but rather to produce instead, "ideal" dream images which slip smoothly into the collective unconscious to perform their roles as symbols. The costume ball was a formal convention where the desire for individualism and extreme originality was not in conflict with the collective performance and its attainment; it was in fact one of its conditions.*
>
> *Together with the beauty contest, it is a rare situation where competition becomes the mirror image of collaboration. At the same time it exposes, as non sequitur, the expressions of languages that are too private: for a costume there is no impact without some "aha" of recognition. The "new" can only be registered if grafted on to the base of the familiar, as a modification which incorporates the rudimentary original. The architects of New York, making their skyscrapers compulsively comparable, turned the entire population into a jury. In the "real," moralistic, modern architecture, the buildings judged the people.[16]*

The masking ends up neither as a playful, carnivalesque condition nor as a factor that pushes things to extremes by subverting their normal condition, but rather as the real face of the skyscrapers embodied by their architects. Basically, the New York architects masked themselves as reality—where reality is the concealment of the multiplication of the vertical, of a wholly economic repetition of the same that takes place behind the façade, inside these skyscrapers. The strongly individual characteristics of each costume (albeit limited to the "tops") are just the illusory, utopian residue that the architects cultivate insofar as it makes their role in the construction of Manhattan still possible. Behind the mask of reality lies the conscious utopia of good intentions; but further behind this lies an unconscious, supremely realistic reality: the acceptance—and therefore the construction—of the conditions of capitalism's existence and reproduction. The suspense is saved only by a competition (the beauty contest for which New York is the jury) that is pure fiction, or that, in any case, does not question the unanimous assumption on which all skyscrapers are founded.

In truth, rather than an amusing masquerade or a full-on beauty contest, this famous photograph portrays a different kind of parade: an American-style police lineup,[17] wherein the seven potential suspects stand side by side, to be scrutinized in the search for a sole culprit. Even if Koolhaas did not reach the same conclusion, he still identified the suspect who differs from the rest—William Van Alen, the Chrysler Building—and casts a shadow on the others. At the same time Van Alen's appearance constitutes a brittle triumph, a swan song, as the Chrysler Building would soon cede its supremacy to the Empire State Building.[18] In any case, Van Alen is suspected of ambiguity: "The Chrysler's status stands revealed: tonight it is easier to imagine it dancing with a man, than with a woman."[19]

Tafuri's comment has a different tenor: "The skyscraper's 'scenic function' is pushed to an extreme at the ball held January 23, 1931, at the Hotel Astoria [sic] in New York, during which the city's principal architects represent 'The New York Skyline,' with costumes and head gear that evoke their works. . . . Architecture explicates itself as theater; its makers unconsciously bring to a close the cycle opened by the expressionist and Dadaist cabarets."[20]

Where Koolhaas saw the multiform traits of a real conflict, just barely mediated by social forces, Tafuri saw the silhouettes of theatrical actors reciting the collective *pièce* of the absurd: Manhattan's skyline. It is no accident that he included the passage above in the section dedicated to "The Adventures of the Avant-Garde: From the Cabaret to the Metropolis," and directly associated it with an analysis of New York–Babylon, reread as a music hall: "In fact, being neither able nor willing to offer themselves as complete 'syntheses,' the skyscrapers of the 'new Manhattan' pose as spectators at a gigantic collective ballet. The subjectivity that the system of big business transfers to the molecules of the crowd—the individuals—it dominates is thus recuperated, in a sort of propitiatory rite, by the 'new subjects' of the city, who advance joyously to the front of the stage of the metropolis transformed into a music hall. The ludic installs itself in the metropolis with masks that lack thickness."[21]

Significantly, Tafuri returns to the same train of thought, just a few pages later, demonstrating the exact opposite: the musical as a serious hermeneutic key to the metropolis:

> In the film Gold Diggers of 1935, *Busby Berkeley inserts a practically independent segment, a film within the film:* Lullaby of Broadway. *The camera begins with a long shot of the singer Wini Shaw, isolating her face against a black background. While Wini performs her song, the camera executes a perpendicular movement, framing the protagonist from above. After a dissolve, Wini's face remains only in profile, within which appears*

an aerial view of Manhattan. The metropolis of sky-scrapers is completely contained in the unconscious of the individual, as it were: the whole and its parts are no longer distinguishable, bound as they are in a relation-ship of complete correspondence. But here we are dealing with a mortal relationship. After an exceptional repre-sentation of "urban chorality"—a musical sequence that assembles a hundred dancers in a gigantic nightclub—Wini falls from the top of a skyscraper, while the camera moves within a Manhattan that indifferently continues its own existence. Once again, the metropolis is superim-posed upon the face of Wini.

In this way, Berkeley demonstrates that the loved-hated big city requires concrete reform in order for the collective festival of the musical to be experienced "au-thentically"; but he also shows that the entire search for "roots," which we have attempted to characterize by iso-lating some examples from the 1920s, is completely su-perfluous. The individual has already internalized the "values" of the urban machine—and they are mortal. The dream will survive: the dance and the choral song of the musical. We are no longer dealing with the gaiety of the Chrysler and Park Avenue buildings.[22]

If the metropolis of skyscrapers is completely contained in the individual's unconscious, then it is precisely this unconscious dimension (both individual and collective) which Koolhaas psy-choanalyzed[23] that produces effects, and not, as Tafuri claims, a mere mortal relationship. Berkeley's choreographic perspec-tive[24] thus appears distorted—or at least reductive—in relation to Koolhaas's crudely realistic perspective. We are dealing with two diametrically opposed perspectives, yet from both points of view the individual has internalized the values of the urban machine. For Tafuri, "they are mortal" only if they do not come to terms with Koolhaas's new metropolitan race.[25] For Koolhaas, and these Metropolitanites, the absence of any and all ideology that is not money and hedonism—and the psychic fractures they lead to—is not at all mortal but, rather, vital.

At this point we need to broaden the discussion beyond the architects' ball, for there are numerous shared themes and illustrations in *Delirious New York* and Tafuri's essays on New York.[26] The reconstruction of the complex events surrounding Rockefeller Center; the focus on figures such as Raymond Hood and Hugh Ferriss (who had previously received little attention); the Zoning Law of 1916; the analysis of works undertaken by the Regional Plan Association of New York; and even the Manhattan-Venice connection—all of these topics constituted just a portion of the liaisons connecting the American works of Tafuri and Koolhaas. If these are examined in greater detail, the coincidences of overlapping interests—which are easily explained, given the importance of the issues—turns out to be quite unique, For example, eight of the twenty-three images related to New York skyscrapers that appear in *The Sphere and the Labyrinth* (including the photograph of the Beaux Arts Ball) also appear in *Delirious New York*. For four of these (the two from Gaudí's project for Manhattan's Grand Hotel; the reproduction of Diego Rivera's mural, *Frozen Assets: A Cross-Section Through the City*, and the view of the Consolidated Edison pavilion at the New York International Exposition in 1939), no explicit comparison can be found in Tafuri's text.[27] Furthermore, the presence of Vriesendorp's *Flagrant délit* unequivocally attests to Tafuri's direct knowledge of Koolhaas's book.[28] While we might be tempted to see a direct relation from *Delirious New York* (1978) to *The Sphere and the Labyrinth* (1980), it is also true that *Delirious New York* established an equal, if not greater, number of relationships with Tafuri's long essay "The Disenchanted Mountain: The Skyscraper and the City" (1973).

Evidently, the question at hand cannot be reduced to a linear relation of actual or presumed affiliations; rather, the problem must be posited in terms of a real coincidence regarding two authors in the same field of study (a coincidence that has no lack of chance occurrences and fully conscious mutual influences). Yet the differences—or rather, the different juxtapositions and developments that each proposed, beginning with their shared themes—seem no less emblematic. Specifically, Koolhaas intertwined Manhattanism with Gaudí, Le Corbusier, Dalí, and Rivera's forays; Tafuri intertwined Americanism with the contemporary European culture—from Wassily Kandinsky's artistic culture to the architectural culture of Adolf Loos, Bruno Taut, Walter Gropius, Ludwig Hilberseimer, Eliel Saarinen, Hans Poelzig, Peter Behrens, Max Berg, Hans Scharoun, and Mies van der Rohe (to name just a few) and the urban-planning culture of Raymond Unwin and Werner Hegemann. In both cases, the focus of such comparisons is on what binds and separates America and Europe. This parameter is almost taken for granted by the Italian historian, as well as by the Dutch architect. Once again, difference counts more than analogy. It is on these retroactive discrepancies, as Koolhaas would say—or, as Tafuri would say, on these different historical projects—that the much greater matter of the interpretation of architecture and contemporary reality hinges. This is also the basis upon which one builds—or tries more or less consciously to build—the direction and orientation toward the future, or, more simply, one's own greater or lesser adherence to it.

In Tafuri's "The Disenchanted Mountain," an apparently monolithic set of skyscrapers is divided into a large number of subsets that expose different problematic faces. The first is revealed between the early twentieth century and the 1920s by the construction of America's major tertiary urban centers. Above all, Tafuri emphasizes the schism between technological innovation and the discrete architectural organism or building (with the consequential "resorting to languages aimed at exalting—through advertising—the concentration of capital, of which the skyscraper itself is the height of expression").[29] Second, he points out the conflict between the speculative nature of single building endeavors and ensuring efficiency within a directed center of multiple integrated functions. (Essentially, it is a matter of controlling the "skyscraper as 'event,' as 'anarchic individual.'")[30] From these two conditions, the "triumph of eclecticism"[31] almost logically descends, as does the expression of a passive attitude with regard to such problems. This is complemented, however, by the idea that architectural language indulges the growth of a building's function and structure. For Tafuri, Cass Gilbert's Woolworth Building is a paradoxical result. Yes, its neo-Gothic adornments are what strike the public imagination, decreeing its success, but they do not have the same importance as its "'telescopic' mass"[32] within the framework of the modern skyscraper. As Tafuri writes: "It is the exact opposite of a formal attitude. Affirming the architectural organism's supremacy over formal superstructures, architectural language is attributed with an instrumental, secondary value, to the point that it appears entirely antithetical to the ideological attributes the European avant-gardes have assigned to the new, nonfigurative syntaxes. In a certain sense, what we are witnessing in America is an ongoing process of architecture's deideologization."[33]

The pragmatic detachment with which American architects view the "'added value' of language"[34] is confirmed by the 1922 competition for the Chicago Tribune Tower. Tafuri's lengthy analysis of the various project submissions was aimed, above all else, at identifying the gap between American and European culture when asked to design "the most beautiful skyscraper in the world." For Tafuri, absolute cynicism dominated the American architects' participation, displayed in a gamut of eclectic proposals.

> *Among its immediate causes, the overall squalor of the American submissions can be attributed to a lack of regard for the urban role of the skyscraper—essentially, a failure to appreciate that role—as, much later on, Le Corbusier ultimately recognized. American architects no longer produce events on a metropolitan scale, but they put great effort into giving formal stability to an architectural object whose intrinsic laws are already largely ignored: the necessary jump in scale—from the object to the control of a highly concentrated structure—given the iron-fisted laws that dominate the profession and the American construction market, is only considered on a zoning level; nor does the dominant pragmatism allow leading architects to venture anywhere beyond projects for restructuring the transportation networks.*[35]

The approach of European architects was quite different. For many of them—from Taut to Clemens Holzmeister—the recourse to "gothicist themes"[36] must not be separated from their resistance to the reduction of the skyscraper to an isolated element, entirely thought within a capitalist logic, as if a toy in the hands of real-estate speculators, and where language is considered a free element. Tafuri writes: "They consider the skyscraper as if it were the bell tower of a precapitalist village, rich in symbolic values . . . such that it could serve as a referential pole for a 'community of subjects.' . . . It is like the regressive utopia of the *small town* that tries to oppose the reality of the metropolis: it is still the opposition of the *Gesellschaft* to the *Gemeinschaft*, of the community to organized society."[37]

Gropius's and Max Taut's projects were no less spoiled by the temptation to create a "symbolic form,"[38] an image that is jealous of its own autonomy—albeit an autonomy quite different from the one sought in the preceding cases. Hilberseimer's proposed skyscraper seems to be "entirely 'free' of any communicative desire,"[39] reduced to pure sign, to a mortal silence.

This complex, nonlinear panorama leads Tafuri to assert that "for now, the European avant-gardes and rear guards have only responded to the false American certainties with a confused debate on the obvious uncertainties: *America as Seen from Europe* seems, judging by these projects, to be an entirely literary myth, more than a structural reality."[40]

And yet in the organic Chicago Tribune proposal by Eliel Saarinen, which in the competition ranked second (much like Hilberseimer's indifferent proposal, albeit with very different accents), there is an effort to link the building to the city, and thereby redeem the skyscraper from its wholly economic vow. All this, it turns out, is unknown and unheard of in American architectural culture. Here, a masquerade is played out, wherein the masks cover a substantially unquestioned structure (which was precisely the case with Howells and Hood's winning proposal). Saarinen's utopian attempt is viewed as the other face, the other side—diametrically opposed—to the absolute, disenchanted realism of the American architects: an enchanted mountain versus disenchanted mountains. If Saarinen's enchantment is the illusion of having a significant, organic influence on the American metropolis, for the American audience it lies instead in the possibility of celebrating the illusory "triumph of architecture over the artificiality of the metropolis"[41] with yet another new mask: "For a few years, Saarinen's severe romanticism fueled the abstract demand for idealistic masks, with which businessmen and corporations thought they could cover up the brutal reality of speculative and financial enterprises tied to urban concentration and to the development of commercial construction."[42]

Tafuri's lucid analysis of Saarinen's development of a project for the Chicago lakefront also holds up in a more general sense:

> *Critiquing, as Saarinen does, the irrational budding of skyscrapers in America's urban centers could have led to the formulation of a global hypothesis for restructuring the construction industry, beginning with skyscrapers: verifying, that is, whether a construction type that presupposes a high concentration of invested capital can or cannot act as a flywheel for technologically innovative experimentation, with induced effects on productive cycles connected to construction. But, in order to launch such research, it would be necessary to free the skyscraper from the ironclad laws that link it to real-estate speculation. Inserting the skyscraper—insofar as it is a privileged element in a highly concentrated city—into a cycle with stimulating effects for technological innovation would have again taken on a utopian character, but at least scaled at the level of real problems. Sure, even Saarinen freed the skyscraper from the contradictory mechanism of American cities' speculative structure. But his liberation was strictly formal: it is the image of a possible liberation, whose conditions are sent back for further analysis—whereupon architecture suddenly comes to a halt.*

> *In other words, with his project for the Chicago lakefront, Saarinen deliberately halts his architectural proposal at an ideological level. The hoped-for control over urban form through a unifying design introducing formal values to convince the community remains a mere*

*schema. In fact, his intuited idea of designing a project
at a new scale of intervention is not elaborated by any
realistic investment plan.* [43]

The failure of Saarinen's attempt does not kill European architects' hope for the possibility "of a synthetic control of the urban
dynamic," [44] even if it is "immediately antithetical to the laws of
growth and the organization of the construction industry in the
American city." [45]

It is highly significant that—when faced with the alternative
between the utopian proposals of Auguste Perret, Le Corbusier,
El Lissitzky, and Mart Stam, and the realistic solutions developed
by American architects—Tafuri chooses to go down a third route,
that of "new utopias, relevant to commercial concentrations . . .
within the attempts at regional planning carried out in the 1920s
and 1930s" [46] in the United States. This choice marks—as we will
clearly see—a significant difference with respect to Koolhaas,
just as, on other occasions, their different interpretive choices
are similarly significant.

From Tafuri's reconstruction of the intricate events surrounding the Regional Plan of New York—and particularly
Thomas Adams's role as development director—a continuous oscillation between mutually contradictory positions emerges.
These positions range from almost Enlightenment stances to
openly speculative ones. In reality, these oscillations are the
fruit of a "series of cautious compromises" [47] made by Adams,
who writes: "It is probable, therefore, that the Utopia of the perfect 'garden city' will influence future urban growth in the New
York region at least as much as the Utopia of the perfect 'skyscraper city' and that the expansion of the city-region will evolve
along lines that will show an attempt, at least, to embrace the
best features of both." [48]

Such a position of faithful compromise is not entirely free of ambiguities. The violent attack Lewis Mumford wages against Adams's ideas helps to clarify them: Adams's failure to substantially rethink the general conditions of New York's development (its political and business institutions) and his proposals' lack of "tools for controlling the territorial dynamics" give the plan an "abstractly 'democratic' tone . . . inadequate for triggering any innovative processes within the American urban economy."[49]

Adams's reasoning, in which "realism and abstraction strangely balance one another"[50] (reasoning that Tafuri understands, if he does not share it), centers upon combining private intervention and public power to obtain a "reasonable speculation,"[51] even though he does not manage to define its exact conditions. It is symptomatic that, alongside the dismissal of Mumford's rigorous idealistic and realistically impracticable position, Adams also argues with Hood, who opposes any hypotheses of public and private collaboration. It is precisely in their evaluations of Hood's role that the distance between Tafuri's and Koolhaas's interpretations can be measured.

Tafuri deems Hood's stylistic eclecticism (from the neo-Gothic Chicago Tribune Tower to the modernist McGraw-Hill Building, not to mention the primitivism of the McCormick Mausoleum) as not only a sign of great unscrupulousness but also a clear professional choice: "between architecture and capitalist development there has to be not only alliance, but close collaboration."[52] The architect is entirely at its service, with his abilities and competence. As such, he is called upon to "successfully assume responsibility and demonstrate that the integration of architectural issues with the heart of financial speculation is advantageous from all points of view."[53] In this light, Hood's antistylistic declarations are emblematic: "A style is developed through imitation and repetition, both of which are lethal to creativity and the criterion—essential in the art of construction—of maximum utility."[54]

If, then, the law of change characteristic of American society is essential for an architect like Hood, nevertheless "in his work there is no ideology of change—the central theme of the European avant-gardes' vitalistic currents—but rather an entirely realistic and commercial consideration of it."[55] His is a pragmatism of convenience, which is not disavowed even, according to Tafuri, by his city-scale projects, City Under a Single Roof and Manhattan 1950. Indeed, the latter two can be read as a "response, from the point of view of a large financial and industrial capital, to proposals for regional decentralization: it is the sign of resistance the purely speculative principle mounts to oppose territorial rationalization."[56] It is true that there is a utopian charge to this, where it implies the possibility of general control of urban form—even on the part of private investors—through "gigantic concentrations of capital . . . with constancy, over time";[57] but for Hood this ultimate, definitive utopia, which is really speculative, only fulfills "vague, abstract cultural desires"[58] that participate in the most "explicit response to the utopias of urban equilibrium that the Regional Plan of New York proposed during those same years":[59] Rockefeller Center.

Tafuri revisits (as does Koolhaas), step by step, the intricate phases of Rockefeller Center's planning: he examines the motivation for its creation; casts light on the various competencies it requires (including a renewed proposal for its operations staff); and, finally, analyzes the many designs for the center before reaching its final configuration. His final judgment after this long examination is eloquent: "The 'realism'—verging on cynicism—that characterizes the events surrounding Rockefeller Center marks the end of any utopia related to the complete controllability, on the part of public power, of City soil."[60]

The *finis terrae* Tafuri thereby ends up glimpsing (which also involves the urban-planning tradition, at least within the confines of American cities) does not straightforwardly coincide with the end of the essay and his historical-critical expertise; rather, it marks—in his view—the effective end of any possibility for further ventures into that territory. Any attempt at such ventures would, for Tafuri, be tantamount to trying to hover in mid-air. Such an operation would be as foolish an ambition as it would be risky, and he cannot but oppose it with a very vehement—and, as far as he is concerned, permanent—admonishment: "The urbanized territory refuses any and all utopias. . . . Every American creation projected on an urban scale" is indelibly marked by "an anti-utopian meaning."[61]

Koolhaas begins precisely where Tafuri leaves off. In *Delirious New York*, the selfsame issues of "The Disenchanted Mountain" are now backlit. What Tafuri sees as an endpoint—one that cannot be revisited any further, and was patent proof of failure—Koolhaas views as a germinal moment, the dawn of a new world of possibilities for architecture and architects.

From this viewpoint Rockefeller Center becomes "the first installment of that final, definitive Manhattan."[62] It represents the collectivity of the undertaking—the fruit not so much of an endless series of compromises, but of the merciless competition between everyone involved, which was indispensable to the final result. The stratification of projects is "the most mature demonstration of Manhattanism's unspoken theory of the simultaneous existence of different programs on a single site, connected only by the common data of elevators, service cores, columns and external envelope."[63] The "sudden suspension of financial gravity"[64] in which the center, due to the crisis of 1929, found itself afloat, was destined to ensure the center a certain "theoretical integrity,"[65] making the committee that oversaw its definition a "forced marriage between capital and art."[66] All this attests not to

Koolhaas's delusions of a hypothetical redemption of Rockefeller Center against the tyranny of speculation, but rather his ability to fix—with great lucidity, but also with extreme detachment—its coexistence between the various components at play, and his ability to read into the various facets of reality, gleaning the aspects that are contradictory but also, in the final analysis, positive.

In this regard, the cases of Hood and Ferriss are enlightening. Hood is seen as an agent of Manhattanism, capable of embracing its inherent contradictions. His buildings apply the stylistic principle of contradiction, while proving the efficacy of the principle of reality: they have room for all Manhattanism's strategies. Alongside this, Hood's theoretical projects play a particularly significant role: a City of Towers and the aforementioned City Under a Single Roof and Manhattan 1950: "They share a premonition of a new age contained in the extrapolation of these trends as they are, grafted onto a continuing devotion to the existing metaphoric infrastructure, a refusal to consider any part of the magic carpet of the Grid as subject to reconsideration."[67]

Basically, in his own way, Hood is the champion of retroactivity: if, on the one hand, this lies in expressing now all that the past has neglected to express, then on the other, Hood's process lies in attributing to the future all that is secretly present in the current state of things. In giving form to his *futurable*, utopian vision, he guarantees the correctness of developing the current state.

There is more. Like all those who have proposed various utopias, Hood overturns the usual order between the level of reality and the level of the ideal projection: "Hood wants to adapt the new age to the real Manhattan, not the reverse."[68] And here Hood shows that he is part of that "mutant kind"[69] that Koolhaas finds in New York's DNA; he is perfectly aware that one can never show his hand in the "Artificial City," where every play is like an act of

7.3
Hugh Ferriss, perspective drawing
of American Radiator Building
by Raymond Hood, 1929. In
The Metropolis of Tomorrow (1929).

double-crossing. Thus, Hood's "discreet, private theory about the Skyscraper"[70]—which at the same time realizes that "in Manhattan, it would be unwise to admit it"—represents less a point of weakness or uncertainty than it does the psychology of his principal strategy: to present a few proposals for New York "as the answer to the condition it is determined to exacerbate."[71] In other words, he makes a show of combating congestion in order to elevate it to an even higher level.

Contrary to this ruthlessly realistic strategy is Le Corbusier's, which Koolhaas presents as a mixture of paranoid activity, naïveté, and sentimentalism: indeed, Corbusier's "'solution' [The Radiant City] drains Manhattan of its lifeblood, congestion."[72]

It is no coincidence that Koolhaas counterposes Le Corbusier and Hood, while Tafuri sets them beside the ambiguous results of European research on the skyscraper. There is a precise logic in both viewpoints. If, in fact, Tafuri tries to make the avant-gardes' dialectics react to the value of the new giants of the mountain as "instruments of economic politics,"[73] to show the avant-garde's ineffectuality over the "paradox of the metropolitan era,"[74] then Koolhaas utilizes the avant-garde's antinomies to bring Manhattanism's manifesto into light, in all its controversial self-evidence—in other words, the triumph of the opportunities offered by the skyscraper and the grid. This change in perspective magically transforms the Tafurian problem of concentration, observed through any remaining ideology of the Regional Plan of New York, into Koolhaas's culture of congestion—and consequently the architecture of Manhattan into *a paradigm for the exploitation of congestion.*[75]

Ferriss provides an integral contribution here. But once again his contribution comes with fundamental differences, depending on one's viewpoint. In Ferriss's drawings Tafuri sees only the work of a "capable conjurer of images,"[76] who at once sings the praises of the skyscraper and propagandizes zoning—and therein also notes the anachronistic coexistence of "mythical, superhuman forces" and an "entirely pre-Enlightenment idea of a *human entity*," full of "futuristic suggestions and Beaux-Arts traditions," "the distressing aura" of "a world upon which the sun has already set."[77] Naturally he lingers on Ferriss's Imaginary Metropolis projects, writing them off as regressive utopias, and late-romantic projects that Koolhaas completely ignores. Analyzed from a utopian perspective, Ferriss's contribution does seem regressive. Yet it looks rather different if evaluated from Koolhaas's realistic perspective. Not that one can neglect to mention the contradictions here: Ferriss is presented as "the greatest theoretician" of the skyscraper, but also, for Koolhaas, as "the greatest obscurantist"[78] regarding the tower's true nature. And yet it is precisely in Ferriss's work as delineator that Koolhaas recognizes the presence of a highly progressive element for New York culture: the "murky *Ferrissian Void*";[79] an "artificial night that renders all architectural events vague and ambiguous"; an "architectural womb . . . [which] absorbs multiple impregnation by any number of alien and foreign influences—Expressionism, Futurism, Constructivism, Surrealism, even Functionalism."[80] The very syncretism Tafuri labels as substantially negative reappears here as the polar opposite: "*Manhattanism* is conceived in Ferriss' womb."[81]

Let us briefly return to the pages of *The Sphere and the Labyrinth* which are dedicated to comparing the European and American positions on the skyscraper. They provide additional elements within the comparative framework we have established here.

Tafuri insistently points out the irreducibility of the skyscraper to the normal experience of old-world architects and planners. From their perspective, the skyscraper schizophrenically wavers between Moloch and avatar,[82] between an incarnation of the dangerous, the monstrous, and the divine; in architectural terms, between an amorphous container and a cathedral. So, on the one hand, old-world architects see the skyscraper "as symbol and threat of total reification, as distressing nightmare produced by the half-sleep of a metropolis that is losing itself as a subject";[83] on the other, they see it "as an *unicum*, as Merzbau, which, upsetting the organization of the stratified city, manages to recover its symbolism, its communicative structure, its *genius loci*, which, ultimately, through an act of extreme violence, manages to purify—by letting it speak—the place of collective assassination, the metropolis."[84] Everything produced in Europe—on the theoretical level—around the 1920s thus reflects this duplicity, wherein "optimism and pessimism end up coinciding."[85] But in both the most radical and most accommodating proposals, "such projects . . . assume a complete control over the ground to be built upon: which is the exact opposite of the condition that generates a proliferation of high office structures in America."[86]

Basically, the European culture cannot break the bewitched, charmed circle of contradiction between opposites, or, practically speaking, noncontradiction between utopia and reality. This is why the question is always posed as an either-or situation: either utopia (the skyscraper as expression of the spirit of synthesis, without regard for the rife economic problems of urban life); or reality ("complex diseconomicity of the 'skyscraper system,'"[87] and therefore its exclusion from plans for development).

The American architects assume a rather different attitude. Tafuri writes: "Paroxystic competition, which invades midtown Manhattan with new commercial skyscrapers, does not need rationalizing interventions from outside the market. The new laissez-faire contains within itself the adequate potential to selfplan: this is the unexpressed ideology that circulates through New York architecture of the 1920s."[88]

There is nothing left to occupy architects save the language in which the new metropolitan colossi are dressed. Yet whether it communicates a sense of speed, exchange, or transience, or searches for new, unexplored, "truly American" roots,[89] for Tafuri, the language of the skyscraper is precisely marked: it must impede perception of the "laws of productive organization"[90] of the metropolis. "This is why 'The New Babylon' must offer itself up as a theater of attractions, as an eccentricity that has become an institution, a collective behavioral mode."[91] This is precisely where the skyscraper's histrionics are let loose, or rather, begin to recite its spectacular assigned script: "No longer a structure as much as a scenic toy rich in playful qualities, the skyscraper renounces the structural matrix imposed upon it by George Post and Ernest Flagg. Its vitalism is [a] response to the relentless speculative race that leads directly to the catastrophe of the Great Depression, and at the same time is a 'mask' overlapping it."[92]

The architectural transcriptions of the linguistic Babel of the New World thus become "just a tool for forcefully obtaining general approval for a paradoxical urban structure that is increasingly bottlenecked by its own growth."[93] It is from this viewpoint—a third possibility!—that the contradictions rearrange themselves, that "utopia gives its hand in marriage to professional opportunism."[94]

Paradoxically, Adolf Behne—in a 1923 article on the skyscraper published in the magazine *Wendingen*—points out not so much the "path to follow for transforming that typology,"[95] as Tafuri maintains, but rather the attitude architects should assume with regard to it: "We should be the keepers of a certain romanticism, even when we hide behind a cold American hyperobjectivity."[96] The path Behne recommends for European architects is, with considerable approximation, the one followed by New York architects over those same years. Significantly, it is also the path Koolhaas identifies: a mixture of cynicism and romanticism, of acknowledging reality and a dream developed despite, and even through it. This is tantamount to bypassing the crisis, or, better still, turning it into a new point of departure, a new beginning. If, for Tafuri, New York fully represents Koolhaas's ironic "Capital of the Perpetual Crisis"[97] (an inescapable crisis, which cannot be surpassed—an innate status quo), a new, unexpected fruit blossoms in the very heart of that crisis.

Utopia, of course, is not of this world (and, least of all, of New York). Koolhaas is perfectly aware of this. Rather, reality, in its most blatant version, is. And yet this awareness does not reduce Koolhaas's analysis to silence, nor affirm that the final shores of crisis can be passed through, as in Tafuri's analysis. Koolhaas still sees shores to linger on, spaces occupied and buildings constructed, in terms of a multifaceted, contradictory, cynical, and nevertheless possible reality; just as—likewise—from here onward he continues to see spaces (both conceptual and physical) to occupy and buildings to construct.

Tafuri's difficulty in following Koolhaas along this path—it must be strongly emphasized—is due not to an insufficient analysis, nor, deep down, to any substantial divergence in the development of each analysis. While the causes that lead to the crisis are largely those that Tafuri identifies, his evaluation of their effects remains totally different from that of Koolhaas.

We will have to return to those effects later. But we cannot proceed without first noting how a point of incidental yet significant contention is their interpretation of the American city and its skyscrapers: a projection screen upon which an even deeper irreconcilability appears, duly enlarged. Yet, upon closer inspection, a deep resemblance also appears.

EPILOGUE: THE DOUBLE LIFE OF CONTRADICTION

Given what we have seen so far, what can we say is Tafuri's legacy? Evaluating a balance sheet of his contemporary-historical construct at this point can only mean placing it in a historical perspective (although such a perspective might well seem disconnected, fragmentary, or even antiperspectival). This means viewing it in light of the culture to which it inevitably belongs—despite the fact that this deeply upsets and shakes Tafuri's construct to its very foundations.

Tafuri and his historical construct—the project of crisis—belong to modern culture. Tafuri truly and completely embodies the twentieth-century man, or the modern. He was, and is, the ultimate "posthumous man," to use the expression Nietzsche coined.[1] As a posthumous man, in fact, Tafuri "has too much reason to be content with a simple truth";[2] as such, "he is understood far less than other contemporary men, but he is listened to more," since "his authority is nothing but this solitary, mute invitation to listen."[3] He understands the "unprecedented strength of *distance*,"[4] and "grasps the event in its most secret fibers, uncovering it from the masks of truth that fix and immobilize it, and he listens to its irreducible polyphony."[5] Like the posthumous men Robert Musil, Ludwig Wittgenstein, Adolf Loos, and Karl Kraus, Tafuri, inasmuch as he is also a posthumous man, inasmuch as his epoch never catches up with him, "does not teach in vain . . . he continues to teach."[6]

As a posthumous man, Tafuri teaches nonlinear history, its irreducibility into overly simplistic explanations—in whose name the universe of architectural discourse pretends to provide a presumed disciplinary autonomy; he teaches "knowing through signs and conjectures . . . not bases and certitudes."[7] He teaches the intrinsic contradictoriness of history, or rather, the coexistence of a multiplicity of tensions within it; but he also shows how such a system of contradictions—and even the historian's procedure itself—far from dissolving into an infinite series of centerless motifs and discourses, are rooted in certain values. These values grow increasingly solid the more they are subjected to perpetual doubt, merciless critique, and self-critique; they grow more evident the more modestly they are held.[8] Renouncing enveloping, rhetorical auras, as well as resisting the temptation to turn them into a discourse; protecting them from the overwhelming ebb and flow of contemporary chitchat; defining their limits; and verifying their conditions—this is all part and parcel of the modern culture that shapes Tafuri. In him, Loos's "need to try and say what we cannot keep silent"[9] is wed to Wittgenstein's "need to keep silent about the unspeakable."[10] While Tafuri always pointedly focuses on the concreteness of the real relationships in which the work of architecture and figurative art, as he demonstrates, are at a complex crossroads, the "unstated, subliminal motivations"[11] that traverse those same works are no less relevant.

Contradiction, for Tafuri, is not a simple framework within which to project relevant phenomena: rather, it is the pillar of a modern line of thought that does not conclude every discourse with a dialectic synthesis; instead, it opens itself to different voices and lines of reasoning—sometimes so different that they reach a point of radical opposition, which nevertheless allows them to coexist in their aporeticity. It is precisely in this aporetic, contradictory way that unease and irony mix in Tafurian thought—as different and necessarily complementary faces.

Tafuri always poses his subjects of study under the sign of unease; an unease that, far from being the unjust intrusion of a personal trait into a scientific context, embodies a deeper nature. It is the unease of things, not just of the gaze cast upon them, the unease that incessantly flashes (and in doing so builds a bridge, but at the same time illuminates the distance) through present and past. As he wrote, "The 'weak power' of analysis . . . is proposed as one moment in a process that allows the unsolved problems of the past to live on, unsettling the present."[12]

The centrality of that unease in Tafuri's historical research—where separately analyzed lines of thought converge—is echoed and emphasized once again by Massimo Cacciari, in an authentically liminal reflection on Tafuri and his work: "Manfredo taught that virtue itself, practice itself, have the same root as the impatience and the restlessness that afflict us, that research and inquiry manifest the principles of that expectation, anxiety, and dissatisfaction from which we would like to free ourselves."[13]

Research and unease turn out to be one and the same, then, for those who manage to make their own the innate risk within a history that is really a construction—a project—rather than a simple reconstruction of events exactly as they happened. Nor, in such a risky line of research—whose results are never taken for granted—does irony appear out of place; rather, it is an essential participant. Cacciari writes: "No one is free from the vicissitude which binds us all, which all of us are. And that vicissitude compels us to continuous practice, to perennial transformations. . . . Of this knowledge, Manfredo was a master. . . . He affirms it with irony, and therefore with all the more rigor: because irony means insistence of inquiry and detachment and moderation of pathos."[14]

Irony is a line of research, then, but irony is also self-awareness,[15] a way of continually testing oneself and one's certainties. Contradiction is thus transformed into a principle of agency, operation, which, as it imposes its own limits, opens up previously unthinkable possibilities.

There is another level on which the contradiction that runs through Tafuri closely intersects with his interpretation of history, when reading both in light of an inexorably modern destiny: inasmuch as he is a posthumous man, Tafuri, says Cacciari, "taught the most difficult thing: the art of disenchantment, together with hope and faith."[16] This type of contradiction is the most arduous to compose, the one that is more intimately lacerating than all others. Cacciari continues: "The disenchantment that comes, suddenly, at the death of hope and faith is easy; and to communicate hope and faith when one has not learned or when one rejects the difficult practice of disenchantment is likewise easy. But to teach disenchantment, hope, and faith in one, to teach that faith and that hope which demand disenchantment, that disenchantment which keeps our gaze free to see hope and faith—this is something of which only the greatest masters, whatever may be their discipline, are capable."[17]

Accepting the tragic necessity of the modern means, precisely, practicing and embodying, in the most sober way, the fatal coincidence—in the selfsame act, the selfsame moment—of disenchantment and expectation, without falling into cynicism or desperation.

Bringing to light the very limits of modern discourse is integral to modernity—and thus also to Tafuri's modernity. Modern, in this sense, must always be understood as *critique of the modern*.[18] Yet while the modern is perfectly capable of identifying and bringing its own moments of crisis to light, mercilessly subjecting them to analysis, it is not capable of surpassing or relativizing them. The ideology to which the modern belongs is ineradicably intrinsic to it: it is its inalienable presupposition, its inalienable given. This makes the modern condition tragic and excruciating, despite all the effort that is made to allow contradictions to exist within it. The forms of conflict that inhabit it are, in any case, reunderstood within a unifying *forma mentis*—or ethos.

Such assertions would risk being equivocal if we were not to lead them back to the earlier conclusion, justifiable in light of Tafuri's line of thinking: the affirmation of crisis as a general form of contemporary reality.[19] Indeed, the validity of such an assertion is in full force within a modern interpretation of reality—and it is final in all regards: that is, it forces a dramatic either-or situation between a perpetual repetition of this clash and a permanent state of checkmate, or silence. Both are theoretically infinite conditions of suspension.

Tafuri tries to maintain both positions simultaneously. This does not allow for noninvolvement, but rather oscillates between—or, more often than not, unifies in a nonconfusing yet contradictory way—a concerned denouncement and reserved display of phenomena that catch his eye as a critical historian. It is equally evident that crisis as a form of reality can be underwritten only by the current champions of what he calls a "disenchanted acceptance of the real, to the point of cynicism"[20] (which perhaps can count Venturi as their forerunner, and Koolhaas as their main champion today), except when used for advantageous, speculative, and noncontradictory operations: in other words, operations aimed, at once and without contradiction, at theory and business.

To call this a postmodern attitude risks more than one misunderstanding. First, it can be potentially misidentified with the architectural postmodern (a label that is even more misleading when Koolhaas's architecture is in question).[21] But that is not what concerns us. Rather, the discussion hinges on bringing a postmodern ideology into focus, much as, earlier on, we tried to identify the thinkable conditions of a modern ideology. It is in precisely this sense that many phenomena can be included under the banner of a *postmodern condition*[22]—including

8.1
Man Ray, *Monument à D.-A.-F. de Sade*, 1940. © Artists Rights Society (ARS), New York.

those that Koolhaas analyzed along with his approach. All in all, the formation of Koolhaas's postmodern attitude parallels the formation of the phenomena that determined the broader postmodern condition, at times even anticipating its officialization.[23] Koolhaas's apologia for the status quo of New York is postmodern—even more so insofar as it assumes the retroactive semblance of a historically based discourse. The enchantment with pragmatism, with disenchantment, that Hood, Lamb, and Harrison display in their architecture—and which Koolhaas displays in its contemporary version—is postmodern. Koolhaas's surfism is postmodern,[24] capable of feeding on contradictions and turning crisis to his advantage. But the omnivorous congestion of New York is also postmodern, and its symbol—not to mention physical locale—is the skyscraper. Insofar as the skyscraper is a "reproduction of the World" and a "glorious whole,"[25] a *"self-contained universe"*[26] (Koolhaas's emphasis), it shares in a utopian tension. But it also projects by that selfsame totalizing tension into the multiform reality, the most extreme tools of which, according to Koolhaas, are an "architectural equivalent of a lobotomy," the clean separation of "exterior and interior architecture,"[27] and the "Vertical Schism, a systematic exploitation of the deliberate disconnection between stories."[28]

Koolhaas becomes the key interpreter of this colossal construction, overcoming the ideology of the modern that is formally manifested in the skyscraper and Manhattan. In fact, through the paradoxical rhythm of this postmodern motif—not through the theatrical, tragicomic cadences Tafuri sees—Koolhaas understands the steps of its particular dance. The interpretive differences that may have seemed to exist strictly within a particular reading of the skyscraper, and to closely connect to its proposed themes, now take the form of a mirror reflecting two radically different ways of thinking: modern and postmodern.

To more precisely define something that otherwise risks becoming an ungraspable abstraction—and to understand the real divisions between recurrent and substantially irreducible interpretations—we must return to and articulate the common element between Tafuri's and Koolhaas's respective thinking. From this dual and curiously speculative perspective, Deleuze and Guattari enter as a useful reference point. With the help of this provocative "reagent," we may not only illuminate—albeit by its differences—the underlying framework of Tafuri's project, but also of Koolhaas's; to give an account of what is by now a triumphant interpretation of contemporaneity.

To date, curiously enough, the not-so-underground relationships that *Delirious New York* shares with *Anti-Oedipus* have not been noted.[29] While the Freudian and Lacanian influences on Koolhaas's text are evident, and in some cases even declared—to the point of making psychoanalysis not only one of the many themes that run through *Delirious New York*, but also a method, a more overarching interpretive key[30]—the influence Deleuze and Guattari's theories had on it are no less important. In fact, they may be even more crucial, beginning with the book's very title. In the 1970s one did not have to be a particularly close reader of *Anti-Oedipus* to grasp its notion of delirium as a social, historical, and political factor: one of the book's three main themes—as Deleuze and Guattari stated—is delirium as understood in the "historical-worldwide sense, not in the familiar sense (races, tribes, continents, cultures, social positions become delirious . . .)."[31] It is only a brief step from that to the delirium of the city—and the delirious character of New York. For an intellect as sharp as Koolhaas's, such a convergence could not go undetected.[32]

On the other hand, the role Koolhaas accorded desire within metropolitan architecture can be traced to the anti-Oedipal conception of desire as a machine that functions and produces; in the case of New York, one that produces the extraordinary desiring machines that are its omnivorous skyscrapers—literal factories of desire, not theaters wherein it is merely represented. (After all, for Deleuze and Guattari, desire and delirium are profoundly one and the same.) More generally speaking, Koolhaas's entire approach to the architectural discourse seems increasingly close to Deleuze and Guattari's conception of the philosophical discourse as a "creation of concepts."[33] Retroactivity. Congestion. Technology of the Fantastic. Artificial. Self-monument. Schism. Lobotomy. These are just a few of the concepts that Koolhaas inscribes—without ever lingering too much to justify them dialectically—into *Delirious New York*. Such concepts are defined through their consistency, self-referentially postulating themselves and their subject in their moment of creation.

A rather different character distinguishes the relationship between Tafuri and Deleuze and Guattari. At first glance, it might superficially appear to be marked by pure negativity, if it does not seem downright nonexistent. And yet it is this negative relation we must confront in order to avoid oversimplification. From Tafuri's few nods to Deleuze and Guattari,[34] his position toward them is clear: whether it is a question of the "metaphysics of desire"[35] or of rhizomes,[36] Tafuri is always suspicious of their promises of false liberations. As Franco Rella notes, behind these reversals lurks a restatement of previous ideas rendered more insidious by their newfound concealment:[37] first of all, ideology and dialectics. Rella emphasizes that "Deleuze and Guattari's model is linked, despite their discourse and its appearances, to the mythology of capitalism. This takes place even when the model seems subtler, and passes through the idealization of the negative: through the conversion of 'bourgeois nonvalue' into 'positive values,' as if they were not the product of the same dominant practices that construct the ideological consensus and reproduction of the labor force."[38]

At times the tone of the critique, and therefore its reasons and motives (Deleuze and Guattari write: "Don't look for roots, follow the channel,"[39] to which Rella ironically replies: "Follow the channel, precisely: free and happy"[40]), closely relate to the debate and political controversy of the time (all for one and one for all: 1977!). Yet it also assumes a more structural character, questioning the very foundations of Deleuze's theories. This is also the case with Cacciari's critiques of desire and play, or the game (critiques that Tafuri appropriates, and which can therefore be considered his position).[41] At the center of such critiques lies the unveiling of Deleuze's (and Foucault's) illusion of contrasting a pure desire—warden of all that is multiform, manifold, complex, and different—against a power that (having declared its immanence in individual, disciplinary fields, its dispersion, and its ability to exert itself within a multiplicity of dispositions, organisms, maneuvers, and functions) is presumed to be absolutely monolithic. This contradictory analysis, according to Cacciari, generates the Deleuzian absolutization of desire as a revolutionary element, and the game as its free practice. In reality, these are synthetic shortcuts that—through the masks of absolute and idealized otherness—elude all serious discussion of the political, its techniques, and its limits.

The problem of limits (the limits of language, of technique) is precisely what interests Tafuri and separates him from Deleuze and Guattari, Foucault, and Lyotard. For Tafuri, as well as for Georg Simmel, the limit, the confine, the border (and, as such, form and history), is the place of contradiction—the place, that is, where the "thing itself and, at the same time, the cessation of the thing . . . are one and the same."[42] At the opposite end are Deleuze and Guattari. The "desiring-production is pure multiplicity, that is to say, an affirmation that is irreducible to any sort of unity":[43] parts, fragments, contradictions without limits. This is precisely where the true distinction lies: for the modern Tafuri, contradiction—although it can be composed of dissonant elements—is characterized by an inseparability of distinct parts. For the postmodern Deleuze and Guattari (and, evidently, not only them), it consists instead of a theoretically infinite accumulation of mere oppositions. This makes Tafuri's reading of contemporary reality critical, insofar as he thinks it cannot be reduced to a complex of contradictions—and that, conversely, makes contemporary reality a happy condition of uprootedness, the place of crisis from the perspective of desire-delirium; a perspective that, as we have seen, is nevertheless inadequate, and is ineffective in the critique of ideology and capitalist mythologies.

To call these two perspectives modern and postmodern is to have a distinct attitude, as opposed to suggesting a chronology. This does not mean that a postmodern attitude has not often been received by a modern attitude as unacceptable, triggering strong opposition on the modern's behalf.[44] Nevertheless these two contradictory attitudes are still not rigidly exclusive; often they touch and overlap, and are mutually influential (at least on specific themes and motifs). To some degree, they even coexist. Tafuri's harking back to the interpretive practices of Foucault, Derrida, Barthes, and Blanchot—along with the critiques launched against them—proves as much. His relationship with Koolhaas can be evaluated in the same way, continually oscillating between suggestions and condemnations, between possible convergences and irreducible distances.

If, to a modern mind, the postmodern discourse represents the opening of perspectives that were previously unthinkable and, in the final analysis, mark the surpassing of a previously unsurpassable limit, then for the postmodern mind, the modern represents an entire universe of discourse it can dip into and draw upon with both hands, albeit conferring a radically different sense upon it. Encountering numerous Tafurian characteristics in Koolhaas's legacy will thus come as no surprise.

And yet, despite this, Koolhaas judges Tafuri harshly:[45] above all, by theoretically declaring (and verifying in a series of studies on contemporary phenomena)[46] the productive function of contradiction. To counter the persistent tendency toward reducing—even demolishing—the fundamental complexity of contemporary architectural culture and urban planning, Koolhaas claims "a more positive position, affirming that you don't have to dissolve contradiction and complexity, but rather exacerbate them."[47] He makes a similar claim elsewhere: "The coherence imposed upon an architect's work is either cosmetic or the result of self-censorship. . . . Contradictions are not avoided."[48]

This proclamation does not function—as one may suspect—to justify sometimes incoherent attitudes. Koolhaas's incoherence is programmatic at best, as is his refusal of utopia: "My work is deliberately nonutopian."[49] This still does not allow for any facile reversal of perspective: "[My work] is critical of that kind of utopian modernism. But it still remains aligned with the force of modernization and the inevitable transformations that are engendered by this project which has been operating for 300 years. In other words, for me the important thing is to align and find an articulation for those forces, again without the kind of purity of a utopian project. In that sense my work is positive vis-à-vis modernization but critical vis-à-vis modernism as an artistic movement."[50]

In this way, what ends up being set into crisis is not one position or another, or an idea of modernism against an idea of postmodernism, but rather a binary system of logic made up of schematically opposed, mutually exclusive positions. Thus, in another context, Koolhaas can declare his propensity for an "absolute rationalism, which is therefore irrational."[51] Irrationality ceases to oppose rationality in a linear way, and instead necessarily descends from it, as its intrinsic implication, as its extreme but nonetheless rigorously inherent limit. Comprehending the effective matrix of this procedure means recognizing Koolhaas as one of the rare architect-theorists who is truly liberated—*Tafurianly*—of all nostalgia.[52]

This leads us back to the theme of reality, where the irreconcilable differences between Koolhaas and Tafuri come to light. Here, the problem cannot be reduced to their being or not being realists—nor can it be reduced, by taking an all-too-easy shortcut, to them both being realists. Instead, the problem—as I tried to demonstrate earlier through an analytical reading of Tafuri's texts[53]—is precisely which type of realism. While the various realisms of contemporary architecture's main protagonists speak to Tafuri, it certainly is not due to their stylistic traits, but rather because they establish a conversation with themselves and with reality, because they put themselves and reality into crisis.

Once again the problem is: which reality? Obviously, if one thing truly differentiates, in the most radical and profound sense, the realism of the 1950s, 1960s, and 1970s from that of our present day, it is precisely the reality in which each is situated. In this sense, Tafuri's realism is as different from Koolhaas's as their respective realities are. But the differences do not end here. They also pertain—above all—to different ways of interpreting the real. In this sense, Tafuri's interpretation is as different from Koolhaas's as the modern is from the postmodern; as much as posthumous men differ from present-day men. Yet this does not make the posthumous man an entirely untimely person. As Cacciari writes:

> The posthumous man is not synonymous with the untimely man. The term untimely makes it sound, albeit unconsciously, as if there is the possibility of becoming timely. The untimely man can always anticipate his time. The posthumous man cannot; he is absolutely protected from the risk of anticipation, he cannot be reached,

*he cannot be understood. His life does not mean his
timeliness, or the affirmation of his reason for being. He
has too many reasons to be able to affirm or establish
himself. . . . The posthumous man has passed through
the end of all subjects. His life, the life he guards, is not
one of affirming or establishing a subject, a timeliness,
but rather that of insignificance, of the superfluousness
of the present day—in which the present truly appears to
be an indecent overestimation of oneself and one's own
language.* [54]

Certainly, even Koolhaas's reality possesses this degree
of complexity, contradiction, and criticality that constitutes
the essence of Tafuri's real. The instrumentation that distinguishes Koolhaas's research—despite its differences from Tafuri—is equally sophisticated, diversified, and pertinent. But
what makes the true difference is the changed point of view of
reality itself. Compare, for example, the following two excerpts,
taken, respectively, from Tafuri's often-quoted examination of
architectural ideology in the capitalist era and then Koolhaas's
research on shopping:

*The arcades and department stores of Paris, like the
great expositions, were certainly the places in which the
crowd, itself become a spectacle, found the spatial and
visual means for a self-education from the point of view
of capital. But throughout the nineteenth century this
recreational-pedagogical experience, precisely in being concentrated in exceptional architectural types, still
dangerously revealed its restricted scope. The ideology of
the public is not, in fact, an end in itself. It is only a moment of the ideology of the city as a productive unity in
the proper sense of the term and, simultaneously, as an*

instrument of coordination of the production-distribu-
tion-consumption cycle.

   This is why the ideology of consumption, far from
constituting an isolated or successive moment of the or-
ganization of production, must be offered to the public as
the ideology of the correct use of the city.[55]

   Not only is shopping melting into everything, but ev-
erything is melting into shopping. Through successive
waves of expansion—each more extensive and perva-
sive than the previous—shopping has methodically en-
croached on a widening spectrum of territories so that it
is now, arguably, the defining activity of public life. Why
has it become such a basic aspect of our existence? Be-
cause it is synonymous with perhaps the most significant
and fundamental development to give form to modern
life: the unfettered growth and acceptance of the market
economy as the dominant global standard. Shopping is
the medium by which the market has solidified its grip
on our spaces, buildings, cities, activities, and lives. It is
the material outcome of the degree to which the market
economy has shaped our surroundings, and ultimately
ourselves.[56]

We are clearly dealing with two different moments in time, two
different stations along the same road: and, indeed, the ideology of consumption and *shopping* constitute two essential steps
within the same capitalist strategy. But this is not what counts
most. Rather, while Tafuri's text is an in-depth and total demystification[57] aimed at the entire cycle of reality—a demystification wherein a maximum awareness of the underlying
dynamics lives disharmoniously alongside the utmost lack of

seductive power—Koolhaas welcomes the real as an already accepted given, isolating and carrying it through to its final consequences—consequences that, without any rhetoric, are truly beyond good and evil, considered in all their potential and effects. Such a method—of which Koolhaas certainly is not the only, but the most lucid exponent today—lies in comprehending those elements of reality that a routine critical reading would consider marginal or second-rate, and dismiss, insofar as they are popular, commercial, or purely spontaneous, lack any intentionality, and completely invert all existing evaluations of reality. To use Rella's terms, this method idealizes the negative. It is not simply a provocative operation, insofar as it aims to draw from reality the maximum possible interpretation, or the maximum available results. Reality does not end up subverted: if anything, it ends up followed, supported, to the extent that it is reread as realistically as possible. This is not tantamount to underestimating, or even denying, the criticality of the real as such; on the contrary, it means exploiting the crisis that pertains to the real, theorizing reality in its most critical aspects.

That the choice of such a critical position now places those who assume it on the victors' side does not necessarily presume a will to "fix what is broken."[58] Any consolation from contemplating the world as it is, any banal apologia of the present, is entirely alien to Koolhaas's analyses. Such realism (much like, on a more general level, contemporary realism) observes—without any pretext of modifying processes currently underway, and therefore without any regret for the potential consequences they create—emergent conditions, as paradoxical and unforeseeable as they might be. In Koolhaas's case, these include instability, the "changes taking place in urban situations."[59] Analyzing them, critiquing them, requires that one accept their reality. And now, more than ever, reality is what exists. The contemporary metropolis exists. Within the contemporary metropolis, crisis and contradiction both have an active role. Koolhaas works precisely within and upon this reality.

The differences between Tafuri's and Koolhaas's discourses do not exist on a different level from their evolution, or as a simple divergence of their interests. What really changes—once again—is the viewpoint from which reality is observed. Anyone today who wishes to judge Tafuri's construct of contemporary history faces the question of viewpoint. Thus, for example, from a postmodern (or current) viewpoint such a construct might perfectly agree with what is by now a generalized, widespread contemporary disenchantment—inexplicably pessimistic in its final outcome. It is also from this viewpoint that Tafuri's historical-critical work might appear to be completed by Koolhaas—that is, Koolhaas may appear to be the one who, more than anyone else, has collected and made use of Tafuri's legacy, the inheritance he left behind. Clearly Koolhaas is not his "legitimate" heir but, rather, the person who most effectively appropriates Tafuri's discourse on the productivity of crisis—going beyond all its limits and making it act, and react, in the present day.[60]

From a strictly modern viewpoint, however, the Tafurian construct cannot be seen as a precursor to Koolhaas—rather, Koolhaas, to state it more exactly, deeply betrays it: a betrayal that in many respects parallels Kahn's betrayal, as well. In other words, from a strictly modern viewpoint Tafuri's project is not at all anticipatory, nor is it prophetic with regard to the evolutionary course of architecture today. Rather, it is an unheeded herald of a catastrophe to be avoided at all costs.

But even this is not the point from which we should try to understand Tafuri's construct. Indeed, it is precisely the modern viewpoint—insofar as it is, at least potentially, "his own"—that Tafuri aims to critique. One should try to observe Tafuri's construct from his own point of view—the viewpoint according to which plunging the real into crisis means continually plunging oneself into crisis. If, then, what now unfolds before our eyes is—with all that Tafuri's project of crisis so long ago predicted— the destiny of the current city and architecture, it is because that destiny is based on a critical and disenchanted analysis, on "a lucid awareness of the situation now underway,"[61] and on its contradictory developmental conditions. Faced with this, Tafuri did not see any possible regret, just as he considered it vain to try to stop things in their tracks. From his point of view, this would be tantamount to setting the situation underway under the sign of the *Fragwürdiges*, of the problematic; this is the same sign, actually, under which *Modern Architecture* has—significantly—situated itself.[62]

The realm of the problematic is the same realm in which the aforementioned weak power of analysis operates to unsettle the present and allow the unsolved problems of the past to live on. It is within the realm of the problematic (not coincidentally, the realm furthest from the contemporary sensibility but—at the same time—what most exactly describes it) that the false choice between the ineffectuality of utopia and the inescapability of the real appears to be avoidable.

This is precisely what Tafuri's historical construct, his project of crisis, taught and continues to teach: *to resist within the problematic*, to continue to question,[63] thereby not dismissing anything as simply past or as simply present. And to do so without promises or guarantees of easy solutions, and without succumbing to overly enthralling current events or trends.

NOTES

PREFACE

1. A comprehensive study of Tafuri is still lacking nearly twenty years after his death. Interesting biographical notes can be found in the special monographic issue of *Casabella* dedicated to Tafuri. In particular, see Giorgio Ciucci, "Gli anni della formazione" [The Formative Years], *Casabella* 59, no. 619–620 (January-February 1995): 12–24. An evaluation of his legacy from an entirely contemporary viewpoint is attempted (albeit with notable biases and blind spots) in a monographic issue of *Any* magazine. See Ignasi de Solà-Morales, "Being Manfredo Tafuri," *Any* 25–26 (February 2000): 10–70. For a historico-critical approach to Tafuri, see Daniel Sherer, "Progetto e ricerca: Manfredo Tafuri come storico e come critico," *Zodiac* 15 (March-August 1996): 32–51. See also Daniel Sherer, "Tafuri's Renaissance: Architecture, Representation, Transgression," *Assemblage* 28 (December 1995): 34–45. An interesting study published after the release of the Italian edition of my book is that of Andrew Leach, *Manfredo Tafuri: Choosing History* (Ghent: A&S Books, 2007). The chapter on Tafuri in Anthony Vidler, *Histories of the Immediate Present: Inventing Architectural Modernism* (Cambridge, MA: MIT Press, 2008), must also be noted.

INTRODUCTION

1. Nikolaus Pevsner, *An Outline of European Architecture* (Harmondsworth, UK: Penguin, 1954), 707.
2. Walter Benjamin, "Theses on the Philosophy of History," trans. Harry Zohn, in *Illuminations*, ed. Hannah Arendt (New York: Schocken, 1976), 257. The phrase Benjamin quotes is from the famous statement by Leopold von Ranke, "wie es wirklich gewesen ist"—the same one used by Pevsner.
3. Ibid., 230.

4. See Friedrich Nietzsche, "On the Use and Abuse of History for Life," in *Untimely Meditations*, trans. R. J. Hollingdale, ed. Daniel Breazeale (Cambridge: Cambridge University Press, 1997).

5. Ibid., 67.

6. Ibid.

7. Ibid., 94.

8. Ibid.

9. Friedrich Nietzsche, *Human, All Too Human: A Book for Free Spirits*, trans. R. J. Hollingdale (Cambridge: Cambridge University Press, 1996), 13.

10. Manfredo Tafuri, *La sfera e il labirinto: Avanguardie e architettura da Piranesi agli anni '70* [The Sphere and the Labyrinth] (Turin: Einaudi, 1980), 6. The Nietzschean passage quoted in the previous note appears on the same page.

11. Ibid., 7.

12. Ibid.

13. Ibid., 8.

14. Ibid., 10.

15. Ibid., 12.

16. Ibid., 17.

17. Ludwig Wittgenstein, *Philosophical Investigations*, trans. G. E. M. Anscombe, 4th edn. (Oxford: Wiley-Blackwell, 2009), 86.

18. Tafuri, *La sfera e il labirinto*, 330.

19. Ibid.

20. At the root of Tafuri's *disintegration-rewriting* are Martin Heidegger's "destruction as the goal of philosophy" in *Being and Time* and the deconstruction of Jacques Derrida, albeit critically rethought.

21. Tafuri, *La sfera e il labirinto*, 330.

22. Ibid.

23. Ibid., 335.

24. Tafuri's "Il 'progetto storico'" appeared for the first time in *Casabella*. See Manfredo Tafuri, "Il 'progetto storico'" [The "Historical Project"], *Casabella* 429 (October 1977): 11–18. It was later published as the introduction to *The Sphere and the Labyrinth* in a longer version. See Tafuri, *La sfera e il labirinto*, 3–30. The introduction was published along with a modified text that previously appeared under the title "Architettura e storiografia: una proposta di metodo." See Manfredo

Tafuri, "Architettura e storiografia: una proposta di metodo," *Arte Veneta* 29 (1975): 276–282. It is to this second version of "Il 'progetto storico'" that I refer. It should be noted that the "conception of history itself as a *project*" was foreseen by Vittorio Gregotti in *Il territorio dell'architettura* (Milan: Feltrinelli, 1966), 137. Quoted by Tafuri in Manfredo Tafuri, *Teorie e storia dell'architettura* [Theories and History of Architecture] (Bari: Laterza, 1968), 73.

25. Tafuri, *La sfera e il labirinto*, 3–4.

26. Henri Focillon, *The Life of Forms in Art*, trans. Charles B. Hogan and George Kubler (New York: Zone Books, 1989), 32.

27. Tafuri, *La sfera e il labirinto*, 4.

28. The inevitable presuppositions of this passage are again included in one of Tafuri's works, and can be considered an adumbration to *The Sphere and the Labyrinth*.

29. Tafuri, *La sfera e il labirinto*, 17–18.

30. Tafuri bases his critique on the absence of spaces of conflict in Foucalt. See Manfredo Tafuri, "Lettura del testo e pratiche discorsive," in Massimo Cacciari, *Il dispositivo Foucault* (Venice: Cluva, 1977), 44.

31. Tafuri, *La sfera e il labirinto*, 5.

32. Ibid.

33. Ibid.

34. Ibid., 11.

35. Ibid., 12.

36. Ibid., 5.

37. Giulio Carlo Argan, *Progetto e destino* (Milan: Il Saggiatore, 1965). See especially pages 9ff. Argan also refers to Emilio Garroni, *La crisi semantica delle arti* (Rome: Officina, 1964). An important text that connects the idea of crisis to architecture is Enzo Paci's "La crisi della cultura e la fenomenologia dell'architettura contemporanea," *La Casa* 6 (1959): 353–365.

38. Massimo Cacciari, "Di alcuni motivi in Walter Benjamin," *Nuova Corrente* 67 (1975): 203–243. This essay was later published in Franco Rella, *Critica e storia. Materiali su Benjamin* (Venice: Cluva, 1980), 41–71. The page numbers cited refer to this edition. It should also be noted that on page seven Rella, in his opening note to the multi-author volume, attributes the concept of a "historical construction as the construction of a critical knowledge" to Benjamin.

39. Cacciari, "Di alcuni motivi in Walter Benjamin," 66.

40. Ibid.

41. Ibid., 67.

42. Ibid.

43. Ibid.

44. Walter Benjamin, "The Author as Producer," trans. Edmund Jephcott, in *Walter Benjamin: Selected Writing*, vol. 2 (Cambridge, MA: Belknap Press, 2005), 770.

45. Tafuri, *La sfera e il labirinto*, 352. On the same page Tafuri includes the excerpt from Benjamin cited in the previous note. The declaration of his intention to respond to Benjamin's question appears on page 22 of the same book.

46. Cacciari, "Di alcuni motivi in Walter Benjamin," 67.

47. Tafuri, *La sfera e il labirinto*, 18.

48. Ibid.

49. Ibid.

50. Ibid., 3. Quoted from Adriano Prosperi and Carlo Ginzburg, *Giochi di pazienza, Un seminario sul "Beneficio di Cristo"* (Turin: Einaudi, 1975), 84.

51. On the assimilation of historical work in Freud's "Analysis Terminable and Interminable," see Tafuri, *La sfera e il labirinto*, 14.–15. The end of historical analysis is given in that light as partial and provisional, although obviously indispensable to practice.

52. Tafuri, *La sfera e il labirinto*, 10.

53. Ibid., 24. It must be emphasized how the same phrase—like the entire context in which it is found—already appears in Tafuri, "Architettura e storiografia," 279. Nevertheless, it lacks any reference to the conflictual nature of many independent histories. In general, "Architettura e storiografia" reaches toward specifying a complex method, multiple histories intertwined, and more than one integrated historical approach. "It proposes a new history of contemporary architecture, based upon a selection of events and protagonists fundamentally different from that carried out in 'classical' histories" (ibid., 280), and a "new historiographic model, alternative to the one that has become canonical" (ibid., 281), where the historical project completely renounces the tendency toward methodological rigidity (but at the same time has a major textual transparency), and omits all cited passages.

54. Tafuri, *La sfera e il labirinto*, 21.

55. Tafuri probably has in mind Bruno Zevi and Paolo Portoghesi's texts on Michelangelo, Francesco Borromini, and Frank Lloyd Wright, but also—on a wholly different level—the appearance of French new criticism, following Roland Barthes's structuralism: figures indefinably oscillating between criticism, narrative, and philosophy, from Maurice Blanchot to Jacques Derrida.

Explicit nods to the dangers of a history subjected to disseminations or understood as infinite diversions are found in Tafuri, *La sfera e il labirinto*, 9, 13, and 345. It is also worth noting that Tafuri took the discussion of a second language directly from Barthes's *Criticism and Truth*. Aside from the cited passage in *Sphere and Labyrinth*, he also developed them in *Theories and History*.

56. Tafuri, *La sfera e il labirinto*, 13.

57. Tafuri, "Architettura e storiografia," 277.

58. Tafuri, *La sfera e il labirinto*, 17.

59. Franco Rella, "Dallo spazio estetico allo spazio dell'interpretazione," *Nuova Corrente* 68–69 (1975–1976): 412. Cited in Tafuri, *La sfera e il labirinto*, 5. Also fundamental to Tafuri's project is Franco Rella, "Nel nome di Freud. Il mito dell'altro," *Quaderni Piacentini* 60–61 (1976): 61–75.

60. Tafuri, *La sfera e il labirinto*, 18.

61. Ibid., 13.

62. Ibid.

63. Tafuri, "Lettura del testo e pratiche discorsive," 44.

64. Ibid., 45.

65. Tafuri, *Teorie e storia dell'architettura*, 161.

66. Ibid., 172.

67. The outlines of this, traced by Tafuri beginning in 1969 with the publication in *Contropiano* of "Toward a Critique of Architectural Ideology" (compare with the chapters following "Critica dell'utopia"), are developed further in *La sfera e il labirinto*.

68. Tafuri, *Teorie e storia dell'architettura*, 179.

69. Friedrich Nietzsche, *Daybreak: Thoughts on the Prejudices of Morality*, trans. R. J. Hollingdale (Cambridge: Cambridge University Press, 1997), 47. Tafuri quotes Nietzsche in *La sfera e il labirinto*, 10.

70. Tafuri, *La sfera e il labirinto*, 11.

71. Tafuri, *Teorie e storia dell'architettura*, 161.

72. "Il mestiere dello storico. Intervista a Manfredo Tafuri," *Domus* 605 (1980): 31.

73. See Tafuri, *La sfera e il labirinto*, 16. See also Manfredo Tafuri, interview by Pietro Corsi, "Per una storia storica," *Casabella* 619–620 (1995): 146. This interview was first published in 1994 in *La Rivista dei Libri*.

74. On operative criticism and Tafuri's position, see Luca Monica, ed., *La critica operativa e l'architettura* (Milan: Unicopoli, 2002). In particular, see Daniel Sherer, "Un colloquio 'inquietante'. Manfredo Tafuri e la critica operativa 1968–1980," in Monica, *La critica operativa e l'architecttura*, 108–120. Sherer nevertheless seems to confuse operative criticism and historical project, not to mention a related contrast between critical analysis and historical research that is completely foreign to Tafuri.

75. Tafuri, *La sfera e il labirinto*, 25.

76. Carlo Olmo, "Il mercato delle interpretazioni," in Monica, *La critica operativa e l'architettura*, 121. "The historian had increasingly retreated (one could try to date this retreat, at least in Italy, to the end of the 1970s) into already claimed procedures and methods in and of themselves, as specific but also autonomous from every other, a more general battle for an idea of architecture (to propose, and thereby fight for and recognize)."

77. Tafuri, *Teorie e storia dell'architettura*, 39.

78. Ibid., 41.

79. Ibid., 46.

80. Walter Benjamin, "The Work of Art in the Age of Its Technological Reproducibility," trans. Edmund Jephcott, in *The Work of Art in the Age of Its Technological Reproducibility, and Other Writings on Media*, ed. Michael W. Jennings, Brigid Doherty, and Thomas Y. Levin (Cambridge, MA: Harvard University Press, 2008).

81. The absolute centrality of Benjamin's essay is postulated by Tafuri not only with regard to the history of criticism in general, but also with regard to his own attempt to rethink the conditions of architecture: "A history that knows how to illuminate the intrinsic possibilities of the tools used by the architect at this point becomes indispensable. Even more so, if you realize that, after the 'great crisis' of the thirties, all the avant-garde' 'design hopes' can do nothing but reveal their ineffectuality. To ignore the limits set on the possibilities of communication, and what new horizons are opened by the means available to architecture, is nothing but an evasive attitude. The analyses of Walter Benjamin on the

semantic, operative, mental, and behavioral consequences unleashed by modern technologies remain an isolated case in the history of contemporary critique: and the suspicion arises that such isolation isn't by chance. The ambiguities and misunderstandings that dominated architectural culture from 1945 to now derive in great part from the interruption of Benjamin's analyses; analyses, it must be emphasized, that were authentically structural, outside of any evasive viewpoint or the fashionable status of the term and concept." Tafuri, *Teorie e storia dell'architettura*, 265.

82. Limits the author also recognized: "At a distance of almost two years from this book's writing we realize that we have remained silent about too many things and that, of those things said, many remain incomplete. Why this is must be immediately clarified: the pages that follow are nothing but the first chapter of an acknowledgment of that which architecture, as an institution, has signified up until now, first as an ideological anticipation or pure petition of principle, then as a process directly included among the modern processes of production and development of the capitalist universe." Tafuri, "Avvertenza alla seconda edizione," in *Teorie e storia dell'architettura*, ix.

83. Tafuri, *Teorie e storia dell'architettura*, 12.

84. "At the moment in which we began this essay we thought we would have to confront such a theme by specifying all the obstacles internal to the discipline, all the unavoidable contradictions, all its institutional ambiguity, in light of the historic, concrete, objective decline of the positive role architecture was entrusted with after the crisis of the programmatic utopianism of the avant-gardes." (Ibid., x.)

85. Luisa Passerini, "History as Project: An Interview with Manfredo Tafuri," *Any* 25–26 (February 2000): 37. This interview, unpublished in Italy, was conducted February 10 and March 28, 1992, in Rome. It is worth mentioning here the quote used by Peter Weiss and used in turn by Tafuri: "SADE: To discern truth from lie / we must know ourselves / I / do not know myself / When I think I have discovered something / I already doubt it / and deny/negate it / Anything we do is just a larva / of what we would like to do . . . // MARAT: We must pull ourselves out of the gutter / by our own bootstraps / turn ourselves inside out / and be capable of seeing / everything with new eyes." Peter Weiss, *La persecuzione e l'assassinio di Jean-Paul Marat* (Turin: Einaudi, 1967), 41, 36.

86. Tafuri, *La sfera e il labirinto*, 61. On this same point, Tafuri speaks of a "lacerating" or "piercing" dialectic (*dialettica lacerante*) in *Teorie e storia dell'architettura*, 36.

87. Tafuri, *Teorie e storia dell'architettura*, 270.

88. Manfredo Tafuri, *Venezia e il Rinascimento* (Turin: Einaudi, 1985), 297.

89. Manfredo Tafuri, *Ricerca del Rinascimento* (Turin: Einaudi, 1992), 67.

90. Ibid., 24.

91. Ibid.

92. Tafuri, *Teorie e storia dell'architettura*, 4.

93. Ibid., 5.

94. The image of the surgeon, contrasted with that of the magician, is taken from Benjamin, "Work of Art," 35. Quoted by Tafuri in *Teorie e storia dell'architettura*, 41.

95. Tafuri, *Teorie e storia dell'architettura*, 7.

96. Ibid., 5.

97. Manfredo Tafuri, interview by Richard Ingersoll, "Non c'è critica, solo storia," *Casabella* 619–620 (1995): 96. This interview was first published in 1986 in *Design Book Review*.

98. Tafuri, *La sfera e il labirinto*, 16. Recall also: "The critic is he who is forced . . . to maintain a balance along a tightrope, while winds that continually change direction do all they can to make him fall." Tafuri, *Teorie e storia dell'architettura*, 5.

99. Tafuri, "Non c'è critica, solo storia," 96.

100. Ibid.

101. The final word, obsessive, quite literally delirious, on the subject of distance and its consequences is that of Roithamer, professor at Cambridge, designer of a unique, extraordinary architecture and its deepest, most merciless critic, the most significant imaginary character from Thomas Bernhard's *Correction*: "We must be removed as far as possible from the scene of our thoughts if we're to think properly, with the greatest intensity, the greatest clarity, always only at the greatest distance from the scene of our thoughts. . . . Always the problem of how to get to the farthest point away from the subject I must consider or think through, in order to consider or think through this subject the best possible way. Approaching the subject makes it increasingly impossible to think through the subject we are approaching. We become absorbed in the subject and can no longer think it through, we can't even grasp it. . . . To think a subject through, one has

to assume a position at the farthest possible remove from the subject. First, approach the subject as an idea, then, take the most distant position possible from this subject which at first we'd approached as an idea, to enable us to evaluate it and think it through, a process leading logically to its resolution. A thorough, logical analysis of a subject, whichever subject, means the resolution of the subject. . . . But . . . we never think with the utmost, analytical rigor, because if we did we'd solve, dissolve everything." Thomas Bernhard, *Correction*, trans. Sophie Wilkins (New York: Random House, 2010), 166–167. This novel, first published in German in 1975, is yet to be adequately reread and analyzed in light of the echoes its protagonist, Roithamer, presents not only of Wittgenstein's house for Gretl but also, in other respects, with the revolutionary French architects, Adolf Loos, Ludwig Mies van der Rohe, Frank Lloyd Wright, Aldo Rossi, and—for the radicalism and coherence of his critical thought—with Tafuri himself.

102. Tafuri, *La sfera e il labirinto*, 3.

103. Ibid., 21.

104. Ibid., 20.

105. Ibid., 19.

1 CRITIQUE OF UTOPIA

1. Manfredo Tafuri, interview with Richard Ingersoll, "Non c'è critica, solo storia," *Casabella* 619–620 (1995): 98.

2. See Manfredo Tafuri, "Per una critica dell'ideologia architettonica" [Toward a Critique of Architectural Ideology], *Contropiano* 1 (1969): 31–79. In reality, *Progetto e utopia* also includes broad excerpts from another of Tafuri's essays. See Manfredo Tafuri, "Lavoro intellettuale e sviluppo capitalistico" [Intellectual Work and Capitalist Development], in *Progetto e utopia: Architettura e sviluppo capitalistico* [Architecture and Utopia] (Rome and Bari: Laterza, 1973). This essay was also published in *Contropiano*. See Tafuri, "Lavoro intellettuale e sviluppo capitalistico," *Contropiano* 2 (1970): 241–281.

3. Tafuri, *Progetto e utopia*, 3. For an English translation of the book, see Manfredo Tafuri, *Architecture and Utopia: Design and Capitalist Development*, trans. Barbara Luigia La Penta (Cambridge, MA: MIT Press, 1976).

4. Tafuri, *Progetto e utopia*, 2. Among the reviews and reactions that followed the publication of *Per una critica dell'ideologia architettonica* and *Progetto e utopia*, see

Paolo Portoghesi, "Autopsia o vivisezione dell'architettura," *Controspazio* 1 (November 1969): 5–7.

5. See Tafuri's letter to Renato De Fusco, published in *Controspazio* 51 (1981): 83–85: "The exception of 'Rossi's sole work, if not even just one of its aspects,' or the 'well-known Tafurian hypothesis that architecture is dead' have to do not with me, but rather with a vulgate I don't even need to distance myself from here. . . . I don't ever recall . . . having sung atop non-existent tombs, nor do I recall tossing lifesavers to anyone. But I certainly have spoken of the extinction of roles in old disciplines" (ibid., 83). This letter was written following the publication of an article in *Controspazio* in January 1981, in which Tafuri's contribution to architectural critique was cast into doubt in the ways indicated in his letter.

6. Massimo Cacciari, "Forme e funzioni dell'utopia nello sviluppo del capitalismo" (course introduction at the Università IUAV in Venice, 1969–1970).

7. Francesco Dal Co, "Note per una critica dell'ideologia dell'architettura moderna: da Weimar a Dessau," *Contropiano* 1 (1968): 155. Dal Co's essay touches upon a series of themes: the abandonment of utopia or its overcoming on the part of modern architecture; architecture and urban planning, and the political role the latter plays in capitalist modes of production. These resurface the following year in Tafuri's essay (which bears an undeniably similar title).

8. Tafuri, *Progetto e utopia*, 2. The visible, as well as physical, "wake" of this ideal appearance is clearly evident in the pages of *Architecture and Utopia*, where there are countless citations and echoes of other essays that appeared in *Contropiano*.

9. Antonio Negri, "La teoria capitalista dello stato nel '29: John M. Keynes," *Contropiano* 1 (1968): 3–40; Mario Tronti, "Estremismo e riformismo," *Contropiano* 1 (1968): 41–58; Alberto Asor Rosa, "Il giovane Lukács teorico dell'arte borghese," *Contropiano* 1 (1968): 59–105; Massimo Cacciari, "Dialettica e tradizione," *Contropiano* 1 (1968): 125–152.

10. An important reference point in the analyses conducted by Tafuri over the course of these years is Franco Fortini. In particular, see Franco Fortini, *Verifica dei poteri* (Milano: Il Saggiatore, 1965). Tafuri would later overcome Fortini's overtly ideological and rhetorical positions.

11. N. Licciardello, "Proletarizzazione e utopia," *Contropiano* 1 (1968): 117.

12. Cacciari, "Dialettica e tradizione," 125–152; Massimo Cacciari, "Sulla genesi del pensiero negativo," *Contropiano* 1 (1969): 131–200. The conjunction between

this—one of Cacciari's most fundamental essays—and Tafuri's *Per una critica dell'ideologia architettonica* has never been sufficiently explored. Not least because of this coincidence, these two texts should be read in parallel.

13. Cacciari, "Sulla genesi del pensiero negativo," 131.

14. Tafuri, *Progetto e utopia*, 50.

15. In particular, see Max Weber, *Methodology of Social Sciences*, trans. Edward A. Shils and Henry A. Finch (1949; repr., New Brunswick, NJ: Transaction Publishers, 2011) and Max Weber, *Max Weber's Complete Writings on Academic and Political Vocations*, trans. Gordon C. Wells (New York: Algora Publishing, 2008).

16. Cacciari, "Sulla genesi del pensiero negativo," 181.

17. Weber, "Politics as a Vocation," in *Max Weber's Complete Writings*, 205. Weber's phrase is strongly echoed by Cacciari in "Sulla genesi del pensiero negativo," 182. The essay was in turn quoted by Tafuri in his passages concerning the Weber-Nietzsche nexus. See Tafuri, *Progetto e utopia*, 53–54.

18. Manfredo Tafuri, "Avvertenza alla seconda edizione," in *Teorie e storia dell'architettura* [Theories and History of Architecture] (Bari: Laterza, 1968), xxiii.

19. Cacciari, "Sulla genesi del pensiero negativo," 135.

20. Tafuri, *Progetto e utopia*, 50.

21. Weber, "Science as a Vocation," in *Max Weber's Complete Writings*, 52. This passage is also quoted in Cacciari, "Sulla genesi del pensiero negativo," 183.

22. Tafuri, *Progetto e utopia*, 3.

23. Ibid., 4.

24. Ibid., 49.

25. Cacciari, "Utopia e socialismo," *Contropiano* 3 (1970): 565. In this sense, "Fourier's 'utopia' is a project of eliminating conflict, which development created and *still* creates—as a hypothesis, alongside Saint-Simon—as a dynamic system."

26. Tafuri, *Progetto e utopia*, 67.

27. In addition to the aforementioned "Per una critica dell'ideologia architettonica" and "Lavoro intellettuale e sviluppo capitalistico," we must note two essays that do not directly enter the corpus of *Progetto e utopia* yet constitute an essential laboratory for its scope. See Tafuri, "Socialdemocrazia e città nella Repubblica di Weimar," *Contropiano* 1 (1971): 207–223; and Tafuri, "Austromarxismo e città: Das rote Wien," *Contropiano* 2 (1971): 259–311. These were later reworked in

Manfredo Tafuri, ed., *Vienna Rossa. La politica residenziale nella Vienna socialista 1919–1933* (Milan: Electa, 1980).

28. Tafuri, *Progetto e utopia*, 5.

29. Ibid., 11.

30. Ibid., 14.

31. Ibid., 16.

32. Ibid.

33. Ibid., 17.

34. Ibid., 20.

35. Ibid., 18.

36. See Max Horkheimer and Theodor Adorno, *Dialectic of Enlightenment*, trans. Edmund Jephcott (2002; repr., Stanford: Stanford University Press, 2007), 63–93.

37. Cacciari, "Dialettica e tradizione," 129.

38. See Manfredo Tafuri, "Giovanni Battista Piranesi: l'architettura come 'utopia negativa,'" *Angelus Novus* 20 (1971): 89–127; and later in "Bernardo Vittone e la disputa fra Classicismo e Barocco nel Settecento," *Atti del Convegno, Accademia delle Scienze, Torino* 1 (1972): 265–319; Tafuri, *La sfera e il labirinto*, 40, 74. In *Progetto e utopia* Tafuri hints at the "negative that lies within Piranesi" (page 22), while in "Per una critica dell'ideologia architettonica" such a reference is absent, as it is from his entire discussion of Piranesi's *Carceri* as well.

39. Tafuri, *Progetto e utopia*, 22.

40. Ibid., 21.

41. See Tafuri, *La sfera e il labirinto*, 47.

42. Ibid., 43.

43. Ibid., 44.

44. Ibid., 49.

45. Ibid., 48.

46. Ibid.

47. Ibid., 51.

48. Tafuri's reference is once again Cacciari, "Dialettica e tradizione," 133.

49. Tafuri, *La sfera e il labirinto*, 48.

50. Ibid., 51.

51. Ibid., 52.

52. Ibid.

53. Ibid., 51.

54. Ibid., 52.

55. Ibid.

56. Ibid., 58.

57. Ibid., 59.

58. Ibid., 40.

59. Ibid., 61–63.

60. Ibid., 68.

61. Ibid.

62. Ibid., 67.

63. Ibid., 74.

64. Ibid.

65. Ibid.

66. Ibid.

67. Ibid., 56.

68. Here Tafuri quotes Michel Foucault, *The Order of Things*, trans. Alan Sheridan (New York: Pantheon, 1970), xviii. For the concept of heterotopia, see Georges Teyssot, "Eterotopie e storie degli spazi," in *Il dispositivo Foucault*, ed. Massimo Cacciari, Franco Rella, and Manfredo Tafuri (Venice: Cluva, 1977), 23–36. See also Michel Foucault, "Spazi altri," in *Spazi altri: I luoghi dell'eterotopia*, trans. Tiziana Villani and Pino Tripodi (Milan: Mimesis, 2002), 19–32. This was from a lecture originally given in 1967 and first published, in French, in 1984.

69. For a critique of Tafuri's assimilation of utopia and heterotopia, see Paul Henninger, "One Portrait of Tafuri: An Interview with Georges Teyssot," in *Any* 25–26 (February 2000): 13–14.

70. Tafuri, *La sfera e il labirinto*, 63.

71. Ibid., 74.

72. Ibid., 75.

73. Tafuri, *Progetto e utopia*, 22.

74. Ibid., 144.

75. Ibid., 133.

76. Ibid., 47.

77. Manfredo Tafuri and Francesco Dal Co, *Architettura contemporanea* [Modern Architecture] (1976; repr., Milan: Electa, 1979), 105.

78. Tafuri, *Progetto e utopia*, 83.

79. Ibid.

80. Ibid., 142.

81. See Manfredo Tafuri, "Il teatro come 'città virtuale'. Dal Cabaret Voltaire al Total-theater," *Bollettino del Centro Internazionale di Studi di Architettura Andrea Palladio* 17 (1975): 361–377; published again, with additions and modifications, in Tafuri, *La sfera e il labirinto*, 113–136.

82. Ibid., 134.

83. Ibid., 136.

84. Tafuri, *Progetto e utopia*, 96.

85. Ibid., 95.

86. Ibid., 99.

87. Ibid., 109.

88. Ibid., 114.

89. Ibid., 117.

90. Ibid., 123.

91. Manfredo Tafuri, "'Machine et mémoire. La città nell'opera di Le Corbusier. 1," *Casabella* 502 (1984): 49.

92. Tafuri and Dal Co, *Architettura contemporanea*, 122.

93. Manfredo Tafuri, "'Machine et mémoire.' La città nell'opera di Le Corbusier. 2," *Casabella* 503 (1984): 45.

94. Ibid., 46.

95. Ibid., 48–49.

96. Ibid., 47.

97. Ibid., 48.

98. Ibid., 49.

99. Ibid., 50.

100. Ibid.

101. Tafuri, *Architecture and Utopia*, 139. Trans. Barbara Luigia La Penta.

102. "Internazionale dell'utopia" is the title of a chapter dedicated to the new vanguards of the 1960s in Tafuri and Dal Co, *Architettura contemporanea*, 347–353.

103. Tafuri, *Progetto e utopia*, 127.

104. Regarding this terminology, it is worth noting the conclusion of one of Tafuri's first essays on the "new utopianism" of the 1970s:

Toward a construction of utopia. Alongside rationalist mannerism and critical rationalism is *the poetics of utopia*: but a utopia quite distant from that which inspired the constructivists of the early twentieth century.

Then, there was hope and tension for a new and different world order, an expression of faith that was perhaps naïve, but full of both positive and premonitory implications. Now there is a kind of pessimism that is more or less concealed and known to its creators, leading toward formulations fraught with unclear and inexplicable symptoms.

But it would be wrong to cast this new utopianism against the codified manner of rationalism without critical clarifications. . . .

Rationalism, too, in its original iterations was born of a utopian inclination, as has been noted, though it was an ideal utopianism, cast in configurations that almost desperately adhered to real conditions—regardless of any consideration of the *scale* of the transformed realities.

In an uncertain world of impending catastrophe, the rationalists *built their "dreams of liberated peoples" at the outskirts of the city*: utopia played the role assigned to their faith in design as redemption and hope.

In a world no less contradictory, yet dominated by new mythologies and a new, more conscious, universalized resistance to the idea that it was racing toward self-destruction, architects *dreamed of structures at the city's heart that are utopian in and of themselves, more than from their underlying ideals—structures that are somehow desperate, on an anxious quest for the never-before-seen, for exhilarating scale—to such a degree that one might even claim they exhibit a form of pessimism that is paradoxically expressed in a sign system completely antithetical to it.*

On closer inspection, the utopianism of these projects is more a question of appearance than of substance, as it is more closely linked to a sense of unease more formalist—rather than idealist—in nature. Whereas rationalism realistically offered new realities that dialectically contrasted extant cities, these projects went right to the heart of the city, designing fantastical structures for realities that, once again, often have little more to them than a thin exterior film.

Today, the utopian path can seem far from evasive, but in what role, with what tools, coherence, and methods can it be fathomed by the architects who champion it and the critics who see its positive, perhaps irreplaceable sides?

Manfredo Tafuri, "Razionalismo critico e nuovo utopismo," *Casabella Continuità* 293 (1964): 22–25. On this same point, there is also a polemical nod to Rogers, who is "guilty" of opening utopia, in the form of a projection of the present "in a possible future, even if its forms are still impossible [to build]." Ernesto N. Rogers, "Utopia della realtà," *Casabella* 259 (1962): 1.

105. Manfredo Tafuri, "Design and Technological Utopia," in *The New Domestic Landscape: Achievements and Problems of Italian Design*, ed. Emilio Ambasz (New York: Museum of Modern Art, 1972), 388–404.

106. Tafuri, *Progetto e utopia*, 130.

107. Tafuri and Dal Co, *Architettura contemporanea*, 353.

108. Ibid., 347.

109. "The nostalgia for a return to childhood seems an irrepressible fact, even in the most progressive research in design" (Tafuri, "Design and Technological Utopia," 388), whether it belongs to the old or the new avant-gardes. But this essay's close is also worth reading: "This does not mean that there will still not be a wide margin for the production of objects and environments that will allow designers bent on 'saving their souls' to carry out their solitary rites of exorcism undisturbed. The nostalgic longing for magic, for the golden age of the bourgeois mystique, still continues to be cherished, even at the most highly developed levels of capitalistic integration, as a typical method of compensation. And this will be the case, as long as the magicians, already transformed into acrobats (as Le Corbusier himself finally realized), agree to the ultimate transformation of themselves into clowns, completely absorbed in their 'artful game' of tightrope-walking." (Ibid., 400.)

110. Tafuri, *Progetto e utopia*, 167.

111. Ibid., 125.

112. Ibid., 169.

113. See the clear, interesting answers Tafuri gave to some of the questions posed by Andrea Branzi and Benedetto Gravagnuolo in the interview published in *Data*

28–29 (1977). Reprinted in Andrea Branzi, *Moderno Postmoderno Millenario. Scritti teorici 1972–1980* (Turin and Milan: Studio Forma Alchymia, 1980), 81–83.

114. Tafuri, *Architecture and Utopia*, 181.

115. Ibid., 182.

116. Tafuri, *Progetto e utopia*, 4.

117. Ibid.

118. Ibid., 168.

119. Ibid., 163.

120. Ibid., 162.

121. Tafuri, *La sfera e il labirinto*, 338.

2 KAHN AS DESTROYER

1. See Nikolaus Pevsner, *Pioneers of Modern Design: From William Morris to Walter Gropius*, 4th edn. (New Haven: Yale University Press, 2005). Curiously, in Pevsner, the modern movement, categorically, preserves its own unity despite the multiplicities and intrinsic contradictions he recognizes: "The Modern Movement in architecture, in order to be fully expressive of the twentieth century, had to possess both qualities, the faith in science and technology, in social science and rational planning, and the romantic faith in speed and the roar of machines" (160).

2. Manfredo Tafuri, interview by Omar Calabrese, "La tecnica delle avantguardie," *Casabella* 463–464 (1980): 101.

3. Much of Tafuri's research toward the end of the 1960s and after was done in collaboration with people who belonged to the Venetian School, first centered at the Istituto di Storia dell'Architettura, then at the Department of Critical and Historical Analysis, and finally at the Department of Architectural History at the IUAV and other universities. Of particular note, among the works Tafuri collaboratively published in this period, are: two on the Soviet Union (Manfredo Tafuri, ed., *Socialismo, città, architettura. URSS 1917–1937: Il contributo degli architetti europei* [Rome: Officina, 1971]; Manfredo Tafuri, Jean-Louis Cohen, and Marco De Michelis, *URSS 1917–1978: la città, l'architettura* [Rome: Officina, 1979]); one on the relationship between the avant-garde and the metropolis (Francesco Dal Co, Massimo Cacciari, and Manfredo Tafuri, *De la vanguardia a la metropoli*

[Barcelona: G. Gili, 1972]); and one on the United States (Giorgio Ciucci and others, *La città americana dalla guerra civile al "New Deal"* [Rome: Laterza, 1973]).

4. Manfredo Tafuri, "Les bijoux indiscrets," in *Five Architects N. Y.* (Rome: Officina, 1977), 7.

5. Manfredo Tafuri, "Storicità di Louis Kahn," *Comunità* 117 (1964): 38.

6. Ibid., 39.

7. Ibid., 40.

8. See Vincent J. Scully, *Louis I. Kahn* (New York: George Braziller, 1962).

9. Tafuri, "Storicità di Louis Kahn," 41.

10. Ibid.

11. Ibid., 43.

12. Ibid.

13. Ibid., 48.

14. Ibid.

15. Clearly the sole aim of this analysis is to bring Tafuri's judgment of Kahn—and its increasing clarity over time—into focus, not to explore the historic judgment of Kahn and his oeuvre as we might formulate it today.

16. Tafuri, "Storicità di Louis Kahn," 49.

17. Ibid.

18. See Manfredo Tafuri, *Teorie e storia dell'architettura* [Theories and History of Architecture] (Rome and Bari: Laterza, 1968).

19. Manfredo Tafuri, foreword to *Teorie e storia dell'architettura*, 4th edn. (Rome and Bari: Laterza, 1976), viii.

20. Tafuri, *Teorie e storia dell'architettura*, 10.

21. Ibid., 10–11.

22. Ibid., 11.

23. Ibid., 75.

24. Ibid.

25. Ibid., 76.

26. Ibid.

27. Ibid., 10.

28. Ibid., 39.

29. Ibid., 122.

30. Also inconclusive is Tafuri's own interpretive "double leap of faith" regarding works such as the capital building in Dacca (often grouped with Paul Rudolph's Boston Government Center, and the Cumbernauld Civic Center by Hugh Wilson and others): "legible diagrams of an intolerable situation," insofar as those works were "obliged to carry out an operation of turning in on themselves: and become a critical discourse on architecture, modeled as investigations into what makes them possible as architecture"; such that "the very same works which make clear the unresolved relationship linking their antihistoricist roots to a present that no longer justifies such antihistoricism, hold within them the meta-language of critique, broadly and loudly announcing the crisis of the very tradition that allows them to exist as new, symbolic objects." Tafuri, *Teorie e storia dell'achitettura*, 116.

31. Manfredo Tafuri and Francesco Dal Co, *Architettura contemporanea* (1976; repr., Milan: Electa, 1979), 370.

32. Tafuri, *Teorie e storia dell'architettura*, 114.

33. Tafuri and Dal Co, *Architettura contemporanea*, 368.

34. Ibid.

35. Tafuri, "Storicità di Louis Kahn," 43.

36. Tafuri, *Teorie e storia dell'architettura*, 11.

37. Tafuri and Dal Co, *Architettura contemporanea*, 370.

38. Ibid., 373.

39. Tafuri, "Les bijoux indiscrets," 7.

40. Tafuri, *Teorie e storia dell'architettura*, 97.

41. This is clearly a reference to the essay by Walter Benjamin, "The Work of Art in the Age of Its Technological Reproducibility," trans. Edmund Jephcott, in *The Work of Art in the Age of Its Technological Reproducibility, and Other Writings on Media* (Cambridge, MA: Harvard University Press, 2008), 62.

42. Tafuri, *Teorie e storia dell'architettura*, 97.

43. Ibid.

44. Ibid.

45. Tafuri and Dal Co, *Architettura contemporanea*, 370.

46. Ibid., 376.

3 THE PULL OF THE VOID

1. Here we encounter a difference more significant than it might initially appear: what Tafuri deems the aporia of modern architecture in *Modern Architecture* becomes the aporia of the modern movement in *The Sphere and the Labyrinth* and "Les bijoux indiscrets."

2. Manfredo Tafuri, *La sfera e il labirinto: Avanguardie e architettura da Piranesi agli anni '70* [The Sphere and the Labyrinth] (Turin: Einaudi, 1980), 358; Manfredo Tafuri, "Les bijoux indiscrets," in *Five Architects N.Y.* (Rome: Officina, 1977), 7–8.

3. It is worth remembering that two of the benchmarks of postmodern architectural interpretation—Peter Blake's *Form Follows Fiasco* and Charles Jencks's *The Language of Post-Modern Architecture*—are dated 1977, the same year in which Tafuri wrote "Les bijoux indiscrets."

4. Tafuri, *La sfera e il labirinto*, 357.

5. Ibid., 358.

6. Manfredo Tafuri, *Teorie e storia dell'architettura* [Theories and History of Architecture] (Bari: Laterza, 1968), 252–253.

7. Ibid., 253.

8. Ibid., 253–256.

9. Tafuri also speaks of the poetics of ambiguity in reference to John Johansen and Charles Moore. See Tafuri, *La sfera e il labirinto*, 331.

10. Ibid., 348.

11. Ibid., 348–349.

12. Ibid., 349.

13. Ibid., 358–359. See also Tafuri, "Les bijoux indiscrets," 8; and—with slight variations—Manfredo Tafuri and Francesco Dal Co, *Architettura contemporanea* [Modern Architecture] (1976; repr., Milan: Electa, 1979), 376.

14. Ibid. This passage was later expunged in "Les bijoux indiscrets" and *Sphere and Labyrinth*.

15. Tafuri, *La sfera e il labirinto*, 348.

16. Ibid., 359.

17. Ibid., 360.

18. Tafuri and Dal Co, *Architetttura contemporanea*, 379.

19. Tafuri, *La sfera e il labirinto*, 349.

20. Ibid.

21. Ibid., 359. And, even more mercilessly, Tafuri writes: "For someone who wanted to overturn Kahn's pseudo-rigorousness, he sure shared many of its underlying motives." Tafuri, "Les bijoux indiscrets," 8.

22. Tafuri, *La sfera e il labirinto*, 359.

23. Ibid., 360.

24. Ibid.

25. Ibid.

26. See in particular Manfredo Tafuri, *Progetto e utopia: Architettura e sviluppo capitalistico* [Architecture and Utopia] (Rome and Bari: Laterza, 1973).

27. Tafuri directly quotes Michel Foucault: see Tafuri, *La sfera e il labirinto*, 360. See also Tafuri, "Les bijoux indiscrets," 9. The passage Tafuri quotes is from Foucault's essay "A Preface to Transgression." See Michel Foucault, "A Preface to Transgression," in *Language, Counter-Memory, Practice*, ed. Donald Bouchard, trans. Donald Bouchard and Sherry Simon (Ithaca: Cornell University Press, 1980), 48.

28. Tafuri, *Teorie e storia dell'architettura*, 91.

29. Here it is worth mentioning Lucy R. Lippard, *Six Years: The Dematerialization of the Art Object* (London: Studio Vista, 1973). It is a fundamental text, published just a few years later, which perhaps further confirms Tafuri's prophetic intuition.

30. Tafuri and Dal Co, *Architettura contemporanea*, 352–353.

31. Tafuri, *La sfera e il labirinto*, 21.

32. Tafuri, *Teorie e storia dell'architettura*, 108–110.

33. Ibid., 110.

34. Gerhard M. Kallmann, quoted in Manfredo Tafuri, "Storicità di Louis Kahn," *Comunità* 117 (1964): 48. See Gerhard Kallmann, "The Action Architecture of a New Generation," *Architectural Forum* 4 (1959): 132–137.

35. Tafuri and Dal Co, *Architettura contemporanea*, 376.

36. Ibid., 379.

37. Ibid.

38. Manfredo Tafuri, interview by Richard Ingersoll, "Non c'è critica, solo storia," *Casabella* 619–620 (1995): 98.

39. *Learning from Las Vegas*, by Robert Venturi, Denise Scott Brown, and Steven Izenour, was published in 1972 and reissued, in a revised edition, in 1977 with

the subtitle *The Forgotten Symbolism of Architectural Form*. For the book's critical success, see the bibliography included in the appendix to the latter edition.

40. Tafuri, "Non c'è critica, solo storia," 98.

41. Tafuri, *La sfera e il labirinto*, 348.

42. This expression, *una disciplina trascurabile*, appears in Manfredo Tafuri, "La montagna disincantata. Il Grattacielo e la City," in Giorgio Ciucci and others, *La città americana dalla guerra civile al "New Deal"* (Rome: Laterza, 1973). The last chapter of *La città americana* is dedicated to this topic: pp. 526–550.

43. Ibid., 546.

44. Ibid.

45. Ibid., 540.

46. Ibid.

47. Tafuri, *Teorie e storia dell'architettura*, 111.

48. Ibid., 112.

49. Ibid.

50. Ibid.

51. Ibid.

52. Ibid., 113.

53. Tafuri and Dal Co, *Architettura contemporanea*, 322.

54. Ibid.

55. Tafuri, *La sfera e il labirinto*, 349.

4 LES BIJOUX DANS LE BOUDOIR

1. Manfredo Tafuri, *Teorie e storia dell'architettura* [Theories and History of Architecture] (Bari: Laterza, 1968), 77. The names Tafuri cites in relation to the Kahn school are Romaldo Giurgola, Tim Vreeland, Gerhard Kallmann, Michael McKinnell, Edward Knowles, and I. M. Pei.

2. Ibid.

3. Manfredo Tafuri, "Les bijoux indiscrets," in *Five Architects N.Y.* (Rome: Officina, 1977), 8. Manfredo Tafuri, *La sfera e il labirinto: Avanguardie e architettura da Piranesi agli anni '70* [The Sphere and the Labyrinth] (Turin: Einaudi, 1980), 359.

4. Tafuri, "Les bijoux indiscrets," 8.

5. It is interesting to reread Tafuri's writing on the final phase of Gropius's career: "T.A.C., subject by its very nature to the laws of the American market, quickly

became a multibranched, anonymous enterprise, equipped to take on heavy professional jobs, and available for any and all public and private commissions." Manfredo Tafuri and Francesco Dal Co, *Architettura contemporanea* [Modern Architecture] (1976; repr., Milan: Electa, 1979), 299. The anonymity and loss of subjectivity inherent to certain American commercial architecture is therefore lucidly pointed out by Tafuri: on the one hand, it is identified as the characters that determine entry into the world; on the other, as the limits that keep it from leaving, from even minimally exceeding the tasks the world has assigned it.

6. See Tafuri, *La sfera e il labirinto*, 359–360.

7. The text by Grosz to which Tafuri refers here is George Grosz, *A Little Yes and a Big No*, trans. Lola Sachs Dorin (New York: Dial Press, 1946).

8. Tafuri, *La sfera e il labirinto*, 360.

9. Ibid.

10. Ibid.

11. Ibid. See Michel Foucault, "A Preface to Transgression," in *Language, Counter-Memory, Practice*, ed. Donald Bouchard, trans. Donald Bouchard and Sherry Simon (Ithaca: Cornell University Press, 1980), 48.

12. See Tafuri, *La sfera e il labirinto*, 361ff. Such considerations, which Tafuri includes in the chapter "Le ceneri di Jefferson" [The Ashes of Jefferson], constitute a return to Tafuri's "Le bijoux indiscrets" (Tafuri, "Les bijoux indiscrets," 7–33)—with a few variations—published on the occasion of the exhibition "Five Architects" in Naples in January 1976. This was a translation, with a few modifications, of the essay: Manfredo Tafuri, "European Graffiti: Five x Five = Twenty-five," *Oppositions* 5 (Summer 1976): 35–74.

13. Tafuri, "Les bijoux indiscrets," 11.

14. Ibid.

15. It is worth remembering that within just a few years, and despite the Five not having a very consistent quantitative output, various critics discussed them, including Kenneth Frampton, Arthur Drexler, Colin Rowe, Rosalind Krauss, and Tafuri.

16. Tafuri, *La sfera e il labirinto*, 323. This expression does not explicitly refer to the Five, but the context within which it appears reveals more than one tangential point of their profile: "Within the current debate, the 'new knights of purity' move forward, brandishing the fragments of utopia as their distinguishing

marks—fragments they keep themselves from observing head on. The avant-garde, once again, is rooted in nostalgia." This persuasive notion is an apt image, if not only for the Five, certainly for them as well.

17. Ibid., 361.

18. Tafuri, "Les bijoux indiscrets," 9.

19. Ibid., 10.

20. Ibid., 9.

21. Ibid., 10.

22. Ibid., 13. Mario Gandelsonas, "Linguistics in Architecture," *Casabella* 374 (February 1973): 22.

23. Gandelsonas, "Linguistics in Architecture," 24.

24. Eisenman discusses conceptual architecture in Peter Eisenman, "Cardboard Architecture," *Casabella* 374 (February 1973): 17–24. See also Peter Eisenman, "Notes on Conceptual Architecture: Toward a Definition," *Design Quarterly* 78–79 (1970): 1–5. Tafuri meanwhile speaks of "architecture as such," or of an architecture entirely resolved in and of itself. Tafuri, "Les bijoux indiscrets," 13.

25. Tafuri, "Les bijoux indiscrets," 16.

26. Ibid.

27. Massimo Cacciari, *Icone della legge* (Milan: Adelphi, 1985), 233.

28. Tafuri, "Les bijoux indiscrets," 14, 29.

29. Ibid., 16.

30. It is worth remembering that Eisenman is the author of a book—announced several times, beginning in the 1970s, and published in 2003—on the work of Terragni. See Peter Eisenman, *Giuseppe Terragni: Transformations, Decompositions, Critiques* (New York: Monacelli Press, 2003). His volume includes an essay by Tafuri, originally conceived as an introduction for the book, and also published, with a few modifications, in *Oppositions*. See Manfredo Tafuri, "Giuseppe Terragni: Subject and the Mask," *Oppositions* 11 (Winter 1977): 1–25.

31. "Without any history, the transformations of Terragni-Eisenman promise an infinite entertainment from which all pleasure as well as all enjoyment is banished." Manfredo Tafuri, "Giuseppe Terragni: Subject and 'Mask,'" in Peter Eisenman, *Giuseppe Terragni*, 292.

32. On Tafuri's relationship to IAUS and *Oppositions*, see Joan Ockman, "Venezia e New York," *Casabella* 619–620 (February 1995): 56–71. See also K. Michael Hays,

ed., "The Oppositions of Autonomy and History," in *Oppositions Reader: Selected Readings from a Journal for Ideas and Criticism in Architecture 1973–1984* (New York: Princeton Architectural Press, 1998), ix–xv. Between 1974 and 1979 Tafuri published five essays in *Oppositions*, two of which dealt directly with the Five: "L'Architecture dans le boudoir: The Language of Criticism and the Criticism of Language," trans. Victor Caliandro, *Oppositions* 3 (1974): 37–62; later reissued, with a few modifications but under the same title, in Tafuri, *La sfera e il labirinto*, 323–354; also Tafuri, "European Graffiti," 35–74. Tafuri also wrote a text solely on Eisenman titled "Peter Eisenman: The Meditations of Icarus," which was later published in Peter Eisenman, *Houses of Cards* (New York: Oxford University Press, 1987), 167–187.

33. Tafuri, "L'Architecture dans le boudoir," 38; Tafuri, *La sfera e il labirinto*, 323. At Princeton—upon the invitation of Diana Agrest—Tafuri met Peter Eisenman, Mario Gandelsonas, Anthony Vidler, and other people involved with IAUS.

34. Ockman, "Venezia e New York," 56. Tafuri's quote is taken from Tafuri, "L'Architecture dans le boudoir," 53. See also Tafuri, *La sfera e il labirinto*, 345.

35. Tafuri, "European Graffiti," 37. The nostalgia for what it never had is the key idea with which Tafuri confronts a consistent part of American culture of the 1970s: a nostalgia for "the European myth of dialectics, as much as—and indifferently— for historicism and antihistoricism, and, in the case of the Five, contrasted, or rather flanked, by a certain detachment."

36. Tafuri, "Les bijoux indiscrets," 11.

37. Tafuri, "L'Architecture dans le boudoir," 51; Tafuri, *La sfera e il labirinto*, 344.

38. Tafuri, "L'Architecture dans le boudoir," 51.

39. The magical attribute—much like suspended tonality, its close correlate—is first used by Tafuri to relate the works of Eisenman and Hejduk to the currents stemming from Terragni and Carlo Belli: "Hejduk and Eisenman's syntactic emphasis lies entirely within 'suspended tonality,' rich as it is in magical and metaphysical ('Stile Novecento') evocations, hints from artistic groups in Como, and some of Adalberto Libera's works (a 'suspended tonality' that film directors like Godard and Bertolucci have understood and made use of much better than most critics have)." Tafuri, "Les bijoux indiscrets," 17.

   The magical is mentioned in relation to Eisenman, in a decisive passage regarding "Graves's magical paths" and the "particular, magical flavor" of certain elements of his architecture, as well as the "magical box that is Whig Hall" by Gwathmey and Siegel. The expression *suspended tonality* is used to define work done by all five of the Five: Eisenman, Hejduk, Graves, Gwathmey, and Meier. Finally, Tafuri uses the term irreality when speaking of the walls of Hejduk's Bye House, and irrealism with regard to Graves's Benacerraf House. Tafuri, "Les bijoux indiscrets."

40. Tafuri uses a Husserlian *epoché* as the bracketing of forms' iconic dimension, by which Eisenman emphasizes syntactic structure. See Tafuri, "European Graffiti," 46. Significantly, this nod to a Husserlian *epoché* is absent from "Les bijoux indiscrets."

41. Tafuri, "Les bijoux indiscrets," 20. In "Peter Eisenman: The Meditations of Icarus," Tafuri returns to the discourse on the utopian in Eisenman's works: "The transparency sought by Eisenman in fact appears to be a sort of 'overly significant' metaphor: it evokes not only mental constructions beyond the realm of the visible, but also a utopia, a utopia of the 'absolute transparency of the sign.'" Manfredo Tafuri, "Peter Eisenman: The Meditations of Icarus," trans. Stephen Sartarelli, in Eisenman, *Houses of Cards*, 175.

42. Tafuri, "Les bijoux indiscrets," 17; Tafuri, "European Graffiti," 50.

43. In *The Sphere and the Labyrinth* the reference to the avant-garde is described by adding the adjective "New York" (Tafuri, *La sfera e il labirinto*, 367). This drastically modifies the original meaning of the passage in "Les bijoux indiscrets."

44. Ibid.

45. Ibid.

46. Tafuri, *La sfera e il labirinto*, 349. See also page 324.

47. Or, as Tafuri writes: "This excludes all attempts to question language as a system of meaning from which the discourse must necessarily be revealed." Ibid, 324.

48. Tafuri, "Les bijoux indiscrets," 11. Here Tafuri refers to Jacques Derrida's introductory essay to Étienne Bonnot de Condillac's *Essai sur l'origine des connaissances humaines*. See Jacques Derrida, "L'archéologie du frivole," in Étienne Bonnot de Condillac, *Essai sur l'origine des connaissances humaines* (Auvers-sur-Oise: Éditions Galilée, 1973).

49. Tafuri, "European Graffiti," 45; Tafuri, "Les bijoux indiscrets," 13.

50. This quote, from Tafuri, "Les bijoux indiscrets," 28, directly concerns Hejduk.

51. See in particular Tafuri and Dal Co, *Architettura contemporanea*, 301–309. The expression quoted here is instead taken from Tafuri, *La sfera e il labirinto*, 332.

52. Massimo Cacciari, "Eupalinos o l'architettura," *Nuova Corrente* 76–77 (1978): 441. Later republished in *Oppositions* 21 (1980): 106–116.

53. Tafuri, "Les bijoux indiscrets," 28.

54. Tafuri, *La sfera e il labirinto*, 367.

55. Tafuri, "Les bijoux indiscrets," 29.

56. "And yet"—Tafuri writes, in a passage that, once again, is absent from the first version of "L'Architecture dans le boudoir"—"the boudoir of the great new writers and creators of architecture, rich as they are in mirrors and tools for pleasure, is no longer the place in which the extreme heights of 'virtuous villainy' burn bright. Modern libertines stand horrified before the inflexibility of any limit. Their vivisections are done [only] after they have wisely anesthetized their patients. The torturer works in muffled operating rooms: the boudoir is sterilized, and has too many emergency exits." Tafuri, *La sfera e il labirinto*, 345.

57. Ibid., 368.

58. Roland Barthes, *The Pleasure of the Text*, trans. Richard Miller (New York: Hill and Wang, 1975), 31. The last few pages of "Les bijoux indiscrets," just like those of *Sphere and Labyrinth*, are dedicated to a discussion and a comparison with Barthes's essay, wherein—incidentally—pleasure and fear, or, better yet, enjoyment and fear, are analyzed in light of their relationship of "proximity."

59. Tafuri, "Les bijoux indiscrets," 30; Tafuri, *La sfera e il labirinto*, 370.

60. Tafuri, "Les bijoux indiscrets," 30; Tafuri, *La sfera e il labirinto*, 370.

61. Tafuri, *La sfera e il labirinto*, 354.

62. Ibid.

63. Tafuri, "L'Architecture dans le boudoir," 38.

64. Tafuri, *La sfera e il labirinto*, 323.

65. Tafuri, "Les bijoux indiscrets," 30. Tafuri, *La sfera e il labirinto*, 371. *The Sphere and the Labyrinth* closes with these same words.

5 FRAGMENT AND SILENCE

1. Manfredo Tafuri, *Storia dell'architettura italiana 1944–1985* [History of Italian Architecture] (Turin: Einaudi, 1986), 139.

2. Another important figure is, obviously, Le Corbusier: for Tafuri, Le Corbusier is, more than any other architect, problematic and contradictory. See, among others, Manfredo Tafuri, "'Machine et mémoire'. La città nell'opera di Le Corbusier," in *Le Corbusier 1887–1965*, ed. H. Allen Brooks (Milan: Electa, 1993), 234–259. In addition to writing a few important critical contributions, for a long time Tafuri also considered writing a monograph on Le Corbusier. Given the complexity of the Corbusierian universe, Tafuri's interpretation merits in-depth analysis and consideration.

3. Manfredo Tafuri, *La sfera e il labirinto: Avanguardie e architettura da Piranesi agli anni '70* [The Sphere and the Labyrinth] (Turin: Einaudi, 1980), 325. The pages dedicated to Stirling later became the introduction to Francesco Dal Co and Tom Muirhead, *I musei di James Stirling Michael Wilford and Associates* (Milan: Electa, 1990), 11–15.

4. Manfredo Tafuri and Francesco Dal Co, *Architettura contemporanea* [Modern Architecture] (1976; repr., Milan: Electa, 1979), 368.

5. Ibid.

6. Tafuri, *La sfera e il labirinto*, 326.

7. Ibid.

8. Ibid., 328.

9. Ibid., 329.

10. Ibid.

11. Ibid., 328–329.

12. Ibid., 326.

13. Ibid., 327.

14. Tafuri and Dal Co, *Architettura contemporanea*, 368.

15. Tafuri, *La sfera e il labirinto*, 329.

16. Tafuri and Dal Co, *Architettura contemporanea*, 368.

17. This expression is Nietzsche's, and appears in Tafuri, *La sfera e il labirinto*, 324. It is also in Manfredo Tafuri, *Progetto e utopia: Architettura e sviluppo capitalistico* [Architecture and Utopia] (Rome and Bari: Laterza, 1973), 133.

18. Manfredo Tafuri, "Il frammento, la 'figura', il gioco. Carlo Scarpa e la cultura architettonica italiana," in Francesco Dal Co and Giuseppe Mazzariol, *Carlo Scarpa. Opera completa* (Milan: Electa, 1984), 77.

19. Ibid.

20. Ibid.

21. Ibid.

22. Maurice Blanchot, *The Infinite Conversation*, trans. Susan Hanson (Minneapolis: University of Minnesota Press, 1993), 308. The emphasis is Tafuri's. Elsewhere, Tafuri expresses critical positions with regard to Blanchot's interpretive method, as it is close to Derrida's disseminative practice. The essay on Scarpa is curiously infested by the term *dissemination*.

23. Tafuri, "Il frammento, la 'figura', il gioco," 86.

24. Ibid., 85.

25. Ibid., 86.

26. Here Tafuri refers to Franco Rella, *Miti e figure del moderno* (Parma: Pratiche, 1981).

27. Tafuri, *Storia dell'architettura italiana*, 143.

28. Tafuri, "Il frammento, la 'figura,' il gioco," 79.

29. Ibid.

30. Ibid., 86.

31. Tafuri, *Storia dell'architettura italiana*, 140.

32. See Tafuri, *Storia dell'architettura italiana*, 143–145. See also Manfredo Tafuri, "Gli anni dell''attesa': 1922–1945," in *Giuseppe Samonà 1923–1975. Cinquant'anni di architetture* (Rome: Officina, 1975), 9–17; and Manfredo Tafuri, "Les 'muses inquiétantes' ou le destin d'une génération de 'Maîtres,'" *L'architecture d'aujourd'hui* 181 (1975): 14–33.

33. Tafuri, *Storia dell'architettura italiana*, 143.

34. Ibid., 144.

35. Ibid., 145.

36. Ibid., 144.

37. Ibid., 145.

38. This is the title of a chapter on Rossi in Tafuri, *Storia dell'architettura italiana*, 166–171.

39. Tafuri, *La sfera e il labirinto*, particularly 21. For a treatment of these themes as understood from a methodological point of view, see the introduction to this book.

40. Ibid., 330.

41. Ibid.

42. Ibid., 330–331.

43. Ibid., 330.

44. Ibid., 331.

45. Ibid.

46. Ibid., 332.

47. Ibid., 333.

48. Ibid., 332.

49. According to Benjamin, "Everything Kraus wrote is like that: a silence turned inside out, a silence that catches the storm of events in its black folds and billows, its livid lining turned outward. . . . The trinity of silence, knowledge, and alertness constitutes the figure of Kraus the polemicist. His silence is a dam before which the reflecting basin of his knowledge is constantly deepened." Walter Benjamin, "Karl Kraus," trans. Edmund Jephcott, in *Walter Benjamin: Selected Writings*, vol. 2 (Cambridge, MA: Belknap Press of Harvard University Press, 2005), 436. Kraus's name turns up repeatedly in Rossi's writings. See Aldo Rossi, *Quaderni azzurri* (Milan: Electa, 1999), in particular, notebooks 18, 28, and 30. See also Aldo Rossi, "Introduction" to Adolf Loos, *La civiltà occidentale* (Bologna: Zanichelli, 1981), 7–16.

50. Tafuri, *La sfera e il labirinto*, 332.

51. Ibid., 333.

52. The difference between the means used here is to a certain degree lessened by Kraus's aptitude for aphorisms, a syntactic-linguistic knot whose contents cannot otherwise be analyzed or untangled. From this point of view, the often inscrutable, elusive (in a strictly logical sense) character of aphorism recalls that of architectural design itself—without ever being translatable in it. Nevertheless, it is significant that Tafuri looks much less to Kraus the aphorist than he does to Kraus the essayist.

53. Tafuri, *La sfera e il labirinto*, 334. The passage from Kraus that Tafuri quotes here appears in Walter Benjamin, "Karl Kraus," in *Reflections* (New York: Harcourt Brace Jovanovich, 1978), 272–273. The emphasis is Tafuri's.

54. Tafuri, *La sfera e il labirinto*, 334.

55. Tafuri and Dal Co, *Architettura contemporanea*, 303. Immediately after these words, Tafuri includes the last sentence from Kraus's earlier excerpt, albeit slightly modified.

56. Ibid., 307.

57. Ibid., 309.

58. Ibid.

59. Tafuri, *La sfera e il labirinto*, 336.

60. Tafuri and Dal Co, *Architettura contemporanea*, 381. This expression refers to Rossi's 1974 design for student housing in Trieste.

61. Tafuri, *Storia dell'architettura italiana*, 169. The reference here is to the interior courtyard of Rossi's school in Fagnano Olona.

62. Tafuri, *La sfera e il labirinto*, 337n 26.

63. Tafuri, *Storia dell'architettura italiana*, 168.

64. Ibid., 170.

65. Tafuri and Dal Co, *Architettura contemporanea*, 381.

66. Ibid.

67. Tafuri, *Storia dell'architettura italiana*, 170. Dal Co writes some inspired pages about this same nostalgia, which representation expresses in the form of a "presence of absence." See Francesco Dal Co, "Ora questo è perduto. Il Teatro del Mondo di Aldo Rossi alla Biennale di Venezia," *Lotus* 25 (1979): 66–70. On the Teatro del Mondo, see also Manfredo Tafuri, "L'Éphémère est éternel. Aldo Rossi a Venezia," *Domus* 602 (1980): 7–11.

68. Tafuri, *Storia dell'architettura italiana*, 168–169.

69. Tafuri, *La sfera e il labirinto*, 345.

70. Tafuri and Dal Co, *Architettura contemporanea*, 381–382.

71. Manfredo Tafuri, letter to Aldo Rossi, October 12, 1971, quoted in Francesco Dal Co, "Il teatro della vita," in Aldo Rossi, *Quaderni azzurri*, xxii. For Rossi's reaction to this letter, see notebook 10 (November 21, 1971–February 13, 1972).

72. Manfredo Tafuri, "Ceci n'est pas une ville," *Lotus* 13 (1976): 12. The same passage is quoted in *Sphere and Labyrinth*, differing only in its first few words: "As logbooks of elliptical voyages into *temps passé*." See Tafuri, *La sfera e il labirinto*, 337–338. The same issue of *Lotus* also contains a text by Rossi. See Rossi, "La città analoga: tavola," *Lotus* 13: 5–8.

73. Carlo Michelstaedter, *Il dialogo della salute* (Milan: Adelphi, 1988), 73.

74. Ibid., 85.

75. Tafuri, "Ceci n'est pas une ville," 12.

76. Tafuri, *La sfera e il labirinto*, 333.

77. Ibid., 338. In "Ceci n'est pas une ville," however, Tafuri uses the word *ideological* instead of *utopian*.

78. Tafuri, *La sfera e il labirinto*, 338. In "Ceci n'est pas une ville," reflected in the mirror beside Mies, the architect "of the silence that reflects only itself," Tafuri also sees Loos, the architect of Café Nihilismus, capable of silently speaking of that silence.

79. Benjamin, "Karl Kraus," 456. See also Walter Benjamin, "Il carattere distruttivo," *Metaphorein* 3 (1978): 10–13; also published in Franco Rella, *Critica e storia. Materiali su Benjamin* (Venice: Cluva, 1980), 201–202.

80. The mistaken notion that there was a direct association between Tafuri and Rossi was encouraged by, among other things, the cover of the American edition of *Architecture and Utopia*, published as Manfredo Tafuri, *Architecture and Utopia: Design and Capitalist Development*, trans. Barbara Luigia La Penta (Cambridge, MA: MIT Press, 1976). This edition included Rossi's 1974 drawing *L'architecture assassinée*, which was expressly and controversially dedicated to Tafuri. For an analysis of the American reception—but more often the misunderstandings—of Tafuri's positions, see Diane Y. Ghirardo, "Manfredo Tafuri and Architectural Theory in the U.S., 1970–2000," *Perspecta* 33 (2002): 38–47.

81. For Tafuri, Benjamin's aforementioned essay on Kraus was absolutely fundamental, and was mentioned more than once in his writings. See, in particular, Tafuri, *La sfera e il labirinto*, 335. Here, Tafuri calls Benjamin's piece "a text rich in reflections, in which the new 'messengers in the old engravings' can find infinite material to mediate on."

82. The terms here and those in the following phrases are liberal citations of Benjamin, "Karl Kraus."

83. This definition was penned by Roberto Calasso, who edited and wrote the preface to the first Italian publication of Kraus's aphorisms. See Karl Kraus, *Detti e contradetti* (Milan: Adelphi, 1972).

84. Here I have adapted, respectively, an aphorism by Kraus (ibid., 364) and an expression by Elias Canetti in reference to Kraus, quoted in Roberto Calasso, "Una muraglia cinese" (ibid., 39).

85. In Tafuri's case, this must not be confused with his conception of history as a project of crisis without any guarantee of absolute validity or definitive solutions. Again, see Tafuri, introduction to *La sfera e il labirinto*, 18. See also the

introduction to this volume. And yet: the voice of the historian who announces the critical construction of the crisis knows no cracks.

86. Kraus was—perhaps not merely by chance—the locus around which Tafuri and Cacciari rarely diverged. See Tafuri, *La sfera e il labirinto*, 334–335n 25. The texts by Cacciari, which Tafuri criticized for "an overly rushed settlement of Kraus," are: Massimo Cacciari, *Krisis* (Milan: Feltrinelli, 1976), 170–180; and "La Vienna di Wittgenstein," *Nuova Corrente* 72–73 (1977): 59ff. "La Vienna di Wittgenstein" was later republished in Massimo Cacciari, *Dallo Steinhof. Prospettive viennesi del primo Novecento* (Milan: Adelphi, 1980), 245–258. It should be remembered that Cacciari's fundamental text *Adolf Loos e il suo Angelo* rereads Loos through Kraus and Benjamin. See Massimo Cacciari, *Adolf Loos e il suo Angelo* (Milan: Electa, 1981).

87. Benjamin, "Karl Kraus," 439.

88. The figure of the "grumbler" (*Nörgler*) appears as the double of its author in Karl Kraus, *The Last Days of Mankind: A Tragedy in Five Acts*, trans. Alexander Gode (New York: Ungar Publishing, 2000). In his foreword to *Ricerca del Rinascimento*, Tafuri writes of original guilt—belonging to both architectural culture, and even more to "contemporary artistic lines of research." See Tafuri, *Ricerca del Rinascimento* (Turin: Einaudi, 1992), xix. On the centrality of the sense of guilt for Tafuri, see Luisa Passerini, "History as Project: An Interview with Manfredo Tafuri," *Any* 25–26 (February 2000): 65. Tafuri says: "I believe the sense of guilt is constitutive."

89. Passerini, "History as Project," 13. Tafuri says: "I tended to appreciate everything that was tragic, almost with a sense of pleasure."

90. Benjamin, "Karl Kraus," 448.

91. Ibid., 456.

92. "Perhaps only when we have gone beyond all undisputed laws—to a place where the 'destructive spirit' manages to construct—will it be possible to question the spirit of law." Tafuri, *Ricerca del Rinascimento*, xxi. The immediate reference is to Mies van der Rohe, Le Corbusier, and Stirling, but this sentence lies in the exact spot where Kraus and Benjamin meet! On the importance of the Benjaminian "destructive character" for Tafuri, and on the role of the intellectual as *pars destruens*, see Passerini, "History as Project: An Interview with Manfredo Tafuri," 40–41. See also Manfredo Tafuri, letter to Renato De Fusco, *Controspazio*

51 (1981): 83: "The sense Benjamin gave to the concept of the destructive character is too dear to me."

93. These are the words with which Benjamin concludes his essay on Kraus and obviously refers to him. See Benjamin, "Karl Kraus," 457.

6 POLITICS OF REALITY

1. Walter Benjamin, "Karl Kraus," trans. Edmund Jephcott, in *Walter Benjamin: Selected Writings*, vol. 2 (Cambridge, MA: Belknap Press of Harvard University Press, 2005), 456.

2. For a reconstruction of the various interconnections between architecture and politics in Italy (albeit limited primarily to the 1950s), see Giovanni Durbiano, *I nuovi maestri. Architetti tra politica e cultura nel dopoguerra* (Venice: Marsilio, 2000).

3. Manfredo Tafuri, *Progetto e utopia: Architettura e sviluppo capitalistico* [Architecture and Utopia] (Rome and Bari: Laterza, 1973), 170. More generally, see the entire preface and last chapter of *Architecture and Utopia*.

4. Manfredo Tafuri, "Architettura e realismo," in Vittorio Magnago Lampugnani, ed., *Architettura moderna. L'avventura delle idee nell'architettura 1750–1980* (Milan: Electa, 1985), 123–145.

5. Ibid., 123.

6. Ibid.

7. On Soviet architecture, see Manfredo Tafuri, "Il socialismo realizzato e la crisi delle avanguardie," in *Socialismo, città, architettura. URSS 1917–1937: Il contributo degli architetti europei* (Rome: Officina, 1971), 41–87. See also Manfredo Tafuri, "Les premières hypothèses de planification urbaine dans la Russie soviétique, 1918–1925," *Archithese*, no. 7 (1973): 31–41; translated into Italian as "Le prime ipotesi di pianificazione urbanistica nell'Unione Sovietica. Mosca, 1918–1924," *Rassegna sovietica* 1 (1974): 80–93; Manfredo Tafuri, "Formalismo e avanguardia fra la NEP e il primo piano quinquennale," in Jean-Louis Cohen, Marco De Michelis, and Manfredo Tafuri, *URSS 1917–1978: La città, l'architettura* (Rome: Officina, 1979), 17–65. See also the chapter "Urss-Berlino 1922: dal populismo all'"internazionale costruttivista,'" in Manfredo Tafuri, *La sfera e il labirinto: Avanguardie e architettura da Piranesi agli anni '70* (Turin: Einaudi, 1980), 141–209.

8. See Manfredo Tafuri, "'Das Rote Wien': Politica e forma della residenza nella Vienna socialista, 1919–1933," in *Vienna Rossa: la politica residenza nella Viena socialista, 1919–1933* (Milan: Electa, 1980), 7–148.

9. On these subjects, see Giorgio Ciucci and others, *La città americana dalla guerra civile al "New Deal"*(Rome: Laterza, 1973). In particular, see Francesco Dal Co, "Dai parchi alla regione. L'ideologia progressista e la riforma della città americana," 149–315.

10. Tafuri, "Architettura e realismo," 130.

11. See in particular György Lukács, *Saggi sul realismo* (Turin: Einaudi, 1950); Lukács, *Scritti sul realismo* (Turin: Einaudi, 1970); and Lukács, *Il significato attuale del realismo critico* (Turin: Einaudi, 1977).

12. Manfredo Tafuri, *Ludovico Quaroni e lo sviluppo dell'architettura moderna in Italia* (Milan: Edizioni di Comunità, 1964). It is worth remembering that, at the time he wrote that book, Tafuri was a teaching assistant for Quaroni's university course in architectural composition.

13. See Manfredo Tafuri and Francesco Dal Co, *Architettura contemporanea* [Modern Architecture] (1976; repr., Milan: Electa, 1979). (See in particular chapters 18–20.) See also Manfredo Tafuri, "Architettura italiana 1944–1981," in *Storia dell'arte italiana*, 7 (Turin: Einaudi, 1982), 425–550. This essay was later revised and expanded in Manfredo Tafuri, *Storia dell'architettura italiana 1944–1985* [History of Italian Architecture] (Turin: Einaudi, 1986). See in particular chapters 1–3.

14. Tafuri, "Architettura e realismo," 133.

15. Tafuri, *Ludovico Quaroni*, 14.

16. Ibid.

17. Ibid., 13–14.

18. Ibid., 10.

19. Ibid., 15.

20. Ibid., 133.

21. Ibid., 16.

22. Ibid., 43.

23. Ibid., 174.

24. Ibid.

25. Ibid., 175.

26. Tafuri, *Storia dell'architettura italiana*, 147.

27. Ibid., 95.

28. Ibid., 107.

29. Ibid., 127. The architecture of Vittorio De Feo can also be traced back to this capacity for self-testing, which is another legacy of Ridolfi's work. For Tafuri, this shows how Ridolfi's legacy can coexist with those of "Kahn and Venturi . . . without falling into the trap that the recent proponents of 'Post-Modernism' will remain tripped up by." On Vittorio De Feo, see also Tafuri, *La sfera e il labirinto*, 340–341.

30. Tafuri, *Storia dell'architettura italiana*, 26.

31. Ibid., 31.

32. Ibid., 27.

33. Ibid.

34. Ibid., 128.

35. Ibid., 44.

36. Ibid., 157.

37. On this point, see the conclusion of "The Years of Reconstruction," the first chapter in Tafuri's *History of Italian Architecture*: "The encirclement of the 'districts' by the speculating city—a predictable and calculated phenomenon—soon revealed that architectural design had not managed to produce even islands of realized utopia. Realism showed itself for what it was, the product of a useless compromise." Tafuri, *Storia dell'architettura italiana*, 33.

38. Tafuri was aware of all the risks that a formalization of reality into a style or school brought with it: since it is true that "on the threshold of the 'economic miracle,' the gradual disappearance of the conditions that had sustained the emergence of this poetic transformed an encounter between the urgency of a subjective need to communicate and the necessities imposed by the historical situation to a coherence that outlived itself by speaking with inappropriate nostalgia of a 'bad' world that had disappeared." Ibid., 20. Also related to this theme, albeit with developments that take a path independent of Tafuri's view, is Antonio Monestiroli, *L'architettura della realtà* (1979; repr., Turin: Allemandi, 1999).

39. Tafuri, *Storia dell'architettura italiana*, 159.

40. Ibid., 48.

41. Ibid., 127.

42. Vittorio Gregotti, *New Directions in Italian Architecture*, trans. Giuseppina Salvadori (New York: George Braziller, 1968), 47–63.

43. Ibid., 63.

44. Manfredo Tafuri, *Vittorio Gregotti. Progetti e architetture* (Milan: Electa, 1982),15. It should also be noted that, early on in his career, Tafuri, alongside Alberto Samonà, Ludovico Quaroni, Carlo Aymonino, and Vieri Quilici, participated in a panel discussion in Rome on the theme *città territorio* (city-territory, a term he probably coined). The proceedings were later published as Carlo Aymonino et al., *La città territorio. Un esperimento didattico sul centro direzionale di Centocelle in Roma* (Bari: Leonardo da Vinci, 1964). See also Manfredo Tafuri, "La città territorio: verso una nuova dimensione," *Casabella continuità* 270 (1962): 16–25.

45. Tafuri, *Storia dell'architettura italiana*, 211.

46. Tafuri, *Vittorio Gregotti*, 29.

47. Ibid., 28.

48. Ibid., 29.

49. Regarding this, one has to wonder about the deeper reasons behind Tafuri's complete dismissal of Renzo Piano (whose name appears only twice in *History of Italian Architecture*, to make explicit the author's perplexities with regard to Piano's architectural research and design). Yet it is Piano's work—centered entirely upon the relationships between project design, place, material, and technique, and conceiving of a building as an organism (without caving in to the temptation of organicism)—that would seem to be paradigmatic of the anti-ideological way of working that Tafuri would (in theory) approve. In this sense, Tafuri seems to express a view that corresponds to the idea of an ideology that is consciously criticized and laboriously, dialectically surpassed. Instead, the idea that ideology is truly absent—as in the work of Piano—seems to lie outside his realm of analysis.

50. Tafuri, *Vittorio Gregotti*, 25.

51. Tafuri, *Storia dell'architettura italiana*, 190.

52. The particular text Tafuri refers to most (ibid., 187–191) is Bernardo Secchi, *Il racconto urbanistico. La politica della casa e del territorio in Italia* (Turin: Einaudi, 1984).

53. Tafuri, *Storia dell'architettura italiana*, 191.

54. Ibid., 184.

55. Manfredo Tafuri, *The Sphere and the Labyrinth*, 4th edn., trans. Pellegrino d'Acierno and Robert Connolly (Cambridge, MA: MIT Press, 1995), 287.

56. Ibid.

57. The figures mentioned are, however, given ample space in Tafuri and Dal Co, *Architettura contemporanea* (esp. chapters 2, 11, and 13). See also Manfredo Tafuri, "E. May e l'urbanistica razionalista," *Comunità*, no. 123 (1964): 66–80. Clarence Stein and Henry Wright, along with Frederick Law Olmsted and Robert Moses, are mentioned as examples of progressive ideology in the distinction Tafuri outlines between the various modes of ideological production. See Tafuri, *La sfera e il labirinto*, 24.

58. Tafuri, *La sfera e il labirinto*, 351.

59. For two ideological approaches, the more realism and utopianism are perceived as polar opposites, the less different they appear to be. This is why sudden switches from one to the other are not infrequent. As, for example, in the way Tafuri writes about the projects for INA-Casa toward the end of the 1950s: "The immersion in realism thus produced the sleep of reason. And demons would soon appear to reverse the mood that had generated the mythologies of the postwar years: the ideology of realism would soon be replaced by a revived quest for utopia." Tafuri, *History of Italian Architecture, 1944–1985*, 2nd edn., trans. Jessica Levine (Cambridge, MA: MIT Press, 1990), 48.

60. Tafuri, *Storia dell'architettura italiana*, 108.

61. Ibid., 119–120.

62. Tafuri, *Ludovico Quaroni*, 170–171.

63. Tafuri, *Progetto e utopia*, 169.

64. Ibid., 28.

65. Ibid.

66. Tafuri, *Storia dell'architettura italiana*, 239. The essays by Massimo Cacciari that Tafuri refers to are: Massimo Cacciari, "Nichilismo e progetto," *Casabella* 483 (1982): 50–51; Massimo Cacciari, "Eupalinos o l'architettura," *Nuovo Corrente* 76–77 (1978); Massimo Cacciari, "Progetto," in *Laboratorio Politico*, no. 2 (1981): 88–119; Massimo Cacciari, *Adolf Loos e il Angelo* (Milan: Electa, 1981), 9–34.

67. Tafuri, *Storia dell'architettura italiana*, 239.

68. Ibid., 240.

69. Ibid., 241.

70. Manfredo Tafuri, *Ricerca del Rinascimento* [Interpreting the Renaissance] (Turin: Einaudi, 1992), 3. Tafuri quotes the version of the *Novella del Grasso legnaiolo* (*The Tale of Grasso the Carpenter*) by Tuccio Manetti, Filippo Brunelleschi's biographer. Brunelleschi, with others, perpetrated the story's practical joke.

71. Ibid., 13.

72. Ibid., 21.

73. Ibid.

74. Thus, for example, for Tafuri, "all of humanist architecture expresses a daring and refined balance between the (re)search for foundation and experimentation" (ibid., 9). Amid the fruitful mines of contradictory, symbiotic, concurrent possibilities he finds in the Renaissance, Venice plays a special role: a case of stunning interests, an "illuminating example" (ibid., 23) of an active, productive contradictoriness, and therefore robbed of any excluding character: Renaissance Venice, "a place in which antitheses are abolished, in which dialectic is not in use, in which tradition and innovation, development and memory, continuity and renovation, sacred and profane, public and private, are not in contradiction." Manfredo Tafuri, *Venezia e il Rinascimento* (Turin: Einaudi, 1985), xviii. And again: "Venice seems to sweep away all other alternatives—yes/no, conservative/progressive, forward/backward, right/left, closed/open—upon which modern paradigms are based." Massimo Cacciari, Francesco Dal Co, and Manfredo Tafuri, "Il mito di Venezia," *Rassegna* 22 (1985): 7.

75. Tafuri, *Ricerca del Rinascimento*, 24.

76. Howard Burns, "Tafuri and the Renaissance," *Casabella* 619–620 (1995): 117. Yet the subject of "retreat" is also the insistent focus of various contributions to *Any* 25–26 (2000), passim. In an interview with Fulvio Irace, Tafuri asserts: "As far as I am concerned, after the effort poured into the essays and other writings [I] published prior to 1980, I believe I concluded, in a certain sense, a phase of [my] work on what is usually called 'contemporary.'" Manfredo Tafuri, interview by Fulvio Irace, *Domus* 653 (1984): 26.

77. As maintained by Georges Teyssot in Paul Henninger, "One Portrait of Tafuri: An Interview with Georges Teyssot," *Any* 25–26 (February 2000): 14–15.

78. See Daniel Sherer, "Progetto e ricerca: Manfredo Tafuri come critico e storico," *Zodiac* 15 (March-August 1996): 34.

79. Tafuri, *Venezia e il Rinascimento*, xix. An evident Benjaminian echo resounds in this expression.

80. The theme of philology in Tafuri's work cannot be fully dealt with here; that said, it clearly recalls the work of Walter Benjamin and Aby Warburg.

81. For the observation that the critique of ideology precedes and determines the discovery of philology, and that between the two there exists an intrinsic, precise nexus, see Alberto Asor Rosa, "Critica dell'ideologia ed esercizio storico," *Casabella* 619–620 (1995): 32. Tafuri himself, on the other hand, connects his own return to Renaissance studies with a few thematic lines present in the seventies and early eighties. See Luisa Passerini, "History as Project: An Interview with Manfredo Tafuri," *Any* 25–26: 61.

82. Regarding this theme, see the introduction to this book.

83. Manfredo Tafuri, *Interpreting the Renaissance*, trans. Daniel Sherer (New Haven: Yale University Press, 2006), 22.

84. Tafuri, *Storia dell'architettura italiana*, 240.

85. Tafuri, *Ricerca del Rinascimento*, 57. The entire second chapter of this book, titled "Cives esse non licere: Nicolas V and Leon Battista Alberti," can be read not only as a pointed analysis of Alberti's disenchanted yet suppressed realism, but also as an emblematic exposition of Tafuri's concept of reality, at the very limits of autobiography.

86. Ibid., 67.

7 GAMES, JOKES, MASKED BALLS

1. Manfredo Tafuri, *La sfera e il labirinto: Avanguardie e architettura da Piranesi agli anni '70* [The Sphere and the Labyrinth] (Turin: Einaudi, 1980), 367. See also chapter 4 above, "Les bijoux dans le boudoir."

2. Ibid., 339, 367.

3. On what Tafuri terms hypermoderns, see Manfredo Tafuri, "La 'gaia erranza': ipermoderni (postmoderni)" ["Gay Errancy": Hypermoderns (Postmoderns)], in *Storia dell'architettura italiana 1944–1985* [History of Italian Architecture] (Turin: Einaudi, 1986), 230–234. He also makes several interesting observations in Manfredo Tafuri, interview by Omar Calabrese, "La tecnica delle avanguardie," *Casabella* 463–464 (1980): 98–101: "[Paolo] Portoghesi's most recent book, *Dopo l'architettura moderna* [After Modern Architecture], is modeled on the

'culture of simulacra' . . . a culture based on the double, on copies that have no referents, without originals. This seems to be a rhetorical game, aimed at covering, with references that belong to a high culture diseased by populism, operations that originated in another way. To me, it seems that the entire 'postmodern' undertaking should be considered more in its market aspects, rather than its theoretical aspects. . . . Postmodernism paradoxically validates . . . another fable, the one created in 1937 [sic] by Nikolaus Pevsner. This means there is a modern movement to which all the ills of metropolitan civilization are now attributed." Ibid., 100.

4. The two sources are Richard Pommer, "The New Architectural Suprematists," *Artforum* (October 1976); and Fulvio Irace, "Le ricerche di architettura più attuali ed insolite," *Op. cit.* 38 (1977): 5–44.

5. See Rem Koolhaas and Elia Zenghelis, "Exodus, or the Voluntary Prisoners of Architecture," *Casabella* 378 (1973): 42–45. The project stemmed from a competition announced by the magazine on the theme of "La città come ambiente significante," or "The city as significant environment."

6. Rem Koolhaas, *Delirious New York: A Retroactive Manifesto for Manhattan* (New York: Monacelli Press, 1994), 300.

7. Ibid., 307.

8. Patrice Goulet, "La deuxième chance de l'architecture moderne . . . , Entretien avec Rem Koolhaas," *L'Architecture d'aujourd'hui* 238 (1985): 4.

9. Here I am paraphrasing Koolhaas, *Delirious New York*, 310.

10. It should be remembered that the first essay Koolhaas published in the United States was about Leonidov and his project for the Ministry of Heavy Industry. See Rem Koolhaas and Gerrit Oorthuys, "Ivan Leonidov's Dom Narkomtjazjprom, Moscow," *Oppositions* 2 (1974): 96–102. Furthermore, in the years he was working on *Delirious New York*, Koolhaas planned to write a book on Leonidov, which remains "unpublished."

11. Rem Koolhaas, "The Architects' Ball—A Vignette, 1931," *Oppositions* 3 (1974): 92–96. Tafuri's essay "L'Architecture dans le boudoir" appeared in the same issue. It is worth noting Koolhaas's ties with the Institute for Architecture and Urban Studies and *Oppositions* at that time. The latter was a true meeting point—in virtual, if not real terms—between Tafuri and Koolhaas.

12. Tafuri, *La sfera e il labirinto*, 231.

13. See Koolhaas, *Delirious New York*, 125–130.

14. Ibid., 127.

15. Koolhaas, "The Architects' Ball," 92.

16. Ibid., 95–96.

17. See Marco Biraghi, *Identification Parade: Manfredo Tafuri and Rem Koolhaas* (Hamburg: Textem-Verlag, 2011).

18. Koolhaas, *Delirious New York*, 130.

19. Koolhaas, "The Architects' Ball," 95. This homophile interpretation of the Chrysler (which Koolhaas deems outclassed in height and virility by the Empire State Building) was later abandoned in *Delirious New York*.

20. Tafuri, *La sfera e il labirinto*, 231n 43. This is where Tafuri explicitly references Koolhaas's article in *Oppositions*.

21. Tafuri, *La sfera e il labirinto*, 231.

22. Ibid., 234.

23. For a reading of *Delirious New York* as historical psychoanalysis or analytical psychohistory, see my afterword to the Italian edition of *Delirious New York*: Marco Biraghi, "Surfin' Manhattan," in Rem Koolhaas, *Delirious New York*, trans. Ruggero Baldasso and Marco Biraghi (Milan: Electa, 2001), 291–303. The tangential relation of that outlook with Tafuri's reflections on the parallels between psychoanalysis and history (see esp. Tafuri, *La sfera e il labirinto*, 12ff.) and "ideologies as 'delirious representations' in the Freudian sense" (ibid., 13) must not be underestimated.

24. Tafuri, *La sfera e il labirinto*, 111. The same book reproduces a still from *Gold Diggers of 1933* and a photograph of the set of *42nd Street*, while another still from the latter film is reproduced in Manfredo Tafuri and Francesco Dal Co, *Architettura contemporanea* [Modern Architecture] (1976; repr., Milan: Electa, 1979), 196.

25. See Koolhaas, *Delirious New York*, 158. This new metropolitan race—the Metropolitanites—is at work on both Coney Island and at the Downtown Athletic Club—and, ultimately, in the skyscrapers, insofar as they are bastions of the antinatural.

26. In addition to the already oft-quoted book *The Sphere and the Labyrinth* (see especially Tafuri, *La sfera e il labirinto*, 211–241), the following are worth mentioning: Manfredo Tafuri, "La montagna disincantata. Il Grattacielo e la City" [The Disenchanted Mountain], in Giorgio Ciucci and others, *La città americana dalla guerra civile al "New Deal"* (Rome: Laterza, 1973), 417–550 (in English in *The American*

City: From the Civil War to the New Deal, trans. Barbara Luigia La Penta [Cambridge, MA: MIT Press, 1979], 389–503); Manfredo Tafuri, "La dialectique de l'absurde. Europa-USA: les avatars de l'idéologie du gratte-ciel (1918–1974)," *L'Architecture d'aujourd'hui* 178 (1975): 1–16; "'New-Babylon': das New York der Zwanzigerjahre und die Suche nach dem Amerikanismus," *Archithese* 20 (1976): 12–24; Manfredo Tafuri, "Dal World Trade Center a Battery Park City (1968–1975)," *Casabella* 457–458 (1980): 86–89. The chapters of *Modern Architecture* dedicated to American architecture (except those addressing the "masters") were edited by Dal Co, who also oversaw the monographic issue of *Casabella* 457–458 (1980) on American skyscrapers.

27. A single, significant reference to Rivera—and the "conflicts that rose up around Lenin" as he was depicted in Rivera's Rockefeller Center paintings (to which Koolhaas dedicated an entire chapter in *Delirious New York*)—can be found in a note in Tafuri, "La montagna disincantata," 505–506.

28. According to Dal Co, to whom I am indebted for his account, Tafuri was very familiar with *Delirious New York*, of which he was a close and highly amused reader. See also Biraghi, "Surfin' Manhattan," 292–293.

29. Tafuri, "La montagna disincantata," 421.

30. Ibid., 418.

31. Ibid., 421.

32. Ibid.

33. Ibid., 424.

34. Ibid., 445.

35. Ibid., 430.

36. Ibid., 435.

37. Ibid., 436.

38. Ibid., 437.

39. Ibid., 440.

40. Ibid., 444.

41. Ibid., 448.

42. Ibid.

43. Ibid., 463.

44. Ibid.

45. Ibid., 465.

46. Ibid., 466.

47. Thomas Adams, *The Building of the City* (New York: Arno Press, 1974), 108. Quoted in Tafuri, "La montagna disincantata," 476.

48. Tafuri, "La montagna disincantata," 477.

49. Ibid., 481.

50. Ibid., 470.

51. Ibid., 476.

52. Ibid., 490.

53. Ibid., 492.

54. Ibid., 494.

55. Ibid.

56. Ibid., 496.

57. Ibid., 532.

58. Ibid., 496.

59. Ibid., 503–504.

60. Ibid., 528.

61. Ibid., 547.

62. Koolhaas, *Delirious New York*, 178.

63. Ibid., 197.

64. Ibid., 184.

65. Ibid.

66. Ibid., 195.

67. Ibid., 174.

68. Ibid.

69. Ibid., 89.

70. Ibid., 164.

71. Ibid., 174.

72. Ibid., 271.

73. Tafuri, *La sfera e il labirinto*, 213.

74. Ibid., 212.

75. Ibid., 8.

76. Tafuri, *La montagna disincantata*, 485.

77. Ibid.

78. Koolhaas, *Delirious New York*, 110.

79. Ibid., 117.

80. Ibid.

81. Ibid.

82. Tafuri speaks of totem and Moloch with regard to the metropolitan malady of the skyscraper (see Tafuri, *La sfera e il labirinto*, 218). "Les avatars de l'idéologie du gratte-ciel" is the subtitle of the essay he published in 1975 in *L'Architecture d'aujourd'hui* ("La dialectique de l'absurde"). Hans van Dijk's interview with Koolhaas is worth mentioning, as he criticizes this very aspect: "In the articles of Tafuri about skyscrapers I have never seen a map. For him the skyscraper is a kind of Totem of the bad side of capitalism and of course he is terrified to discover that there is something else going on." Hans van Dijk, "Rem Koolhaas Interview," *Wonen-TA/BK* 11 (November 1978): 18.

83. Tafuri, *La sfera e il labirinto*, 213.

84. Ibid., 215.

85. Ibid., 213.

86. Ibid., 218.

87. Ibid., 221.

88. Ibid., 223.

89. Ibid., 232.

90. Ibid., 224.

91. Ibid.

92. Ibid., 225.

93. Ibid., 233.

94. Ibid., 234. It is interesting to note how Dal Co assigns to a more conflicted and conflicting position "skyscrapers' decorative incrustations . . . inspired by the most varied traditions. . . . How can one not imagine that, behind the redundancy that comes along with the blossoming of the most imaginative urbanistic proposals and vast programs for 'reform,' there lurks a mediated controversy against the fundamental mechanism that regulates the organic cycles of the great American megalopolis? How can one help but relate all that to an increasingly generalized state of malaise that is felt when one is faced with the rigid uniformity imposed by the function of the urban *grid*? Where the rule of repetition reigns supreme, isn't it precisely the Art Deco skyscraper that—splitting itself in two, multiplying, and breaking apart—alludes to a hypothetical plurality that the

metropolis seems to negate?" Francesco Dal Co, "L'evanescenza della trasgressione," *Casabella* 457–458 (1980): 17.

95. Tafuri, *La sfera e il labirinto*, 217.

96. Ibid.

97. Koolhaas, *Delirious New York*, 11. Koolhaas's reference here is intentionally ironic. Pay close attention: the intention of the book is, instead, to go beyond—and even *subvert*—this reading.

EPILOGUE: THE DOUBLE LIFE OF CONTRADICTION

1. The expression "posthumous man" appears in Friedrich Nietzsche, *The Gay Science*, ed. Bernard Williams, trans. Josephine Nauckhoff (Cambridge: Cambridge University Press, 2001), 229–230; and in Friedrich Nietzsche, *Twilight of the Idols*, trans. Duncan Large (New York: Oxford University Press, 1998), 6. His connection to Tafuri was first outlined by Mario Tronti.

2. Massimo Cacciari, *Dallo Steinhof. Prospettive viennesi del primo Novecento* (Milan: Adelphi, 1980), 16. Many of the expressions Cacciari uses here and later paraphrase passages of the Nietzsche text mentioned in note 1.

3. Cacciari, *Dallo Steinhof*, 17.

4. Ibid., 18.

5. Ibid. It is no coincidence that for Cacciari the posthumous men *par excellence* are Robert Musil and Ludwig Wittgenstein, both on a par with Karl Kraus as the great Viennese of language, or the ruthless critique thereof. For Tafuri's spiritual proximity to Wittgenstein, see Luisa Passerini, "History as Project: An Interview with Manfredo Tafuri," *Any* 25–26 (February 2000): 50. For his elective affinity with Musil, see Paul Henninger, "One Portrait of Tafuri: An Interview with Georges Teyssot," *Any* 25–26 (February 2000): 16.

6. Massimo Cacciari, preface to *Adolf Loos e il suo Angelo*, new edn. (Milan: Electa, 2002), 5. Cacciari's words refer to Loos.

7. Massimo Cacciari, "Quid tum," *Domus* 762 (July 1994): 37. This was originally a memorial speech given on the occasion of Manfredo Tafuri's funeral, February 25, 1994, Tolentini courtyard, Venice.

8. One could, in this regard, see a similarity between Tafuri's discourse and Mies's position against multiple, formulaic "aesthetic cultures," in which the "absence of a center [is] held up as a new centrality," "vague, truthless wandering is held

up as a new kind of abode," and "*Wertfreiheit* [neutrality, the quality of being free of values] is transformed into a new law decreeing the end of all values." Massimo Cacciari, "Res aedificatoria. Il classico di Mies van der Rohe," *Paradosso* 9 (1994): 23–24. Reprinted in *Casabella* 629 (1995): 3.

9. Cacciari, preface to *Adolf Loos e il suo Angelo*, 4.

10. Ibid.

11. James S. Ackerman, "In Memoriam: Manfredo Tafuri, 1935–1994," *Journal of the Society of Architectural Historians* 53, no. 2 (June 1994): 138. For an explicit acknowledgment of the relationship between psychoanalysis and historical inquiry (including autobiographical reflections), see Passerini, "History as Project," 45–48, 61.

12. Manfredo Tafuri, *Ricerca del Rinascimento* [Interpreting the Renaissance] (Turin: Einaudi, 1992), xxi.

13. Cacciari, "Quid tum," 37.

14. Ibid.

15. Tafuri, *Ricerca del Rinascimento*, 52. This refers to Robert Klein.

16. Cacciari, "Quid tum," 37.

17. Ibid.

18. For an analysis of the key terms of modernity and its limits—as they refer exclusively to the architectural world—see Francesco Dal Co, *Abitare nel moderno* (Rome and Bari: Laterza, 1982).

19. See chapter 6 above, "Politics of Reality."

20. Manfredo Tafuri, *La sfera e il labirinto: Avanguardie e architettura da Piranesi agli anni '70* [The Sphere and the Labyrinth] (Turin: Einaudi, 1980), 349. See chapter 3 above, "The Pull of the Void."

21. Although in the 1980s Koolhaas's work showed significant points of convergence with the postmodern condition, it nevertheless kept an unequivocal stylistic distance from postmodern architecture. On this point, see, among others, Jacques Lucan, *OMA–Rem Koolhaas: Architecture 1970–1990* (New York: Princeton Architectural Press, 1991).

22. See the "foundational" text by Jean-François Lyotard, *The Postmodern Condition: A Report on Knowledge* (Minneapolis: University of Minnesota Press, 1984)—and, among others, Zygmunt Bauman, *Postmodernity and Its Discontents* (New York: New York University Press, 1997).

23. Lyotard's *The Postmodern Condition*, first published in France in 1979, explicitly presents itself as a "report" on a "conception of knowledge in the most highly developed societies" (Lyotard, *The Postmodern Condition*, 18) that was evidently elaborated during an earlier period. Among the other discourses, Lyotard's discussion of a "search for instabilities" on the part of postmodernist science (ibid., 98ff.) has a parallel in the concept of "definitive instabilities" that Koolhaas outlined in *Delirious New York*. Koolhaas's strategy of retroactivity is a precursor—capturing the sense—of the theoreticization of postmodernity as anamnesis or the return to something forgotten, as an elaboration upon an initial oblivion; see Jean-François Lyotard, "Ripetizione, complessità, anamnesi," *Casabella* 517 (1985): 44–45. The idea of postmodernity also includes Koolhaas's idea of giving modernity a second chance, having duly cleansed it of all utopian and ethical (or, in his view, moralistic) components that were part of the first appearance of the modern.

24. See Marco Biraghi, "Surfin' Manhattan," in Rem Koolhaas, *Delirious New York*, trans. Ruggero Baldasso and Marco Biraghi (Milan: Electa, 2001), 302.

25. Rem Koolhaas, *Delirious New York*, 2nd edn. (New York: Monacelli Press, 1994), 82.

26. Ibid., 93.

27. Ibid., 100–101.

28. Ibid., 105.

29. Gilles Deleuze and Félix Guattari, *Anti-Oedipus*, trans. Robert Hurley, Mark Seem, and Helen R. Lane (1984; repr., New York and London: Continuum, 2004). The original French edition was published in 1972.

30. See Biraghi, "Surfin' Manhattan," 291–303, as well as chapter 7 above, "Games, Jokes, Masked Balls."

31. Gilles Deleuze and Félix Guattari, preface to the Italian edition of the book, in *Mille piani. Capitalismo e schizofrenia* [A Thousand Plateaus] (Rome: Cooper Castelvecchi, 2003), 30. See also Gilles Deleuze, "Relazione," in Armando Verdiglione, ed., *Psicoanalisi e politica*, congress catalog (Milan: Feltrinelli, 1973), 8.

32. On numerous occasions Koolhaas has declared the debts he owes to the French philosophers, particularly Roland Barthes. See, for example, François Chaslin, *Architettura© della Tabula Rasa©. Due conversazioni con Rem Koolhaas, ecc.* (Mi-

lan: Electa, 2003), 54. In that same text, on page 70, Koolhaas makes explicit reference to Deleuze and Guattari's *A Thousand Plateaus*.

33. See Gilles Deleuze and Félix Guattari, *What Is Philosophy?*, trans. Graham Burchell and Hugh Tomlinson, 4th edn. (London: Verso, 1994). The authors also point out that Nietzsche was the first to explicitly champion the idea of philosophy as the production of concepts.

34. Curiously, Tafuri's rare nods to Deleuze and Guattari—as well as to Derrida and Blanchot—seem to determine these authors' debuts on the American architectural scene. See Diane Y. Ghirardo, "Manfredo Tafuri and Architectural Theory in the U.S.," *Perspecta* 33 (2002): 44, 37n.

35. Tafuri, *La sfera e il labirinto*, 9.

36. Ibid., 15.

37. See Franco Rella, "Nel nome di Freud. Il mito dell'altro," *Quaderni Piacentini* 60–61 (1976), 67.

38. Franco Rella, introduction to Massimo Cacciari and others, *Il dispositivo Foucault* (Venice: Cluva, 1977), 18. Significantly, Rella (as well as Cacciari) draws a parallel between the discourses of Deleuze and Guattari and Lyotard, which are all considered "a sort of vulgarization" of Foucault (ibid., 22).

39. Gilles Deleuze and Félix Guattari, *A Thousand Plateaus*, trans. Brian Massumi (1984; repr., New York and London: Continuum, 2004), 21.

40. Rella, introduction to *Il dispositivo Foucault*, 18.

41. See Massimo Cacciari, "Il problema del Politico in Deleuze e Foucault (sul pensiero di "Autonomia" e "Gioco"), in Cacciari and others, *Il dispositivo Foucault*, 57–69; Massimo Cacciari, "'Razionalità' e 'Irrazionalità' nella critica del Politico in Deleuze e Foucault," *aut-aut* 161 (1977): 119–133. Both essays are cited in Tafuri, *La sfera e il labirinto*, 11 and 15.

42. Georg Simmel, "Metafisica della morte," in *Arte e civiltà* (Milan: ISEDI, 1976), 67. This quote appears again in Tafuri, *La sfera e il labirinto*, 8.

43. Deleuze and Guattari, *Anti-Oedipus*, 45.

44. In this sense it would be interesting to investigate the reasons for the lack of a warm welcome—among the Italian culture of the late 1970s and early 1980s—for two books as important as *A Thousand Plateaus* and *Delirious New York*, which were only translated into Italian years after their initial publication, in 2003 and 2001, respectively.

45. It is interesting to read the following passages from the 1978 Koolhaas interview:

> Hans van Dijk: You [in *Delirious New York*] mystify Manhattan deliberately. This makes it an attack on the critics and architects who, before they do anything, want to get to the tabula rasa, want to demystify everything first.

> Rem Koolhaas: You mean people like Tafuri? Sure, irritation and anger about their work has been an important source of energy.

> H. v. D.: Is that because from that corner, the judgment of each architectural enterprise gets placed within an economic and social context? For example, the question from Benjamin of what position the intellectual work of the architect should take within the context of production, or the question whether it gives functionality to means of production (to use the words of Brecht)?

> R. K.: I have always found it nearly physically impossible to think in those terms and to talk in that manner. I have a strong impression that Tafuri and his co-thinkers hate architecture. They declare architecture dead. For them architecture is a set of corpses in the morgue. But they do not leave the corpses in peace: they are vain enough to want to be the experts of the morgue. They do name-dropping in the morgue. Now and then they take out a corpse, say something about it, and put it back again; but altogether it is impossible. Except, for unexplainable reasons, for Aldo Rossi.

> H. v. D.: Who also speaks against Tafuri.

> R. K.: Yes, if you remain the only one left for someone who declares the others dead, I would feel uncomfortable as well.

Hans van Dijk, "Rem Koolhaas Interview," *Wonen-TA/BK* 11 (November 1978): 18.

46. This research began with *Delirious New York*, and often touched upon urban themes, or subjects otherwise connected to what is usually called the city. See R. Koolhaas, S. Boeri, S. Kwinter, N. Tanzi, and H. U. Obrist, *Mutations*, exh. cat. (Barcelona: Actar, 2000); C. J. Chung, J. Inaba, R. Koolhaas, and S. T. Leong, eds., *Great Leap Forward: Harvard Design School Project on the City* 1 (Cologne: Taschen, 2001); C. J. Chung, J. Inaba, R. Koolhaas, and S. T. Leong, eds.,

Harvard Design School Guide to Shopping: Harvard Design School Project on the City 2
(Cologne: Taschen, 2001). Other research done under the auspices of *Project on the City*—directed by Koolhaas and carried out by a vast number of collaborators—are dedicated to Lagos, capital of Nigeria, and the imperial Roman city.

47. Chaslin, *Architettura© della Tabula Rasa©*, 45. Compare—not despite but, rather, in light of the vast distance that separates their respective sociopolitical contexts—the following phrase by Tronti to the one just quoted: "From the worker's point of view, the contradictions of capital are to be neither refused nor resolved, but rather to be used. And in order to use them, they must be exacerbated." Mario Tronti, *Operai e capitale* [Workers and Capital] (Turin: Einaudi, 1966), 23–24. Tafuri himself affirmed the need for an "exacerbation of the antitheses, a head-on collision of these positions, the accentuation of the contradictions." Manfredo Tafuri, *Teorie e storia dell'architettura* [Theories and History of Architecture] (Bari: Laterza, 1968), 270.

48. Rem Koolhaas, introduction to OMA, Rem Koolhaas, and Bruce Mau, *S, M, L, XL*, 2nd edn. (New York: Monacelli Press, 1998), xix.

49. Rem Koolhaas, "Seminar 1/21/91," in Sanford Kwinter, ed., *Rem Koolhaas: Conversations with Students* (New York: Princeton Architectural Press, 1996), 65. The seminar took place at Rice University School of Architecture in 1991.

50. Ibid.

51. Chaslin, *Architettura© della Tabula Rasa©*, 32.

52. For his denouncement of nostalgic analyses and points of view that are still widespread among architects, see Koolhaas, "Seminar 1/21/91," 42–43. Instead, Koolhaas's entire production—both architectural and theoretical—is imprinted with a total absence of nostalgia, and therefore possesses a deep sense of disenchantment.

53. See chapter 6 above, "Politics of Reality."

54. Cacciari, *Dallo Steinhof*, 17–18.

55. Manfredo Tafuri, *Architecture and Utopia: Design and Capitalist Development*, trans. Barbara Luigia La Penta (1973; repr., Cambridge, MA: MIT Press, 1979), 83–84.

56. S. T. Leong, *Harvard Design School Guide to Shopping*, 129.

57. "A coherent Marxist critique of architectural and urban-planning ideology cannot but demystify the contingent and historical realities—realities that are

anything but objective or universal—that are hidden behind the unifying categories of the terms art, architecture, and city." Manfredo Tafuri, *Progetto e utopia: Architettura e sviluppo capitalistico* [Architecture and Utopia] (Rome and Bari: Laterza, 1973), 168. The aim of this critique is to recognize and confront the new levels of capitalist development. It is interesting that the latter consideration substitutes the much more intransigent passage present in the original version of that same text: "[By] assuming its own historic and objective role of class criticism, architectural criticism has to become a criticism of urban ideology, and completely avoids taking part in progressive conversations with the techniques of rationalization of capital's contradictions." See Manfredo Tafuri, "Per una critica dell'ideologia architettonica" [Toward a Critique of Architectural Ideology], *Contropiano* 1 (1969): 78.

58. The reference here is to Tafuri's words previously quoted in chapter 6 above, "Politics of Reality."

59. "These changes unfold right before our eyes, but are not always adequately understood. Above all because, when faced with the imposing task of speculating about the city's state of becoming, one does not much wonder about its actual state, and it is rare that any precise information about its current conditions is collected." Chaslin, *Architettura© della Tabula Rasa©*, 61.

60. Mark Wigley hypothesized, albeit without specifying any names, that Tafuri's legacy could now lie in the hands of research not directly influenced by him, or even in "writing that he would have no doubted have hated." Mark Wigley, "Post-Operative History," *Any* 25–26 (February 2000): 53.

61. Tafuri, *Progetto e utopia*, 3.

62. See Massimo Cacciari, "Eupalinos or Architecture," trans. Stephen Sartarelli, *Oppositions* 21 (Summer 1980): 106–116. This is a review essay dedicated to the book *Modern Architecture* by Tafuri and Dal Co. Cacciari writes: "Manfredo Tafuri and Francesco Dal Co's book *Architettura contemporanea* (*Modern Architecture*) ends with the name of Heidegger. 'Difference' and 'renunciation' constitute the *tragic* point of view from which the developments of this architecture are described. The book therefore has nothing to do with 'history'—but rather with the problem of modern architecture, with its *Fragwürdiges [problematic]*: its fundamental relation to the world and to things, its language as the existence of such a relation" (ibid., 106). It is worth noting that, according to Tafuri and Dal Co, it is not the history of an ideology that *Modern Architecture* sounds out and investigates, but rather "[the history of] many ideologies, as well as how they were born of the work of a few architects, [and] of the interactions between the real and utopia." Manfredo Tafuri and Francesco Dal Co, *Architettura contemporanea* [Modern Architecture] (1976; repr., Milan: Electa, 1979), 382.

63. Tafuri, *Ricerca del Rinascimento*, 24.

BIBLIOGRAPHY

As an Italian author, Marco Birgahi quotes from the Italian editions of Manfredo Tafuri's works, as cited in the notes to this book. Many of these are also available in English, as noted here.

Ciucci, Giorgio, Francesco Dal Co, Mario Manieri-Elia, and Manfredo Tafuri. *The American City: From the Civil War to the New Deal*. Translated by Barbara Luigia La Penta. Cambridge, MA: MIT Press, 1979.

Tafuri, Manfredo. *Architecture and Utopia: Design and Capitalist Development*. Translated by Barbara Luigia La Penta. Cambridge, MA: MIT Press, 1976.

Tafuri, Manfredo. *History of Italian Architecture, 1944–1985*. Translated by Jessica Levine. Cambridge, MA: MIT Press. 1989.

Tafuri, Manfredo. *Interpreting the Renaissance: Princes, Cities, Architects*. Translated with an introduction by Daniel Sherer. New Haven: Yale University Press, 2006.

Tafuri, Manfredo. *The Sphere and the Labyrinth: Avant-Gardes and Architecture from Piranesi to the 1970s*. Translated by Pellegrino d'Acierno and Robert Connolly. Cambridge, MA: MIT Press, 1987.

Tafuri, Manfredo. *Theories and History of Architecture*. Translated by Giorgio Verrecchia. London: Granada, 1980.

Tafuri, Manfredo. *Venice and the Renaissance*. Translated by Jessica Levine. Cambridge, MA: MIT Press, 1985.

Tafuri, Manfredo, and Francesco Dal Co. *Modern Architecture*. Translated by Robert Erich Wolf. New York: Harry N. Abrams, 1979.

INDEX

Printed in the United States
by Baker & Taylor Publisher Services